D1522778

DOSTOEVSKI AND THE HUMAN CONDITION AFTER A CENTURY

Recent Titles in
Contributions to the Study of World Literature
Series Adviser: Leif Sjoberg

Aksel Sandemose: Exile in Search of a Home
Randi Birn

Edith Sodergran: Modernist Poet in Finland
George C. Schoolfield

Sigurd Hoel's Fiction: Cultural Criticism and Tragic Vision
Sverre Lyngstad

Per Olov Enquist: A Critical Study
Ross Shideler

Images in Transition: The English Jew in English Literature, 1660-1830
Abba Rubin

Per Olof Sundman: Writer of the North
Lars G. Warme

Quests for a Promised Land: The Works of Martin Andersen Nexø
Faith Ingwersen and Niels Ingwersen

Elmer Diktonius
George C. Schoolfield

Jens Bjørneboe: Prophet Without Honor
Janet Garton

Klaus Rifbjerg
Charlotte Schiander Gray

Scenarios of Modernist Disintegration: Tryggve Andersen's Prose Fiction
Timothy Schiff

Guido Gezelle: Flemish Poet-Priest
Hermine J. van Nuis

Voices of the Storyteller: Cuba's Lino Novás Calvo
Lorraine Elena Roses

Lessing and the Enlightenment
Alexej Ugrinsky, editor

DOSTOEVSKI AND THE HUMAN CONDITION AFTER A CENTURY

Edited by
ALEXEJ UGRINSKY,
FRANK S. LAMBASA,
and
VALIJA K. OZOLINS

Prepared under the auspices of Hofstra University

Contributions to the Study of World Literature, Number 16

Greenwood Press
New York • Westport, Connecticut • London

Library of Congress Cataloging-in-Publication Data

Dostoevski and the human condition after a century.
  (Contributions to the study of world literature,
ISSN 0738-9345 ; no. 16)
  Bibliography: p.
  Includes index.
  1. Dostoyevsky, Fyodor, 1821-1881—Criticism and
interpretation—Addresses, essays, lectures.
I. Ugrinsky, Alexej. II. Lambasa, Frank S. III. Ozolins,
Valija K. IV. Hofstra University. V. Series.
PG3328.Z6D57 1986   891.73′3   86-362
ISBN 0-313-25379-X (lib. bdg. : alk. paper)

Library of Congress Catalog Card Number: 86-362
ISBN: 0-313-25379-X
ISSN: 0738-9345

First published in 1986

Greenwood Press, Inc.
88 Post Road West, Westport, Connecticut 06881

Printed in the United States of America

The paper used in this book complies with the
Permanent Paper Standard issued by the National
Information Standards Organization (Z39.48-1984).

10 9 8 7 6 5 4 3 2 1

Copyright Acknowledgment

The editors and publisher are grateful to the following for granting the
use of their material:

Excerpts from Fyodor Dostoevski, *The Double*, trans. George Bird
(Bloomington: Indiana University Press, 1966) are reprinted
courtesy of Collins Publishers, London.

Contents

1. Introduction. Dostoevski and the Human Condition after a Century: The Poet and the City
   Pete Hamill   1

Part I   Textual and Conceptual Interpretations   11

2. The Legend of the Grand Inquisitor: The Death Struggle of Ideologies
   Thelma Z. Lavine   13

3. Murder and Suicide in *The Brothers Karamazov*: The Double Rebellion of Pavel Smerdiakov
   N. Norman Shneidman   23

4. The Dynamics of the Idea of Napoleon in *Crime and Punishment*
   Shoshana M. Knapp   31

5. The Nature of Referentiality in *The Double*
   Asya Pekurovskaya   41

6. *The Idiot*: A Feminist Reading
   Olga Matich   53

7. Narcissus Inverted: Fantastic-Realism as a Way of Knowing in *The Idiot*
   Dennis Patrick Slattery   61

8. *Notes from the Underground*: One Hundred Years After the Author's Death
   Rado Pribic   71

9. Kirillov, Stavrogin, and Suicide
   Roger L. Cox   79

10. The Demon of Irony: Stavrogin the Adversary at Tihon's
    Reed Merrill   87

11. The Concept of Beauty in *The Possessed*
    Valija K. Ozolins   99

Part II   Keynote Essay   113

12. The French Face of Dostoevski
    Henri Peyre   115

Part III   Comparative and Interdisciplinary Studies   131

13. The Russian Iconic Representation of the Christian Madonna:
    A Feminine Archetype in *Notes from Underground*
    Patricia Flanagan Behrendt   133

14. Dostoevski and Jean-Luc Godard: Kirillov's Return in
    La Chinoise
    Peter G. Christensen   145

15. Dostoevski and Vladimir Nabokov: The Case of *Despair*
    Julian W. Connolly   155

16. Dostoevski and Richard Wright: From St. Petersburg
    to Chicago
    Dasha Culic Nisula   163

17. Dostoevski and the Catholic Pax Romana
    Dennis Dirscherl   171

18. Rebirth and the Cognitive Dream: From Dostoevski to
    Hermann Hesse and C. G. Jung
    Phyllis Berdt Kenevan   181

19. Between Heaven and Hell: The Dialectic of Dostoevski's
    Tragic Vision
    Anthony S. Magistrale   191

20. Dostoevski and George Sand: Two Opponents of the Anthill
    Isabelle Naginski   199

    Program of Conference   211

    Index
    Darla Kowalski   227

    About the Editors and Contributors   235

DOSTOEVSKI AND THE HUMAN CONDITION AFTER A CENTURY

1.
Introduction. Dostoevski and the Human Condition after a Century: The Poet and the City

PETE HAMILL

The other night, on the West Side of Manhattan, I saw Raskolnikov again. He was standing in a doorway beside a bookshop, unshaven, the collar of his overcoat pulled high on his neck. When I passed him, his hand moved to his helmet of unruly hair as if to cover his face. But I knew him immediately from the blazing eyes. He was staring past me at the city that had spawned him.

I had seen him before, of course. In the sixties, he was everywhere: on the silent edge of gigantic crowds chanting against the Pentagon in Washington; tramping the streets of Haight-Ashbury in the flower summer; lurking near the sound trucks of Altamont, while the Rolling Stones began their dance of death. He was always silent and removed, as if ruled by sneering ironies. Once I even saw him in Saigon, on the wrong side of the river, in the Chinese joints where the deserters and hookers come to listen to Aretha Franklin records, or to ride the white horse of heroin. I have seen him too often in the upstairs squad rooms of police stations, waiting behind a wire fence, while a detective typed with two fingers on a battered Remington. His face was always different. The clothes always changed. He never used precisely the same language. But I always knew him: he was Rodion Raskolnikov.

Over one hundred years have now passed since Fedor Dostoevski came to the end of his life, and was returned to the Russian earth. But the city of his dark vision remains alive for all of us, peopled by the characters of his imagination. Prince Myshkin wanders that city searching for goodness; Stavrogin inhales the city's violence, trying to avoid "the final deception in an endless series of deceptions"; Fedor Karamazov is murdered every Saturday night, and the Grand Inquisitor mocks us from the shadows, in league with the underground man. Dostoevski made a city in which all of us continue to live.

In one sense, of course, that city was a literal one: the St. Petersburg that Dostoevski first saw in May 1837, when he arrived there with his brother Mikhail, to prepare for entrance to the Chief Engineering Academy, a military school that trained cadets for the Czar's army. This was

the capital city of all the Russias, but to the
16-year-old Fedor, drunk on literature, it was above all
the city made holy by the presence of Pushkin. Moving out
of his room overlooking the Fontanka Canal, he devoured
the city, making a daily reconnaissance of its streets,
seeing it through the filters of art: Racine and
Corneille, Balzac and Schiller. In St. Petersburg, when
Dostoevski is still only a boy, we begin to see the first
rough sketch of Prince Myshkin, the man "who is altogether
foreign." At eighteen, he wrote a letter to his brother
that stated with extraordinary certainty the goals he was
setting for himself: "Man is mystery. This mystery must
be solved, and even if you pass your entire life solving
it, do not say you have wasted your time. I occupy myself
with this mystery, since I want to be a man."

In August 1844, his mother long dead, his father
apparently murdered by his own serfs (the truth was never
discovered), Dostoevski passed his examinations with
honors and was supposed to enter the army full-time. He
decided instead to resign. He explained his reasons in
another letter to his brother: "I couldn't stand it
anymore. It disgusted me to waste the best years of my
life in this way. They wanted to send me to the provinces." And then, the key sentence: "For heaven's sake,
what would happen to me without St. Petersburg?"

What would have happened to all of us without that
St. Petersburg that lives on in the pages of Dostoevski?
A St. Petersburg that for more than a hundred years has
survived politics and war, revolution and invasion, Hitler
and Stalin, and even Constance Garnett? By choosing to
stay in the city, by choosing art, that young man decided
to speak directly to all of us, crossing all frontiers,
transcending all languages, defeating the inexorability of
time and death. He was to become, of course, one of the
most unpleasant men in the history of literature. His
rages, feuds, betrayals, obsessions, xenophobia are
familiar to most of us. Who would not prefer lunch with
the urbane Turgenev to a weekend with Dostoevski? But
forced to make a brutal choice, we would probably
surrender all of the finely-drawn modest art of Turgenev
in order to preserve only a portion of the volcanic
furies, the dark terrifying urban art of Dostoevski.

That art was shaped by St. Petersburg, by its marble
palaces and wooden slums, its hot dusty summer streets and
dank winter smells. Rats crawled from the city's canals
into sinister fogs. Horses often died in its muddy
streets, their bodies swelling until children used them as
ghastly trampolines. The only sidewalks were in the
network of boulevards around the Winter Palace, and there
were evil inns in the sidestreets where the vodka flowed,
prostitutes waited for their customers, and violence was
always on the menu.

This was a city that Dostoevski embraced with such
ferocious passion. Sometimes its violence was
self-inflicted; hardly a day went by without some fresh
body being dragged from the Neva. There was repression
too: the golden spire of the Peter and Paul Fortress
dominated the sky, simultaneously housing the bodies of

dead Czars and living political prisoners. It was a city
populated by a tiny ruling class of immense wealth, a
ragged bureaucracy, and the broad sullen mass of the poor.
In 1846, with publication of his first novel, Poor Folk,
Dostoevski claimed that city for himself; he continues to
own it today, as Dickens owns London, Balzac owns Paris,
and Raymond Chandler owns Los Angeles. Three years after
staking his literary claim, the Peter and Paul Fortress
claimed Fedor Mikhailovich himself. He was charged with
treason, for the terrible crimes of discussing with others
emancipation of the serfs, judicial reform, socialism, and
revolution. Russian rulers continue to fear words more
than almost any other nation on earth does.
     His death sentence, mock execution, and deportation
to Siberia are all familiar parts of the Dostoevski legend
now. But sometimes I think about him on that last night,
embarking on his terrible journey to the east. Ten-pound
weights were shackled to his ankles; the Cathedral bells
were tolling for Christmas. But Dostoevski must have been
most upset because he was leaving St. Petersburg, the
city, for the house of the dead. He was then 28 years
old. He was never again young.
     But in the stockade near Omsk, Dostoevski went to
graduate school as an artist. Deprived of literature, he
was forced to look at man. Most of his fellow prisoners
were common criminals, murderers, thieves. Others had
been jailed for their ideas. The crude democracy of penal
degradation forced them to look at each other with the
wary distrustful eye that was later to distinguish
Dostoevski from all of his literary contemporaries. From
his jailers, he began to truly understand the tyranny that
man is capable of when granted arbitrary power. From his
fellow prisoners, and himself, he began to understand
man's darkest instincts, particularly for murder.
     In a way, the basic ideas about man that permeate his
four greatest novels were most clearly stated in the
following passage from The House of the Dead, written
after Dostoevski had returned from Siberia to the city of
the living:

> A man is living quite calmly and peacefully. He
> has a hard life, but he is resigned to his fate.
> He may be a peasant, a domestic serf, a townsman
> or a soldier. Suddenly something gives way
> within him, and he plunges his knife into his
> oppressor or his enemy, and from that moment
> begins the strange part of the affair. Suddenly
> he goes beyond all measure. The first victim is
> his oppressor, the enemy, and the crime is
> perfectly understandable, because there is a
> demonstrable cause. But afterwards he goes on
> to kill others who are not his oppressors or his
> enemies, killing them indiscriminately for the
> pure pleasure of killing for an abusive word or
> an unpleasant look, or simply to make the number
> of his victims equal, or merely because someone
> is standing in his way.

He is now behaving like a drunken man, like
someone in delirium. It was as though he had
passed some fatal line, and was elated to
discover that nothing was sacred for him
anymore. Some inner urge causes him to break
all laws, defy all powers, and enjoy the
sensation of boundless freedom. He enjoys the
turmoil of his own heart and the terror he
inspires. He knows too, that a dreadful
punishment lies in store for him. His
sensations are like those of a man on a high
tower as he stares at the abyss yawning below,
and would be happy to hurl himself headlong if
only to hasten his end. Such things happen to
the most quiet and inconspicuous people. There
are some, of course, who dramatize themselves in
their delirium, and the more they were
downtrodden before, the more they bluster and
put on airs. They glory in the fear and
revulsion they inspire. They affect desperation
to the point where punishment comes as a relief
from the strain of keeping up the game. The
curious thing is that the excitement only lasts
until the moment when they are punished, as
though some unknown law measured the extent of
their exaltation. After that, the thread is
cut, and they become suddenly calm, limp,
drained of courage, and they implore pardon from
the people.

That vision of man going "beyond all measure" informs
Crime and Punishment and The Possessed, The Idiot, and The
Brothers Karamazov. But it also is part of the Son of Sam
story, the Hillside Strangler, the FLAN, Omega Seven; the
words could describe Stalin and Idi Amin; they could
explain why we went to Vietnam, and even how Richard
Nixon, enjoying "the sensation of boundless freedom,"
could have presided over the multiple crimes of Watergate.
Dostoevski was not, of course, a prophet. But his
life in exile taught him to look closely, at human beings,
and then to move even more deeply, into the scary regions
of the self. He often did not like what he found. When,
after ten years away, Dostoevski was allowed at last to
return to St. Petersburg, he was a different man: a
fawning monarchist, a political conservative, a believer
in orthodox religion. He had also suffered the epileptic
seizures that would plague him for the rest of his life,
and had married Mariya Dmitrievna Isayeva, a tubercular
widow with one son. Said biographer Ronald Hingley of
Mariya: "Seductive to him as an object for pity, she was
doubly so through her perverse temperament. This might
have repelled another man, but he was overjoyed to find so
accomplished a sufferer and purveyor of suffering."
Mariya was as much a part of his postgraduate studies as
jail and exile. The man Dostoevski was now fully formed;
the artist, stained with dark knowledge, had just begun to
live.

When Dostoevski made his first trip to Europe in 1862, he was alone, his talent for hatred at full maturity. He might be the only writer in recorded history to have loathed Paris. Certainly he hated the French, their materialism, the narcissism of French women, their obsession with money and style and fashion. His misery and melancholy seem to have been relieved only by a trip to the Pantheon, where he roared with laughter, pointing out to a guide that Voltaire once had called Rousseau a liar, and Rousseau had called Voltaire an imbecile, and here they were at the end, lying in honor, side by side.

If Paris was silly and decadent, London appealed to his love of the demonic. In one sense, he was literature's police reporter, and the beat was purgatory. His description of London, full of sardonic praise, easily could apply to sections of the American city today: "In the presence of such majesty, of the far-ranging pride of the sovereign spirit, of the triumphant perfection of the creations brought into being by that spirit, even the thirsting soul must find itself terrified: it humbles itself, and submits, and seeks salvation in gin and debauchery, and believes that everything is for the best."

Everything is for the best: the coda of modern urban fatalism. How I wish that he had somehow managed to see Boss Tweed's New York, when I read him about London:

How different it is from Paris in all outward respects! A city as unfathomable as the seas, never-resting by day and night; the roar and pandemonium of machines; the railroads running above the houses (and soon they will be running under them); that spirit of bold enterprise; the apparent disorder which is actually the highest kind of bourgeois order; the polluted Thames; the air saturated with coal dust; the splendid gardens and parks; those sinister places like Whitechapel with its half-naked, savage and hungry people; a city populated by millions with a commerce stretching across the world. . . . .

For a few years, Dostoevski circled his subject matter, feinting and experimenting, writing thousand words of journalism, comparing all of the world to St. Petersburg and finding it lacking. He gambled too much; he humiliated himself, scrounging for money; he fell into a disastrous love affair with Appollinariya Suslova. And then, back home in his own city, he fell back, regrouped, and then in the spring of 1864, he plunged into the dark night of his own soul, and ours. He began to write Notes from Underground.

"Established by his early 40s as a writer notable and original indeed, yet still of the second rank," writes Hingley, Dostoevski pivoted on Notes from Underground to become the supreme master that we know."

A month after the birth of the underground man, his wife Mariya died of tuberculosis. In the letter, he said of this unhappy marriage: "She and I were decidedly unhappy together owing to her weird, pernickety and

pathologically fantastic character. But we could not stop
loving each other. The unhappier we were, actually, the
more attached we became to each other." With her death,
Dostoevski ostensibly was free, but he was not happy.
City men almost never are.

In a way, happiness, serenity, bourgeois safety were
no longer important; the wedding of experience, thought,
technique that makes a great artist had taken place. The
great work began to flow. It is with us still.

Dostoevski did not, of course, use words like an
engraver's tool, delineating every detail of the world he
presented to us. His technique was at once less precise
and more powerful. His characters for example, are almost
never drawn specifically as are those of Dickens; he tells
us they are fair or dark, or young or aging, short, tall,
but very little more. As a result, the reader must take
part in the act of creation. Dostoevski's light resembles
that of Rembrandt: glancing in direct, casting thick
impasto shadows, but seeming to smolder with a mysterious
inner glow. We never see the bucolic open landscapes of
Turgenev, the vast historical spaces of Tolstoi; when we
follow Dostoevski, we seem always to be in cramped rooms,
devoid of furniture, standing in badly-lit hallways,
waiting in seedy ginmills, or hurrying along the Nevsky
Prospect. We see people in rags, but not very specific
rags; he forces us to look at human beings one at a time,
but usually he only reveals their eyes to us, as if their
eyes were windows through which we might glimpse their
souls.

These people move in a cityscape as bare as a play by
Pinter or Beckett: high walls, a river, a police station,
a dark cold room at the top of stairs. There are no
Zolaesque catalogs of the objects of the reportable world,
no excursions into history. Dostoevski's city seems to
exist in a dream, and Arkady, in A Raw Youth, saw it
exactly that way: "And often I am haunted by another
question, which is utterly senseless: Here everything is
flitting to and fro, but how can one tell, perhaps it is
someone's dream, and there is not one real person here,
nor one real action. Someone who is dreaming all this
will suddenly wake up--and everything will suddenly
disappear."

Dostoevski loved the moment of dusk, which is a
fearful hour in many cities; the day dies, and the
night--that little death--envelops the world. That moment
when everything suddently disappears was most lovingly
described in Dostoevski's short story, The Faint Heart;

It was already dusk when Arkady returned home.
As he approached the Neva he stood still for a
minute and turned a keen glance down the river
into the smokey distance, hazy with frost,
suddenly flushed with the last crimson glow of
the blood-red sun, slowly sinking on the misty
horizon. Night lay over the city, and the vast
expanse of the Neva boundless, and swollen with
frozen snow-shone in the last gleams of the sun
with myriads of sparks form the silver needles

of hoarfrost. The temperature had fallen to
twenty below zero. Clouds of frozen steam rose
from the hard-driven horses and pedestrians
hurrying along the streets. The thin air
quivered with the slightest sound, and columns
of smoke rose up like giants from all the roofs
on both sides of the river, and they streamed
upwards into the cold sky, twining and untwining
as they soared, so that it seemed that new
buildings were rising above the old, and a new
city was taking shape in the air. In this hour
of twilight it seemed that all this world with
all its inhabitants, the strong and the weak,
with all their habitations, the hovels of the
poor and the gilded palaces which are the solace
of the powerful in this world, was like a
phantasm, magical and illusory, a dream which
vanishes in a moment and fades away like smoke
in the dark blue sky."

What is always clear in this city of Dostoevski is
the strange and erratic movements of the human heart. He
could be described, in a way, as the inventor of a cinema
of the psyche: he shows us a long shot, he comes closer
with a medium shot, he ends up in the tightest, most
agonizing of close-ups. Along the way, we are lifted,
dropped, and hurled about. Over and over again, as
readers (and participants in the imagining of the novel)
we are placed in a state of delirium. Hunger puts in
delirium, or drink, or passion, or guilt. And when we
call for help, when we reach out for something concrete
and stable, all we find is the bridge, the police station,
the dark room at the top of the stairs.
    In that spare city, and in ours, the dominant
emotions are pity and terror. Dark humor moves through
much of Dostoevski, of course; the undergroud man cackles
at the absurdity of humanity, at all belief in utopian
abstractions, at ambition, at human folly. But the
driving engine of these urban novels is terror. Men are
in flight. Men are pursued. Demons swarm through their
night thoughts, and there is no place of refuge. The
protagonists are of the city, but separated from it too.
In Notes from Underground, St. Petersburg is described as
"the most abstract, the most deviously-minded city on this
terrestial sphere of ours." But it is one concrete
reality of that city that sends the narrator off on his
voyage. Specifically, the weather: "It is snowing just
now, in wet, dingy, swirling flakes. It was snowing
yesterday too, and the day before as well. I think it was
the sleet that reminded me of the incident that now
refuses to leave me alone. So let this be a story apropos
of the falling sleet."
    Sleet is always falling in the hearts of Dostoevski's
city dwellers. In the century since he placed them on
stage, they have been claimed by Marxists and
existentialists, reactionaries and religious fanatics,
Freudians and Jungians but Dostoevski saw them in his own
special way. In the notebooks for A Raw Youth he wrote:

"I alone have evoked the tragic condition of the
underground man, the tragedy of his sufferings, of his
self-punishment, of his aspirations towards the ideal and
his incapacity to attain it; I alone have evoked the lucid
insight these wretched beings possess into the fatality of
their condition, a fatality such that it would be useless
to react against it."

Even in The Idiot, Dostoevski's great novel of
redemption, there is a brooding sense that nothing can be
done about that fatal destiny. When action is taken, it
is almost always extreme. In a way, the most
extraordinary of all Dostoevski characters was Joseph
Stalin. When I read of Stalin's bloody crimes, I always
think of that speech of Prince Myshkin, in which he
assails the Russians for acting out thoughts which would
be confined to art or philosophy in the West: "If one of
us becomes a Catholic, he is bound to become a Jesuit, and
one of the most subterranean. If one of us becomes an
atheist, he is bound to demand the uprooting of faith in
God by force, that is, of course, by the sword!... And our
people don't simply become atheists, they infallibly
believe in atheism."

Dostoevski recognized the extremism of his fellow
citizens because he also found it in himself. In one
letter, he wrote: "Everywhere and in everything, I go to
the ultimate limit. All my life I have crossed beyond the
frontier."

Perhaps that is why his fiction remains so fresh and
relevant in our century, a hundred years after his death,
and most particularly to Americans. We are a wild and
bloody country, afflicted now with such deep brooding
fatalism that the shooting of a President is a story that
lasts three days in the newspapers, evoking man's sighs of
helplessness from those leaders who could take steps to
prevent such actions in the future. As Americans, we live
in extremes, repeatedly crossing our own psychic
frontiers. In a way, the underground man is a brother of
Ralph Ellison's Invisible Man: existing on the margin,
seeing power and ambition more clearly than the men who
are driven by them, his separation itself an act of
extremism. Our cities are full of Raskolnikovs; murder is
our basic subject, our tabloids overflowing with those
lurid melodramas that so obsessed Dostoevski and which he
transformed into such high and durable art.

Who can recall of the Atlanta murders without
remembering the words of Ivan Karamazov, in his mighty
challenge ot the alleged harmonies of God: "Listen! If
all must suffer to pay for the eternal harmony, what have
children to do with it, tell me, please?"

He recites a catalog of atrocities against children
that could have come from any American newspaper, and then
says:

    They must be atoned for, or there can be no
    harmony. But how? How are you going to atone
    for them? Is it possible? By their being
    avenged? But what do I care for avenging them?
    What do I care for a hell of oppressors? What

good can hell do, since those children have
already been tortured? And what becomes of
harmony, if there is hell? I want to forgive.
I want to embrace. I don't want more suffering.
And if the sufferings of children go to swell
the sum of sufferings which was necessary to pay
for truth, then, I protest that the truth is not
worth such a price.

Such words echoed around Atlanta each time another
child was dragged from a river. They apply equally to all
the children of this century who ended up waiting on lines
in Dachau and Auschwitz, all those we saw running on roads
in Vietnam, with the napalm still burning on their flesh,
all those who were taken by the lunatics of Cambodia to
die in the hills of the new Kampuchean paradise. "What
good can hell do, since these children have already been
tortured?" There are some who have glibly dismissed
Dostoevski as an iron reactionary. But we know this about
him: he would not have spent a second of his life drawing
up lists of names to be sent to the gallows, the gas
chambers, or the boneheaps of history. Ivan Karamazov no
longer believes in God, but he does believe in life.
Sometimes against the best--or worst--evidence. "I live,"
he says, "in spite of logic."
    Later, he expands on that theme: "If I no longer had
any faith in life, if I doubted a woman I loved, or the
universal order of things, if I were persuaded, on the
contrary, that everything was only an infernal and
accursed chaos--even then I would want to live."
    Today Dostoevski lives. I wish his work was read
more widely in the fantastic cities in which all of us now
live. I hope that his art does not end up as part of a
literary museum, tended by scholars and curators. Most of
all, I wish that the great novels could be absorbed and
experienced by all those American children who have grown
numb with the banalities of television. Dostoevski gave
us himself, as all great artists do. But he also showed
his readers their own darkest places--I saw Raskolnikov
the other night. I see him each time I glance in a
mirror.

Part I

Textual and Conceptual Interpretations

2.
The Legend of the Grand Inquisitor: The Death Struggle of Ideologies

THELMA Z. LAVINE

The Legend of the Grand Inquisitor, which appears as
Chapter Five of Book Five of The Brothers Karamazov, is
now 100 years old. It has become a kind of icon, in some
respects similar to the icons of the Eastern Orthodox
church, those richly symbolic and evocative portrayals,
painted or enameled in vivid colors, of sacred persons and
objects. An icon presents a unique clustering of symbols,
images, and representations; the icon which is constituted
by the Legend of the Grand Inquisitor is just such a
configuration of awesome personages, symbols, and
representations and it burns as brightly now as it did one
hundred years ago.
     When late in the night the Inquisitor goes to the
prison cell where Christ has been taken, he asks, "Is it
Thou? . . . Why . . . art Thou come to hinder us? . . .
Tomorrow I shall condemn Thee and burn Thee at the stake
as the worst of heretics." And then there ensues that
famous dialogue in which the Inquisitor points out that
Christ's kingdom--the kingdom that He intended--has been
destroyed, of course, and that He is responsible for that.
He is responsible because He insisted that He came to make
men free. He gave them a terrible gift in that freedom
because human beings are naturally rebels, weak and
sinful, and His offer of freedom in place of the ancient,
rigid laws, had created havoc among them. Moreover, says
the Inquisitor, what human beings want is not freedom but
bread: "In the end they will lay their freedom at our
feet, and say to us, 'Make us your slaves, but feed us.'
They will understand themselves, at last, that freedom and
bread enough for all are inconceivable together. . . ."(1)
In ages to come, the Inquisitor continues, in dreadful
prophecy of what is indeed to come, humanity will cry out
from the lips of their sages that "there is no crime, and
therefore no sin; there is only hunger."(2) (In the age
to come of the mid-twentieth century Jean-Paul Sartre, the
reigning intellectual of France, existentialist and
Marxist, proclaimed these words of the Grand Inquisitor
and also their corollary, invoked from Bertolt Brecht:
"Feed men and then ask of them virtue!"(3))
     The Inquisitor admonished Christ that where His
church stood, one day the Tower of Babel will be built:

> Freedom, free thought and science will lead them
> to such straights and will bring them face to
> face with such marvels and insoluble mysteries
> that some of them, the fierce and rebellious,
> will destroy themselves; others, rebellious but
> weak, will destroy one another, while the rest,
> weak and unhappy, will crawl fawning to our feet
> and whine to us: 'Yes, you were right, you
> alone possess His mystery, and we come back to
> you, save us from ourselves.(4)

What we propose to do, the Inquisitor announces, is to
feed the sinful millions who seek only bread, and to do
so falsely in Christ's name. They will marvel at us as
gods, they will be happy when they are led like sheep.
You, Christ, he says, rejected the three powers that could
bind men forever: miracles, mystery, and authority. But
we have founded our rule upon them. We are not working
with you but with the Anti-Christ:

> We shall triumph and be Caesars and plan the
> universal happiness of man . . . all that man
> seeks on earth: someone to keep his conscience,
> and some means of uniting all in one unanimous
> and harmonious ant heap. . . .(5)

> Too, too well they know the value of complete
> submission! And until men know that, they will
> be unhappy. Who is most to blame for their not
> knowing it, speak? . . . But the flock will come
> together again and will submit once more, and
> then it will be once for all.(6)

> What I say to Thee will come to pass, and our
> domain will be built up. . . . If anyone has
> ever deserved our fires, it is Thou. Tomorrow I
> shall burn Thee.(7)

The Inquisitor ended his terrifying speech: "Dixi," I
have spoken. but when in reply Christ softly kissed him
on the lips, the Inquisitor shuddered, opened the door,
and said "Go, and come no more. . . .Come not at all,
never, never!"
     This fearful legend is a prophetic vision. It is the
vision of an ant heap which is a demonized,
pseudo-Christian socialism. The vision incorporates and
synthesizes two themes. One is the theme of Old and New
Testament apocalypse,(8) the concept of the approach of
the Last Days in great horrors prior to a reversal and a
culmination in a Day of Light; the greatest miseries,
catastrophies, and degradations of human beings will be
endured before the coming of the Messiah, the New
Jerusalem, the End of Days, and the Last Judgment.
Incorporated also in the vision and synthesized with the
apocalyptic theme is the theme of communism, specifically,
the conception that the New Jerusalem will appear in the
form of communism, and its characteristic materialism,
mechanization, bureaucratization, and despiritualization.

And thus the vision is a prophecy of the ideology of what
has become one of the greatest mass movements in history,
namely the ideology of Marxism, embraced by the communist
movement. It was Marxism that indeed commanded the power
of this stupendous vision and combined the force of its
two elements: Biblical apocalypse and communism. The
Biblical mythos of great battles waged by the Saints of
God against a series of corrupt earthly empires is
appropriated by Marx and invested with communist symbols:
the great battles are the Marxist class conflicts which
have led to the overturning of the historical and
necessary series of unjust economic modes of production.
With the last revolution at hand, the proletariat, the new
Saints of God, will overturn capitalism and bring an end
to worldly injustice by equalizing bread for all. For
this, the price will be the surrender of freedom to a
dictatorship in the name of the proleteriat, which will
eventuate post-historically into a New Jerusalem for a new
Adam, a species-man who will have no need for spiritual
freedom. One hundred years ago Dostoevski perceived that
the key to the appeal of Marxism among Christian peoples
is that Marxist symbolism presents communist revolution
(with its loss of spiritual and political freedom, and its
enforced submission to a secular, materialistic
dictatorship) as a righteous Judeo-Christian apocalypse,
the work of the modern Saints of God.

We must raise at this point the question: How was
Dostoevski able to develop and express this prophetic
vision? How did he arrive at this? In part, it was that
he had come to perceive the revolutionary potential of
Hegelianism, and of developing socialist theories,
including Marxism, and to identify them as distorted and
intellectualized forms of Christianity. As a young
successful author, he had assimilated socialist theory
from those extraordinary Russians who initiated the
Russian intellectual culture into the growing socialist
movement of the West. He had ties to these innovators,
among whom were Alexander Herzen, Mikhail Bakunin,
Vissarion Belinski and various other followers of the
German Young Hegelians and of the French socialists.(9)
In 1847 at the age of twenty-six, Dostoevski began to
attend the meetings of the "Petrashevsky Circle," a group
whose members were studying the forbidden books from the
West--especially the French socialists and left-wing
Hegelians. The Petrashevsky Circle was itself swept up in
the excited effort of Russian intellectuals to grasp
left-Hegelianism and French socialism, to interpret their
applicability to the Russian scene. For consorting with
this illegal revolutionary group, Dostoevski paid with
nine years of his life in dehumanizing confinement in the
penal colony of Omsk, in Siberia.

The effect of these years of brutalization upon
Dostoevski was a conversion. Whereas Bakunin's
imprisonment in the Fortress of Peter and Paul intensified
his radicalism, the conversion of Dostoevski was away from
socialism, away from the Petrashevsky Circle, and in
particular away from Vissarion Belinsky who in memory
became the one clear embodiment of what Dostoevski now

regarded as the manifold evil of the West.(10) The
intuitive genius of Dostoevski probed the powerful appeal
which this Western evil, the form of Hegelian and
socialist thought, held for the radical circles at the
University of Moscow and in St. Petersburg.

In the East, rather than in the industrialized West,
in Russia itself, which had never gone beyond feudal
autocracy and theocracy, the theocratic and autocratic
central power of the Czar--here, Dostoevski saw, there was
fertile territory for the spread of the new theocracy and
centralized power of communism. Here in Russia, there was
misery that was ripe for revolution, for the redress of
centuries of bitter grievances. Ideologically, Russia was
in a state of slave mentality primed for revolt against
the old feudal masters in a seemingly Christian
apocalypse,(11) and primed for the acceptance of new
masters in a socialist apocalypse. Had Marx been more of
a psychologist and less committed to economic explanations
of human phenomena, he would not have predicted falsely
that the development of dictatorial communism would take
place in the industrialized West with its liberal
traditions of democracy, individualism, and due process;
he would instead have predicted that the development of
communism would take place, as it did, in the feudal East,
where the traditional legitimations of Czarist theocratic
authority were available for transfer to the absolute
authority of the Communist Party. It was Dostoevski who
discovered the conceptual and structural affinity of the
theocratic autocracy of traditional Russia and the
pseudo-theocratic centralized power of communism, as well
as the affinity between Christian and communist
apocalypticism.(12) And, thus, we can understand how
Dostoevski was able to originate the conception of a new
politics that was to appear within Russia herself. The
Legend of the Grand Inquisitor provides for us his fearful
prophecy of a new dictatorial politics and a new
pseudo-Christian salvation which was to become the reality
of twentieth century Russian communism.

Specifically with respect to the Russian climate of
opinion in which Dostoevski wrote, the prophetic new
politics synthesizes the conflicting ideals of the
Slavophiles and the Westernizers with regard to the
destiny of Russia. It incorporates the Slavophiles'
intense love for the Russian people and their historic
culture, and also the Slavophile cult of nationalism,
spiritual unity, and solidarity against the world. And it
includes the concept of salvation through great bloodshed,
crime, and suffering, even to the killings of thousands,
in order that the final apocalpyse would come. These
Slavophile themes are combined in the Legend of the Grand
Inquisitor with the themes of the Westernizers: the
fascination with Western philosophical skepticism; with
Western science, technology, industrialization, and
organization; and with the theory of socialist apocalypse
which will provide what is needed in Russia: bread in
place of spirit.

The conflict between the Slavophiles and the
Westernizers is a personal conflict "writ large," it is

the struggle between the two sides of Ivan Karamazov's warring self--between his Slavophile orthodox Christian nationalism and his hankering after Western science, skepticism, and socialism. And the new politics and the new conception of universal salvation which the Legend of the Grand Inquisitor presents are Ivan's attempt to find a reconciliation for this personal and cultural conflict. But the politics of salvation through an Anti-Christ is too horrible for Ivan to accept and when his brother, Alesha, pales at hearing the Legend, Ivan seeks to comfort him and says it is all nonsense. "It's only a senseless poem of a senseless student. . . ." And Alesha says, "With such a hell in your heart and head, how can you [live?]"(13) The answer is, of course, that he cannot--he escapes from life by madness. In Ivan Karamazov's legend, Dostoevski has presented the notion of the future dominion of Anti-Christ which will use pseudo-Christian symbolism to organize humanity until the end of days in a communist totalitarian rule to satisfy the brute needs of all for bread.

There is one remaining question for us: Where, in this prophetic myth, is the ideology of the West? We have before us the formidable, burning symbolism of the icon of the Legend of the Grand Inquisitor which presents the synthesis of Christian apocalypticism and communism. Where then is the ideology of the Western world in the icon of the Grand Inquisitor? The answer is that Dostoevski has assimilated Western politics into the prophetic new politics of the legend, and he perceives Western politics only through the distorting lens of his synthesis of communist and Christian apocalyptic. More specifically, Dostoevski presents two ideologies. One is a demonized Christian communism--the demonic ideology envisioned in the legend. Although demonic, nevertheless, this ideology still exists within an apocalyptic framework. It expresses the politics of the Anti-Christ, but it is the Anti-Christ as the evil that finally will yield to a higher good: the Second Coming and the Last Judgment. In Dostoevski's legend, this demonized Christian socialism thus enjoys a position superior to the ideology which Dostoevski concedes to the politics of the West.

The politics of the West, Western Liberalism, is the second ideology he presents, and it is for Dostoevski a demonized ideology in two ways. It is demonized intellectually as prideful humanism, skepticism, negativity, corrosion of the sacred beliefs of Christianity, atheism, nihilism, anarchism, and the death of the spirit. It is demonized institutionally as the domain of materialistic, secularistic science, technology, bureaucratic organization and social engineering. As far as the first, the intellectual-philosophical aspect of the politics of the West is concerned, it is, he points out, weak and ineffectual, without power or spirit. It is corrosive of all beliefs, not exclusively of the beliefs of Christian orthodoxy. It makes no substantive contribution; it is merely Euclidian understanding. Western liberalism offers no home for the human spirit; it

fails to see the spiritual dimension of mankind; it is the
death of the spirit. As for the second aspect of
Dostoevski's demonizing of liberalism, in terms of its
dominant institutions--materialistic science, technology,
massive industrialization and bureaucratic organi-
zation--in this demonized component of Western liberalism,
the West does indeed have power. It has the power of
science, technology, organization, bureaucracy to exercise
control over man and nature. But, here, where he concedes
that Western liberalism has power, Dostoevski views this
power as in fact assimilated by demonized Christian
communism. It is Marxism that indeed takes over from the
demon world of capitalism all of its science, its
technology, its organizational power, its bureaucratic
structure, its power to control and marshal nature and
human life. And, thus, where Western liberalism has power
this power is assimilated by Dostoevski into his view of
Marxism as demonized Christian socialism. Where he
perceives liberalism to have no power, he scorns it as a
pernicious mode of despiritualization.

Dostoevski's treatment of Western liberalism
indicates that in a spiritual sense, Dostoevski lived
still in the penal colony of Omsk. He does not see that
Western liberalism is an ideology that provides a way out
of the master-slave relation in which he views all
politics. What he does not see is that liberalism as an
ideology transcends the notion that all ideology or
politics is that of the ascendancy of the master or the
slave. Western liberalism grounds itself upon a hard-won
development of principles for politics, that will permit
the escape from the choice that Dostoevski leaves us: the
choice between infantile dependency upon some form of
authority or infantile rebellion against it. What
liberalism permits for the human race is to escape from
the master-slave, domination-rebellion syndrome, into a
founding of politics upon universal principles that will
appeal universally to human intuitive reason. What
liberalism provides is precisely the hard-earned, bitterly
learned political principles of human freedom: the
superordination of the individual to the state; democracy;
egalitarianism; the inalienability of human rights; par-
liamentary procedure; due process of law. These
principles are derived from a sober yet modestly trusting
view of human nature, and the "natural light" of its
reason and its capacity for reasonableness in coping with
the passions. And these Enlightenment principles, forged
and fought for by Western liberalism, constitute the only
shelter for human freedom which human efforts at
government have ever constructed.(14)

However, Dostoevski perceives none of this.
Dostoevski comprehends all principles of politics and law
in the tradition in which Hegel and Marx have understood
them--namely, by way of assimilating the principles of
morality and politics to will, to the will of the master,
or of God, the King, the Czar, the nation, or a selected
social or political group. Thus, for Dostoevski, as for
the long tradition of voluntarism of which Hegel and Marx
are our greatest examples, the ground of truth is the will

of a master. So it is, as Dostoevski portentously says,
that if God does not exist, everything is permitted
because the only ground of moral truth is God's will that
it be true. And if God's will does not command, there
results self-will, rebellion, and finally nihilism. But
in opposition to the conception that refers all moral and
political truths to the will of some master, there stands
the oldest tradition of Western rationalism, which appears
in the Euthyphro, one of the earliest dialogues of the
philosopher Plato, where the question is asked: Is the
moral law moral because the gods command it or do the gods
command it because it is moral? And the clear answer is
that indeed the moral law is commanded by the gods because
it is intrinsically moral. From Athens to Jerusalem the
answer is the same. In the Judeo-Christian tradition the
moral laws are accepted both as the will of God and as
intrinsic in their moral truth.
     There is clearly a need for the contemporary
intellectual culture to rescue the demonized, distorted
version of Western liberalism from the icon of the Legend
of the Grand Inquisitor and from Marxist ideology. There
is a need at the present time to recognize the principles
of Western liberalism as providing the substantive truths
and practical shelter on behalf of human freedom which
constitute the Westen political heritage. One of the
limitations of Western liberalism as an ideology of
universal principles is that it does not foster the making
of icons of sacred personages and objects. Nevertheless,
as the highest achievement of the human struggle for
freedom the universal principles of Western liberalism are
sacred to humanity and command our devotion and reverence.
The configuration of these principles of freedom forms an
icon which burns as brightly now as it did three hundred
years ago at the beginning of the Age of Enlightenment.

CONCLUSION

     1. The Legend of the Grand Inquisitor has become an
icon. It reveals a prophetic vision of a Marxist Russia,
as a synthesis of Christian apocalypse with communist
dialectical materialism.
     2. It was the intuitive genius of Dostoevski which
discovered the isomorphism of Christian and Marxist
apocalypse, in which the proletariat is legitimated as the
modern Saints of God, destroying the Babylon of
capitalism, and ushering in the New Jerusalem of the
Dictatorship of the Proletariat and of a post-historical
World to Come. With insight into this isomorphism,
Dostoevski was able further to predict the appeal of
communism to the slave mentality prevailing in feudal,
agrarian Russia, rather than to the industrialized and
democratized West, as Marx had falsely predicted.
     3. The presentation of the conflict between
Slavophiles and Westernizers, which Ivan Karamazov has
internalized, reflects Dostoevski's distortion of the
ideology of the West. Dostoevski demonizes Western
liberalism as itself spiritually weak, and as perniciously
delegitimating spiritual beliefs and values; its strength

is confined to its technological and bureaucratic mechanisms of control over nature and human life--a strength which demonized communism takes over from demonized capitalism. Dostoevski distorts Western liberalism by viewing it in the Hegelian-Marxian tradition in which all politics expresses the master-slave relation, as the choice between submission to authority or rebellion against it. Dostoevski does not see that Western liberalism, through its principles of individualism and democracy, inalienable human rights and due process of law, provides an escape from the master-slave relation and a shelter for human freedom. Moreover, Dostoevski distorts Western liberalism by grounding truth also in the master-slave relation. But if truth is the will of the master, and if the will of God, as the ultimate master, is not acknowledged as establishing truth by Western liberalism, then there is no truth, according to Dostoevski; "everything is permitted," and the world is plunged into rebellion and nihilism. Dostoevski does not see that Western liberalism provides liberation from truth as willed by any master (God, class, or nation): Western liberalism derives from the oldest tradition of Western rationalism in Plato's claim that the moral law is moral, not because it is commanded by the gods but because it has intrinsic, knowable moral truth.

4. The rescue of Western liberalism from its distorted and demonized version in the icon of the Legend of the Grand Inquisitor leads to the perception that the configuration of the universal principles of Western liberalism, which are the highest achievement of the human struggle for freedom, form an icon which has been revered since the beginning of the Age of Enlightenment.

NOTES

1. Fyodor Dostoevski, The Brothers Karamazov, trans. Constance Garnett (New York: Modern Library, 1950), Book V, Chapter V, p. 300.

2. Ibid.

3. "But I discovered suddenly that alienation, exploitation of man by man, under-nourishment, relegated to the background metaphysical evil which is a luxury. Hunger is an evil: period . . . I believe, I desire, that social and economic ills may be remedied. With a little luck that epoch may arrive. I am on the side of those who think that things will go better when the world has changed." Jean-Paul Sartre, Encounter, June 1964, pp. 61-62. See also Sartre, unpublished notes, quoted in Simone de Beauvoir, La Force des Choses (Paris: Gallimard, 1963), p. 218: "This year [1949] Sartre abandoned his morality properly so-called, because he became convinced that a moral attitude appears when technical and social conditions make a positive behavior impossible. Morality is an ensemble of idealistic tricks which help you to live in the way the lack of resources and techniques compels you to live."

4. Dostoevski, <u>Brothers Karamazov</u>, pp. 306-307.

5. Ibid., 305-306.

6. Ibid., 307.

7. Ibid., 309.

8. Dan., 7; Rev. 13, 19, 20, and 21. See also, Norman Cohn, "Jewish and Early Christian Apocalyptic," in <u>The Pursuit of the Millennium</u> (New York: Harper and Row, 1961), pp. 1-13.

9. See Martin Malia, <u>Alexander Herzen and the Birth of Russian Socialism</u> (Cambridge, Mass.: Harvard University Press, 1961; reprint New York: Grosset and Dunlap, 1971), Chapter X, XII, XIII. See also Joseph Frank, "Belinsky and Dostoevsky," in <u>Dostoevsky: The Seeds of Revolt 1821-1849</u> (Princeton N.J.: Princeton University Press, 1976).

10. "I insulted Belinsky more as a phenomenon of Russian life than as a personality." <u>Pisma</u> 2 (May 1871); 364. Cited in Joseph Frank, "Belinsky and Dostoevski," p. 183. See Victor Terras, <u>Belinsky and Russian Literary Criticism: The Heritage of Organic Aesthetics</u> (Madison: University of Wisconsin Press, 1974), Chapter 3, especially pp. 59-76; Chapter 4, especially pp. 91-126; Chapter 7, especially pp. 222-226.

11. Cf. Ellis Sandoz, "The Legend as Political Apocalypse," in <u>Political Apocalypse: A Study of Dostoevsky's Grand Inquisitor</u> (Baton Rouge: Louisiana State University Press, 1971), pp. 75-100.

12. See Irving Howe, "Dostoevsky: The Politics of Salvation," in Rene Welleck, ed., <u>Dostoevsky: A Collection of Critical Essays</u>. (Englewood Cliffs: Prentice-Hall, 1962), p. 56: "He [Dostoevski] 'translated' the political radicalism of the 1840s . . . into Christian terms. . . ." But it is important to note that whereas Feuerbach "translated" Hegel into Christian terms, and Marx "translated" Hegel into economic terms, Dostoevski penetrates to the isomorphic logic which makes the translation he performs possible.

13. Dostoevski, <u>The Brothers Karamazov</u>, Book V, Chapter V, p. 312.

14. See, Barrington Moore, <u>Reflections on the Causes of Human Misery</u> (Boston: Beacon Press, 1970), pp. 192-193.

3.
Murder and Suicide in *The Brothers Karamazov*: The Double Rebellion of Pavel Smerdiakov

N. NORMAN SHNEIDMAN

Pavel Smerdiakov, the illegitimate son of Fedor, is often considered a secondary character in The Brothers Karamazov. Yet much of the tragic tension, the intrigue and suspense in the novel are generated by his actions. Smerdiakov is a man of few words, but his actions, abrupt and extreme, propel the movement of the plot.

Dostoevski describes Smerdiakov's traits of character at great length, yet the real Smerdiakov eludes us. Dostoevski compares Smerdiakov with the little peasant in Kramskoi's remarkable picture, "The Contemplator." Smerdiakov could stop dead any place, any time, and contemplate something no one could fathom. He would keep his accumulating sensations and impressions hidden from outsiders, even from himself. But these perceptions which were the product of his psychological make up and of his life experience, penetrated his subconscious and guided, at times, his actions and movements.

Smerdiakov, the son of Fedor and the idiot-girl Lizaveta Smerdiashchaia, was brought up by Karamazov's servants Grigorii and Marfa. He was by now a young man of twenty-four in the service of Fedor Karamazov who sent him to Moscow to be trained as a cook. Smerdiakov was extraordinarily unsociable, taciturn, and secretive. He had a supercilious character and seemed to despise everyone. He was vain, vindictive, and could never forget or forgive an insult. He was an epileptic and he exhibited an inborn disposition to sadism. As a boy he was fond of hanging cats and burying them with ceremony. Later in his life he taught the little Iliusha Snegirov a beastly trick, to take a piece of soft bread, stick a pin into it, and throw it to some stray dog and then watch for what would happen.

Smerdiakov hated all those who reminded him of his origin and he rebelled against his own birth. He once told Grigorii that he would let himself "be killed in the womb rather than come into the world at all."(1) Smerdiakov was always aware of the fact that he was an offspring of the Karamazov kin, but since he was an illegitimate child he belonged to a lower social stratum than his brothers, whom he treated with hidden disdain. One of Smerdiakov's prime concerns was the task of running away from himself. He had a high opinion of himself with

exaggerated aspirations and expectations from life. He
was sly and mean, sure that once people fail to recognize
his social background, he could advance in society and
assume the place that was due to him. He dreamed of
opening a cafe-restaurant in Moscow, but even then, deep
in his heart, he was afraid that his Skotoprigonevsk fame
will follow him. It appears that old Russia was too small
for him and that there was no place to which Smerdiakov
could escape from his past. He hated Russia and despaired
that the French did not conquer it in 1812. He said: "A
clever nation. . . would have conquered a stupid one and
annexed it. Things would have been different then."(2)

The image of Smerdiakov's mother, Lizaveta
Smerdiashchaia, appears first in the drafts to A Raw
Youth.(3) At the early stages of Dostoevski's work on The
Brothers Karamazov, as long as Ivan is still referred to
as "the killer," Smerdiakov's name is not mentioned. His
name appears for the first time in the drafts when it is
inserted next to a notation: "He struck with a knife,"(4)
an ominous foreboding which points to Smerdiakov's later
role as a parricide. The name Smerdiakov has been
selected for the illegitimate child by Fedor Karamazov
himself. This name foreshadows, in a way, the future
relationship between father and son, because it points to
the father's contempt for his son, a fact never forgotten
or forgiven by Smerdiakov. The origin and the meaning of
the name Smerdiakov reflect also on the negative ethical
and psychological qualities of Smerdiakov's character
which are to develop fully in the course of his
relationship with his father and brothers.

It is evident that Smerdiakov lives in a state of
constant inner rebellion against, what N.M. Chirkov calls,
his "source of life."(5) He despises and feels no moral
ties with his father, nor does he identify with his
brothers. He is an outcast and a coward doomed to
vegetate in Skotoprigonevsk. The spark which turns
Smerdiakov's passive inner rebellion into an act of
murderous aggression is ignited by his sudden ethical and
spiritual identification with his half-brother Ivan.
Smerdiakov accepts fully Ivan's atheistic philosophy of
life, merging the latter's ideas with his own bloodthirsty
intentions.

The psychological make up of Smerdiakov's character
is such that he is capable of any action without
experiencing any pangs of conscience. Until he identifies
completely with his spiritual brother, Ivan, Smerdiakov
seems apathetic and resigned to his fate. Ivan's
proposition that if there is no God then everything is
permitted, an idea which harmonizes beautifully with
Smerdiakov's own notions about life and God, sets on fire
Smerdiakov's smouldering hatred towards his father and
turns his inward passive rebellion into a violent act of
murder. Smerdiakov is now ready now to act because he
seems confident of Ivan's moral support. His rebellion
against his father no longer appears to him as a cowardly
act of revenge against his roots, but as an expression of
a higher ideal; as an act justified by an elevated notion
of life, and by his right to overstep the confines

established for him by fate. By murdering his father
Smerdiakov severs his connections with his past life line
and he aspires to new heights along the path indicated by
Ivan.

Smerdiakov goes through with the murder of Karamazov.
He even shrewdly manages to conceal his act, but he
finally breaks down and goes to defeat. He realizes
that his new communion and spiritual unity with Ivan,
moulded allegedly by the blood of their dead father, is a
delusion. It is a dream that turns into a nightmare.
During his last encounter with Smerdiakov, Ivan begins to
appreciate the slyness and surprising intelligence of his
half-brother, saying "no you're not stupid. You're much
cleverer than I thought."(6) At this meeting Smerdiakov
discloses to Ivan all the horrifying details of his crime
and tells him that he--Ivan--murdered his father. "You
are the chief murderer. I was only your accomplice, your
loyal page, and I [have] done it because you told me
to."(7) Smerdiakov perceived Ivan's subconscious wish for
Fedor Karamazov's death, a wish which the rational Ivan
was afraid to admit even to himself. Smerdiakov acted as
an obedient tool of his intellectual mentor and accepted
Ivan's departure from town as a tacit approval for the
forthcoming murder of Karamazov.

The third interview of Ivan and Smerdiakov leads to
Ivan's mental disintegration. Only then does Ivan begin
to realize the extent of his guilt as an inspirer of
parricide. According to Dostoevski evil ideas are even
worse than evil deeds. Every individual is "no less
responsible for the consequences of the ideas he spreads
and propagates than for his own actions."(8) That does
not mean in the least that Dostoevski absolves Smerdiakov
from his guilt. It shows only that sinful ideas are to
Dostoevski no more venial than evil deeds. Indeed, there
are indications that Dostoevski intended to punish
Smerdiakov for his crime. Dmitrii's exclamation, during
his meeting with Alesha prior to the trial, that "God will
kill him, you will see,"(9) is very ominous in this
respect.

Parricide and the miscarriage of justice are at the
centre of The Brothers Karamazov. These are the problems
which receive most attention in literary scholarship. The
suicide of Smerdiakov, however, surprisingly receives
little notice in the critical literature on the novel.
Most critics seem to view Smerdiakov's suicide as an
occurrence of little significance to the main plot of the
novel. Such a conclusion is hasty and ill-founded. The
suicide of Smerdiakov has, on the one hand, deep symbolic
meaning; on the other hand, it makes possible the
development of the plot and the conclusion of the novel
along the lines envisaged by the author.

Had Smerdiakov remained alive and been tried for his
crime instead of Dmitrii, the symbolic significance
attached by Dostoevski to the conclusion of the Karamazov
family drama would have been lost to the reader.
Dmitrii's murderous passion, Ivan's murderous ideas,
Alesha's indifference, have been transformed into
Smerdiakov's murderous act. Dmitrii, Dostoevski's great

tragic hero, accepts the collective responsibility for all
his brothers. His readiness to accept suffering for the
sins of others and his willingness to seek regeneration,
are an expression of Zosima's basic ethical doctrine of
man's responsibility for all and his answer to all other
social, hereditary, and environmental theories.

Had Smerdiakov not confessed to Ivan his crime, the
mystery of parricide would not have been clarified, and
the evolution of Ivan's character would not have received
full expression. Ivan is Dostoevski's greatest
intellectual, but his tragedy is expressed in that he
cannot accept the limitations of his thought.
Smerdiakov's confession leads to Ivan's mental
disintegration. After their third interview, the
devil--Ivan's hallucination--appears, and Ivan is driven
to insanity by the realization of his own guilt.

The devil, who is Ivan's double, is the projection of
Smerdiakov and a reflection of Ivan. Ivan is bothered and
depressed all the time by Smerdiakov because the latter is
the embodiment of what Ivan sees in himself: a projection
of Ivan's sense of guilt. Ivan's mental anguish and
breakdown are a confession of the bankruptcy of his ideas
and the first step in his future possible regeneration.
According to Dostoevski, regeneration is a matter of inner
emotion and only a person who spiritually recognizes
something beyond himself is able to regenerate. Ivan, an
atheist who is absorbed in constant reasoning and who is
consumed by a sense of unjust suffering of the innocent,
could not regenerate easily. His experiences might lead
him, however, along the path envisaged by Dostoevski for
Raskolnikov, if not to full regeneration, then at least
towards a reassessment of his position in life.

The suicide of Smerdiakov is for Dostoevski not only
an artistic necessity, it is also an expression of
Dostoevski's ethics and of his understanding of the nature
of man. In the third interview with Ivan we encounter a
greatly changed Smerdiakov. "His face had grown very thin
and sallow. His eyes were sunken and there were blue
patches under them."(10) Smerdiakov returns the stolen
money to Ivan and tells him in a shaking voice: "I don't
want it at all. . . . I did have an idea of starting a new
life in Moscow or, better still, abroad with the money,
but that was just a dream, sir, and mostly because 'everything is permitted.' This you did teach me, sir, for you
talked to me a lot about such things: for if there's no
everlasting God, there's no such thing as virtue, and
there's no need of it at all."(11)

It is evident that Ivan underestimated Smerdiakov's
shrewdness. At the same time Smerdiakov overestimated
Ivan's strength of character and his ability to witness
peacefully his murderous ideas put into action. To
discuss abstract ethical and religious principles at the
Karamazov dinner table it is one thing, but it is a
totally different thing to see these principles tested in
real life. Smerdiakov's dream of a better life, which is
based on Ivan's ideals, and which is to be built on the
shattered foundations of the Karamazov family edifice, has
been destroyed by Ivan's amazement at, and disapproval of,

Smerdiakov's actions. Ivan's rejection of Smerdiakov does
not change, however, the latter's approach to life. He
still refuses to believe in God, and he views his murder
of Fedor Karamazov as a test of his ability to overstep,
as in the case of Raskolnikov, the commonly defined and
accepted boundaries of religious and social ethics. By
embracing Ivan's abstract notion that if there is no God
or immortality there is no virtue and "everything is
permitted," Smerdiakov exemplifies the proposition that
ideas once expressed can assume a new life of their own
and precipitate actions often unexpected even by those who
initiate them.

     It appears that Smerdiakov is essentially the
creation of Ivan. Ivan's ideas gave the necessary impulse
to his evil deeds. When Ivan rejects him there is little
left for Smerdiakov but death. The changing appearance of
Smerdiakov, his state of mind and his total openness with
Ivan during their last interview are an indication of his
disillusionment with Ivan and of his disappointment with
life; a life which has been inspired by Ivan's ideas.
Indeed, soon after Ivan's departure Smerdiakov hangs
himself.

     It is suggested that "being killed is the extreme form
of submission just as killing is the extreme form of
aggression."(12) Smerdiakov's suicide, however, is not an
act of submission. Rather, it is an act of spiteful
rebellion against his brothers. For all practical
purposes Smerdiakov avenges himself on his blood and kin
twice. The first time he avenges himself on his father
for bringing him into this world and for placing him in an
inferior social position. The second time he avenges
himself on his brothers who hate him and treat him with
the contempt worthy of a lower human creature.
Smerdiakov's rebellion against his father leads to
parricide. The rebellion against his brothers leads to
suicide, resulting in the conviction of Dmitrii, hastening
at the same time the mental disintegration of Ivan.

     A. H. Lyngstad points out that Smerdiakov's double
crime of murder and suicide "are covered by Franz Moor's
analogy between the 'itch' which leads to the conception
of a child and the 'itch' to murder; in each case there is
nothing but bestiality. If a man's life originates in a
'bestial impulse,' who Franz asks, would have any qualms
about the 'denial of birth.'"(13) In The Brothers
Karamazov there are three legitimate brothers and one
bastard. In "The Robbers" by Schiller there are only two
brothers. The older impulsive and dissolute brother, Karl
Moor, reminds us of the passionate nature of Dmitrii
Karamazov, while the vicious and greedy Franz is more
reminiscent of the intellectual Ivan. Yet it is possible
to suggest that both Ivan and Smerdiakov inherit certain
character traits from Schiller's hero. Ivan inherits, in
a way, Franz's ideas, while Smerdiakov follows Franz's
examples in action. Smerdiakov is Ivan's murderous tool.
Franz Moor puts his ideas into action himself. First he
is instrumental in the death of his father, then he
strangles himself.(14)

The Freudian analyst Karl Menninger suggests that suicide must be regarded as a peculiar kind of death which entails three internal elements: the wish to kill, the wish to be killed, and the wish to die.(15) Smerdiakov certainly has the wish to kill. He calculates the murder of Karamazov with cold-blooded aloofness. The wish to be killed, which is paradoxically not always tantamount with the wish to die, is expressed in Smerdiakov's defiance of his own being and of his roots.

The wish to be killed, which is an assertion of Smerdiakov's revolt against his own life and of his rebellion against his brothers, leads to his suicide; the final act of defiance and the expression of extreme self-will. The death of Smerdiakov illustrates the proposition that the social decay, expressed in the depraved essence of the Karamazov family, and the spiritual corruption exemplified by Smerdiakov's vacuous nature, lead to biological disintegration symbolized in Smerdiakov's death. Symbolically the suicide of Smerdiakov is an example that the violation of the code of ethics which separates man from beast and which makes the cohabitation of men on this planet possible leads to punishment. The death of Smerdiakov signifies symbolically the defeat of evil. Even Smerdiakov who, as George Steiner suggests, is in his outward design "repeatedly associated with Judas,"(16) cannot overcome the impelling power of the law of ethics. No one can build his happiness on the misfortunes of others. There are many, according to Dostoevski, who dare to overstep the boundaries of these unwritten laws, but there are very few who are capable of bearing the guilt and responsibility of their crimes and sins. Down deep there are traces of a hidden conscience in everyone; a conscience which may sometimes rebel against the rational wishes of its bearer. Even a creature like Smerdiakov has been created in the image of man and he is subject to the same laws which govern the life of all people.

NOTES

1. Fyodor Dostoyevsky, The Brothers Karamazov, trans. and Intro. David Magarshack (Harmondsworth: Penguin, 1963), p. 262.

2. Ibid.

3. F. M. Dostoevsky, Polnoe Sobranie sochinenii v tridtsati tomakh, Vol. XVI (Leningrad: Nauka, 1976), pp. 137-38, 179.

4. Dostoevski, Polnoe sobranie sochinenii, Vol. XV (Leningrad: Nauka, 1976), p. 212.

5 N. M. Chirkov, O stile Dostoevskogo (Moscow: Akademiia Nank, 1967), p. 238.

6. Dostoevski, Brothers Karamazov, p. 741.

7. Ibid., pp. 731-732.

8. E. I. Kiiko, "Iz istorii sozdaniia 'Brat'ev Karamazovykh,'" in Dostoevsky, Materialy i issledovaniia, Vol. II (Leningrad: Akademiia Nank, 1976), p. 129.

9. Dostoevski, Brothers Karamazov, p. 693.

10. Ibid., p. 730.

11. Ibid., p. 743.

12. Karl A. Menninger, Man Against Himself (New York: Harcourt, Brace, 1938), p. 50.

13. Alexandra H. Lyngstad, Dostoevskij and Schiller (The Hague, Paris; Mouton 1975), p. 56.

14. J. Ch. F. von Schiller, Schillers Werke. Nationalausgabe. Dritter Band (Weimar: Akademie Verlag, 1953), p. 126.

15. Menninger, Man Against Himself, pp. 24-83.

16. George Steiner, Tolstoy or Dostoevsky (London: Knopf, 1967), p. 278.

4.
The Dynamics of the Idea of Napoleon in *Crime and Punishment*
SHOSHANA M. KNAPP

The hero of <u>Crime and Punishment</u> is like the hero of
Pushkin's "The Queen of Spades" and the hero of Stendhal's
<u>The Red and the Black</u>. All three are latter-day
Napoleons--driven, inspired, and ultimately destroyed by
an obsession with Napoleon. Developing an obsession with
Napoleon, however, is not the same as formulating an idea
about him; for neither Hermann nor Julien Sorel does
Napoleon become more than a cryptic point of reference.
In Dostoevski's novel, on the other hand, Napoleon gives
rise to a complex idea that itself seems to take on a life
of its own, becoming an object of artistic representation,
a living event, discussed by many voices, enacted by many
characters, explored by many minds. The idea of Napoleon
is tested against innocence (Sonya), against experience
(Svidrigailov), and against everything in between.

Some critics have reduced the idea to the simple
formula of "the rights of genius"; others, like Mochulsky,
have seen in the multiple forms of the idea a regrettable
confusion of authorial intention.(1) I would rather view
the complexity of the idea as the conscious achievement of
the artist and as a challenge to the critic. I propose to
examine here the dynamics of the idea of Napoleon, as it
is defined, maligned, defended, and developed in the
course of the novel.

The idea of Napoleon, throughout the transformations
it undergoes, is in essence polemical; it is a defense of
the extraordinary man who commits acts that invite
criticism. The extraordinary man is theoretically
justified in doing that which is forbidden to the lesser
man, the ordinary man. There are at least six versions of
the idea, presented here in the order in which they are
discussed in the text:

1. The extraordinary man may do whatever his great heart
    desires.
2. The extraordinary man is bound and obliged, by his
    nature, to commit crimes.
3. The extraordinary man may commit crimes only for the
    fulfillment of his ideas.
4. The extraordinary man may commit crimes only for
    altruistic reasons.

5. The extraordinary man may commit one crime, as a first
    step, to begin his career, so that he will later be
    able to fulfill his ideas.
6. The extraordinary man may commit a single altruistic
    crime.

All of these versions, let us note, apply only to the
extraordinary person, the Napoleon. Ordinary people, on
the other hand, are not permitted to commit crimes and
will not get away with the crimes they commit. If a
criminal is revealed to be an ordinary man, then, it is
possible to condemn his deed without abandoning the
theory--and the novel, at some points, in fact does so.
In the course of Crime and Punishment, as we shall
observe, these six ideas are subject to myriad
expositions, counter-expositions, objections, and
modifications.
    The theory of the rights of genius, of course, was
not new, nor was it linked exclusively with Napoleon; it
was, however, a major topic for progessive European
journalists in the mid-1860s. Napoleon III had written a
straightforward history of Rome, with a notorious
introduction. Calling attention to the ability of
geniuses to survive destruction, he said that Providence
makes use of extraordinary men in order to achieve in a
few years the work of centuries. Although he did not say
exactly what the great men were entitled to do, the mere
mention of Providence in connection with extraordinary man
was inflammatory. Few readers noticed that he also said
great men needed clean hands in order to perform their
glorious deeds, and perhaps they were not intended to
notice. Napoleon III, it was assumed, was trying to
justify the immortality of extraordinary men such as
Caesar, Christ, and Napoleon--and the debate was on.(2)
    Several references in Dostoevski's notebooks for
Crime and Punishment show his response to this debate. He
expresses the most extreme version of the theory, without
necessarily endorsing it: for a great man, crime as such
does not exist, and he is permitted to trample on the law
(Version 1). Dostoevski also expresses a more moderate
form of the idea: the great man takes power only for a
good end (Version 4). In the notebooks, Dostoevski begins
to outline the dynamics of the idea in the proposed
fictional setting. The idea itself, he plans to show, can
make one ask if the theory is valid in principle and if it
is applicable in practice to a particular crime performed
by a particular criminal.(3)
    A key scene at the midpoint of the novel includes
several references to Napoleon, as well as the first
sustained discussion of the idea. Raskolnikov, who knows
he is suspected of killing the pawnbroker and her sister,
goes with his friend Razumikhin, on a trivial pretext, to
see the prosecutor, Porfiry Petrovich. The prosecutor, it
seems, has read the article in which Raskolnikov has
developed his theory, and is prepared to provide his own
interpretation: "The point is that in his article people
are divided into two classes. The "ordinary" and the
"extraordinary." The ordinary ones must live in

submission and have no right to transgress the laws because, you see, they are ordinary. And the extraordinary have the right to commit any crime and break every kind of law just because they are extraordinary.(4)

Perceiving the discussion as a trap, Raskolnikov begins by denying a position somewhat different from the one attributed to him by Porfiry. No, says Raskolnikov, the extraordinary man may not commit any crime he happens to want to commit (a denial of Version 1). Nor is he absolutely bound and obliged to commit crimes (a denial of Version 2, which the prosecutor has not expressed). Even the extraordinary man, says Raskolnikov, is permitted (not required) to commit a crime "only in the event that his ideas (which may sometimes be salutary for all mankind) require it for their fulfillment." Raskolnikov thus affirms Version 3 and suggests Version 4.

In explaining what he means by ideas that require fulfillment, however, Raskolnikov yokes together two very different concepts. The first one, which is not particularly dangerous or even original, is that people who create are, by that very fact, also destroyers. All law-givers are law-breakers; "in making a new law they _ipso facto_ broke an old one...." (This statement, we observe, is an innocent variant of Version 2, which says that all extraordinary people are also criminals--a version Raskolnikov denies.) The second concept is more ominous. Geniuses, he says--men such as Lycurgus, Solon, Mohammed, and Napoleon--are frequently murderers: "of course, they did not stop short of shedding blood, provided only that the blood (however innocent and however heroically shed in defiance of the concrete law) was shed to their advantage. It is remarkable that the greater part of these benefactors and law-givers of humanity were particularly blood-thirsty." Remarkable indeed. His observation depends on a willingness to characterize certain men as benefactors in spite of the harm they seem to do. The best example for the concept of the destructive law-giver is Newton; the best example for the concept of the murderous benefactor, however, is Napoleon.

Raskolnikov believes that a genius like Napoleon may "in all conscience authorize himself to wade through blood--in proportion, however, to his idea and the degree of its importance." The ordinary people should obey "because that is their destiny"; they exist only for the sake of the geniuses. A law of nature determines who the geniuses are, and who the ordinary people are. If the ordinary people mistake themselves for Napoleon, they will be overcome by guilt as they become aware of their error. Raskolnikov's theory is a comprehensive system; by defending the right of the genius to break civil and religious laws, he admits that ordinary people have no such right, under any circumstances. This admission is significant.

If, at this point, Raskolnikov wished to surrender to stress and doubt, if he wished to admit that he should not have killed two women, he would not necessarily be obligated to abandon the theory at the same time. He has two escape routes, two ways to protect his theory. He

could say, first of all, that an extraordinary person is
allowed to commit a crime only to further the fulfillment
of his ideas, and that this crime did not meet the
requirement. Since he did not even keep the money for
which he murdered the pawnbroker, he has murdered for
nothing. The crime, then, does not correspond to the
conditions of Raskolnikov's theory as he has expressed it
(Versions 3 and 4), although the crime could easily meet
the more lenient requirements of Porfiry's variation
(Version 1, that extraordinary people can commit any crime
they choose), a formulation Raskolnikov has rejected. By
correcting the prosecutor's exposition of this point,
therefore, Raskolnikov can be seen, by us, as defending
his idea, yet leaving his behavior open to attack.
Raskolnikov himself, however, does not really seem to take
seriously this way of reconciling his firm beliefs with
his feelings of inadequacy.

He has a second escape route, one that appeals to him
for very different reasons. Without being inconsistent,
Raskolnikov could say that an extraordinary person might
have committed this very crime, but that he himself was
unqualified, by his nature and his destiny, to exemplify
the extraordinary criminal of his theory. His emotions,
as we shall see, make him feel unworthy. The act is
perfectly all right; he himself, however, is all wrong.

Raskolnikov is indeed tortured by the possibility
that he might be ordinary. Observe: sooner than
relinquish his theory about extraordinary men or his
conception of Napoleon as its exemplar, Raskolnikov is
willing to doubt his essential value as a human being. In
the conversation with Porfiry, Raskolnikov has expressed
his theory; in the following chapter (III, 6), he goes on
to voice his self-doubt. As he lies alone in his room, he
sinks into despair.

He seems to think he has shown himself to be unlike
Napoleon in two ways, of varying weight. The first way is
more basic: Napoleon is a being of an essentially
different nature, permitted to perform acts Raskolnikov
should have known he has no right to attempt: "No, these
people are not made like this; the real ruler, to whom
everything is permitted, destroys Toulon, butchers in
Paris, forgets an army in Egypt, expends half a million
men in a Moscow campaign, shakes himself free with a pun
in Wilno, and when he is dead they put up statues to him;
everything is permitted to him." To him, but not to all.
Not to Raskolnikov.

The difference between the ordinary and the
extraordinary is both dramatic and absolute. There are no
part-time Napoleons. The ability to kill without guilt or
apology or punishment--the ability to get away with
murder--marks the difference between Napoleon and ordinary
people.(5) Painfully conscious of his physical debility
and mental confusion, excessively preoccupied with the
possibility of witnesses and evidence, Raskolnikov feels
sure that he is not one to whom everything is permitted,
that he should have known better, and that, in fact, he
did.

He is also unlike Napoleon in a purely aesthetic
sense; he has committed a singularly undignified crime:
"Napoleon, the pyramids, Waterloo--and a vile, withered,
old woman, a moneylender, with a red box under her
bed--what a mishmash even for somebody like Porfiry
Petrovich to digest! . . . How could he, indeed?
Aesthetic considerations forbid. "Does a Napoleon crawl
under an old woman's bed?" he will say." Raskolnikov
feels that he has become ridiculous in the eyes of the
prosecutor and in his own eyes as well. He then begins,
perversely, to enjoy the sensation.

Raskolnikov seems to take "malicious" pleasure in
enumerating the reasons he is, "aesthetically speaking," a
louse, or the least valuable of the ordinary people. But
his reasons go back to the basic differences between
himself and Napoleon (a man to whom everything is
permitted because he can smile away bloodshed with an
epigram) and not to the aesthetic differences he has been
considering (Does a Napoleon crawl under an old woman's
bed?). All four reasons are psychological. Introspection
tells him he is unfit, psychologically, to be Napoleon
because he has to ask himself if he is, because he claimed
an altruistic purpose that was not in fact in his mind,
because he calculated the profits of his crime as
precisely as he did, and, finally, because he knew
beforehand he would come to despise himself. We should
observe that no one else knows, or could know, that he is
a louse for these purely private reasons. And no one else
ever has to know how he feels. The real crime, then, is
known only to him; by talking about himself and his
theory, by affirming his theory at the expense of his
freedom, he gives himself away as he gives himself up.
The novel could, with justice, be called "Crime and
Incrimination."

Raskolnikov further incriminates himself when he
confesses to Sonya, who has, by becoming a prostitute,
also stepped over a barrier (V, 4). Even as he confesses,
though, he shows his confusion. Although he ends by
admitting that he committed the crime to see if Napoleon
could indeed be his model, he begins by saying that he was
merely trying to follow Napoleon's example.

> The point is this: on one occasion, I put this
> question to myself: what if, for example,
> Napoleon had found himself in my shoes, with no
> Toulon, no Egypt, no crossing of Mount Blanc, to
> give his career a start, but, instead of those
> monumental things, with simply one ridiculus old
> woman, who must be killed to get money from her
> trunk (for that career of his, you
> understand?)--well, would he have made up his
> mind to do it if there was no other way? Would
> he have shrunk from it, because it was so
> unmonumental and . . . and so sinful? . . . I
> realized (quite suddenly) that not only would he
> not shrink, but the idea would never even enter
> his head that it was not monumental. . . . And
> if there had been no other way open to him, he

would have strangled her, without giving her a
chance to squeak, and without a moment's
hesitation! . . . Well, I also . . . stopped
hesitating . . . strangled her . . . following
the example of my authority . . . and that is
exactly how it was!

Certainly that is not exactly how it was. For one
thing, the murder method here was not strangulation.
Following the example of his authority, furthermore, pre-
supposes the goal Raskolnikov wanted to accomplish. Only
if he had already made himself Napoleon could it have been
right for him to imitate his authority. Yet, as he speaks
to Sonya, he somehow seems to have become Napoleon after
all. He assumes he was entitled, as Napoleon would have
been, to commit a crime in order to start his career;
Napoleon would have gone ahead and killed an old woman, as
Raskolnikov feels he has had to do. This formulation is
not, to be sure, the logical result of the article as we
have heard it discussed. It is, instead, Version 5 of the
idea: great men are entitled to commit a single crime as
a first step. This is what Raskolnikov wants to believe
he has done.
His explanation, however, is inadequate and
inappropriate. The genuinely Napoleonic response to the
"un-monumental" nature of the crime would be to ignore
it--which Raskolnikov has found it impossible to do.
Another problem lies in his growing disorientation, his
mental confusion, his preoccupation with his subjective
inner life at the expense of the objective fact of the
murder. He cannot think or speak coherently about what he
has done. After the conversation with Porfiry, he had
said to himself: "I killed not a human being, but a
principle." Talking to Sonya, he says: "Well, killing
the old woman, of course . . . that was wrong. . . . Well,
that's enough!" It is, however, far from enough, given
that the fact is not yet real to him. He himself is
surprised that he rarely thinks about the death of the
pawnbroker's sister, Lizaveta; he never thinks about her
probable pregnancy, either. He is responsible for three
human deaths, yet he denies that he has killed even one
person. "I only killed a louse, Sonya, a useless, vile,
pernicious louse." He then rejects his "first step"
explanation as "all wrong," as not "the truth," and he
tries again.
His second explanation ignores all the subtle
distinctions we have made in contrasting the different
versions of the idea; at this point, the only distinction
that matters is the one between the ordinary and the
extraordinary man. This late explanation also amounts to
a rejection of altruism as even a partial motivation.
Realizing that most people are stupid and that this is
"the law of their nature," he wanted, or so he says, to
learn the law of his own nature, to see whether he had the
courage to "stoop" and take power. (The "stoop" is
revealing.) "I wanted to dare, Sonya, that was the only
reason!" He did not want the money for his family, for
his "first step," or for the untold benefits his genius

might one day bring to humanity. His former interest in
ideas that "may sometimes be salutary for all mankind,"
his image of himself as a benefactor on a small or large
scale, his regard for Dunya's honor--all generous motives
are now dismissed as irrelevant. "I murdered for myself,
for myself alone," and the real motive was to test
himself: "what I needed to find out then, and find out as
soon as possible, was whether I was a louse like everybody
else or a man, whether I was capable of stepping over the
barrier or not."   But this explanation, like the first
one, is not entirely clear or satisfactory. The mere act
of killing, after all, does not mark the difference
between a louse and a man. And if Raskolnikov were to
follow the same course again, he says, he might not commit
murder. Why, then, was the murder a test? What did he
hope to accomplish?

He wanted to find a private equivalent for the public
acclaim granted to the extraordinary man. His theory,
after all, does not admit the existence of closet
Napoleons. Supremacy is conditional, he says, dependent
on the perceptions and the submission of the ordinary
people. "And I know now, Sonya, that the man of strong
and powerful mind and spirit is their master [nad nimi
vlastelin]! The man who dares much is right in their
eyes. The man who tramples on the greatest number of
things is their law-giver, and whoever is most audacious
is most certainly right. The Russian makes the point even
clearer: the ruler is powerful in relation to the
non-rulers who acknowledge his sway. But the project of
murder, in most cases, is not one that invites public
recognition.

Raskolnikov, then, appears to be playing two roles,
and his very name refers to the split within the self. He
acts and watches himself in action; he is both the hero
despising the louse, and the louse worshipping the hero.
This double role is a subterfuge, a device for which
Napoleon himself has no need. On some level, Raskolnikov
knows that. Disturbed by this further discrepancy between
himself and his model, Raskolnikov clings to the murder
itself as a kind of solution.

Napoleon, Raskolnikov feels, had only a single self;
he did not need to ask himself questions or give an
accounting of himself to himself. Since Raskolnikov has
in fact had to ask himself questions, he is by definition,
not Napoleon:

> You don't think, either, that I didn't know, for
> example, that if I began questioning and
> cross-examining myself about whether I had the
> right to take power, that meant I hadn't any
> such right? Or that, if I asked myself, "Is a
> man a louse?" it meant that for me he was not,
> although he might be one for a man to whom the
> question never occurred, and who would march
> straight ahead without asking any questions at
> all? . . . If I worried for so long about
> whether Napoleon would have done it or not, it

must be because I felt clearly that I was not
Napoleon. . . .

To need the test is to fail it, in that the test involves
a questioner and an answerer, a split self. But suppose
one finds a way to cheat, to use one self to fool the
other. By committing the act, and interpreting the act as
a Napoleonic one, he ends the debate and gives his
"ordinary" self an "extraordinary" hero to acclaim. "I
endured all the torment of the endless debating, Sonya,
and I longed to shake it off; I longed to kill without
casuistry, to kill for my own benefit, and for that
alone." By committing the murder, he tried to deny the
awful fact that he had never been Napoleon and the more
awful fact that he had known it all along.

The life of Napoleon, however, made it possible for
him to sustain the illusion as long as he did. Of all the
extraordinary men he imagines, Napoleon is the closest to
him in time and circumstances. Napoleon was once an
ambitious student like him, brooding in a tiny room in a
large city, with a widowed mother to worry about. The
resemblance did not end there--or so Raskolnikov hoped.
By committing a murder, he planned to make the theory
apply to his life. If he did just what he thought
Napoleon would have had the right to do, he would be able
to show, by exercising the "right" to kill, that this
right was genuinely his.

The plan failed. Exercising his right to kill, as we
have seen, has made him feel even less Napoleonic than
before. Yet when Sonya asks him to say aloud that he has
committed murder, he clings more tenaciously to his theory
and even believes that it still applies. "Perhaps I am
still a man and not a louse, and I was in too much of a
hurry to condemn myself. . . . Perhaps I can still put up
a fight." An extraordinary person, after all, would not
surrender, in spite of recurrent doubts. Raskolnikov is
still trying to convince himself that the killing proved
what he wanted to prove. He will try to believe that he
is getting away with murder, psychologically, as long as
he can continue to get away with it, legally. He renews
his determination, ironically, through discussing his
ideas with Sonya, who completely rejects his theory and
who asks him to interpret his act as she does: as a crime
that needs to be punished.

Still later, he listens to the prosecutor's attempt
to induce a confession, an attempt that is tainted by
Porfiry's own longings to play Napoleon. You could have
done much worse with your theory, says Porfiry--a tempting
distortion (VI, 2). Svidrigailov, explaining
Raskolnikov's idea to Dunya, commits another distortion.
Whereas Raskolnikov usually says that geniuses are
justified in wading through blood, Svidrigailov presents a
simplified variation (Version 6): the extraordinary man
may commit a single altruistic crime. Svidrigailov thus
dilutes Raskolnikov's position--and Raskolnikov himself
then follows suit. After testing himself and his idea
against reality, after committing the act and dissecting
the theory, he reconsiders his thinking one more time.

When Raskolnikov goes to see Dunya, he defends his
convictions, denies his criminality, and expresses
Svidrigailov's version of his theory, a formulation that
has never before been unequivocally his. "I myself wanted
to benefit men, and I would have done hundreds, thousands
of good deeds, to make up for that one piece of
stupidity--not even stupidity, but simple clumsiness. . .
. I understand less than ever why what I did is a crime!"
(VI, 7). He does not understand anything new, but he has
discovered a new escape clause. His theory was fine, he
thinks, and it applied to this deed and to him. Although
he lacked the technical skill to commit murder with
impunity, he had the right. Although he was, admittedly,
clumsy, he got away with murder in the way that matters
most to him. Raskolnikov acknowledges failure in his
ability to practice the theory, but he does not abjure the
theory itself.

He never does in fact reexamine his ideas; he simply
puts them aside as he follows the advice he has been
offered. He comes for Sonya's crosses, as she wished. He
stops philosophizing, as Porfiry suggested, and plunges
straight ahead. "Suddenly he felt conclusively that he
need ask himself no more questions" (VI, 8). He confesses
to the police clerk: "It was I who killed the old woman
and her sister, Lizaveta, with an axe and robbed them."
His statement is precise, circumstantial, and pertinent.
After prolonged evasion of his crime, he finally
identifies his act in the proper fashion for the benefit
of the proper audience. He killed two women--not an idea,
not a louse, not himself. But although he boldly
confesses this act, he never admits that the crime itself
was wrong.

The concluding pages of the novel do not seem to deal
with Napoleon at all. The epilogue replaces the theory
with the religion and love of Sonya, who accompanies
Raskolnikov into exile. "Life had taken the place of
logic, and something quite different must be worked out in
his mind." Even his deed is wiped out, along with his
discarded theory. "Everything, even his crime, even his
sentence and his exile, seemed to him now, in the first
rush of emotion, to be something external and strange, as
if it had not happened at all." The idea is dissolved
without being resolved.

And yet Raskolnikov has remained true to his model.
The man who inspired his theory and his crime now provides
as well the blueprint for "something quite different."
Just as Napoleon, after Waterloo, departed for St. Helena
with a devoted entourage, Raskolnikov goes, unrepentant,
into exile accompanied by a loyal woman. Napoleon's exile
produced the exculpatory memoirs of friends such as
Bertrand and Las Cases, books known collectively as "the
Gospels of St. Helena." From Raskolnikov's exile, too,
then breathes a hint of grace. His salvation seems to
require not a repudiation of his crime--any more than
Napoleon felt compelled to admit wrongdoing--but instead,
as for Napoleon, an adoption of new values. If the St.
Helena Gospels are to be believed, Napoleon was speaking a
new language during the final years. He considered

himself, he said, a man of peace. He had wanted a
glorious federation, a United States of Europe. If only
the other nations had not forced him to go to war. . . .
For Raskolnikov, too, we are told that exile holds the
prospect of a "new life" and "a new story, the story of
the gradual renewal of a man."
     The epilogue is the final form of the idea.
Dostoevski has shown us how the idea of Napoleon can be
defined, debated, denounced, and defended. Raskolnikov,
in despair and in pain, has maintained his theory at the
cost of his freedom and his self-respect. Yet, at the
end, after admitting that he is not, after all, the
extraordinary man of his theory, Raskolnikov experiences
his own St. Helena. Life has taken the place of logic.
The idea of Napoleon is dead. Nevertheless, long live
Napoleon.

NOTES

     1. Konstantin Mochulsky, Dostoevsky: His Life and
Work, trans. and intro. Michael A. Minihan from the 1947
Russian edition (Princeton: Princeton University Press,
1967), pp. 280-285.

     2. Napoleon III, L'Histoire de Jules Cesar, I
(Paris: Plon, 1865, p. i-vii, 306-308). See also, F. I.
Evnin, "Roman 'Prestuplenie i nakazanie,'" in N. Stepanov,
ed., Tvorcestvo F. M. Dostoevskogo (Moscow: Akdemija
nauk, 1959), pp. 153-157.

     3. Feodor Dostoevski, Notebooks for "Crime and
Punishment", trans. and ed. Edward Wasiolek from the 1931
Russian edition (Chicago: University of Chicago Press,
1967), pp. 57-58, 81, 84, 88, 176-177, 198.

     4. Feodor Dostoevski, Crime and Punishment, trans.
Jesse Coulson, and ed. George Gibian, 2d. (New York:
Norton, 1975), p. 219 (part III, Chapter 5). Subsequent
chapter references appear in the text. This translation
has been compared with Prestuplenie i nakazanie, ed. V. V.
Vinogradov, Vol. VI of Polnoe sobranie socinenij, ed. V.
G. Bazanov (Leningrad: "Nauka," 1973).

     5. It is clear in this scene that Napoleon, more
than the other extraordinary men Raskolnikov has named,
expresses the pure essence of the theory. Raskolnikov
says that Mohammed invoked the will of Allah, thus relying
on an authority and a justification beyond his
extraordinary self. Although Raskolnikov does not
identify Mohammed's statement as a compromise, the
compromise is implicit in the example. A reference to
Napoleon could not have encompassed the hinted compromise,
which appears only here. That is why Mohammed is cited
only briefly and occasionally, while Napoleon is the most
frequent exemplar of the theory.

5.
The Nature of Referentiality in *The Double*

ASYA PEKUROVSKAYA

With a notable persistence (more than thirty times)(1) number "two," both cardinal and ordinal, appears in Dostoevski's narrative as the most explicit tool of executing the theme of the double referred to by the title of the novel. If his persistence is not gratuitous, which is a matter of simple certainty, one should be able to speak of some laws, governing the multiple usage and meaning of the word-sign "two." And indeed the list of textual reference just reproduced suggests, not without an accord with the general concept of "two," that all word-signs pertaining to the notion of "two," denote either a simultaneity ("two gentlemen," "two rows," "both chairs," "a twin") or a sequence ("two hours," "two steps," "second floor"). Yet, no general concept of two supports the idea that all these word-signs denote either spatiality or temporality, respectively, the former manifested by a precise figure: mathematical symbol (2) or a collective linguistic word-sign ("a couple," "a twin"), whereas the latter--by a pendulate integer susceptible to a confusion with its closest integers, "one" and "three" ("a thing or two," "two or three officers") as well as with the figure of spatiality.(2)

The lack of a clear-cut distinction between the basic functions of the word-sign "two" was presumably the source of a general belief that the theme of the double was introduced into modern discourse as a borrowing from Romanticism. Yet a close textual reading with a provisional view as to a heterogeneity of the "two"-concept, leads to an observation that to a certain type of discourse, no matter whether it is regarded as romantic or modern by tradition, the theme of the double, understood as a simultaneity concept,(3) will be foreign. Let us call a discourse which dispenses with the notion of simultaneity in favor of sequence a modern text and, hence, let us question its historically determined continuity with the concept of the "Doppelganger." It will appear then that the theme of the double is appropriated by the modern text not as a borrowing from romanticism accountable in descriptive terms, but as an usurpation which can be described in dialectical terms, encroaching upon the romantic notion of referentiality.(4)

It appears thus, that to speak of romantic referentiality in modern terms means already to discard the notion of referent in favor of the notion of non-referent, insofar as the latter notion constitutes the perspective from which modern man invariably commences his reading of literature. Let us observe The Double from the perspective of its (non)referentiality.

The narrative strategy can be described by a term of replication which points to the fact that parts of the narrative are to reappear as if in order to make more sense than their counterparts. For example, Golyadkin's monologue, recorded in Chapter 2 as an undecipherable "confession" to Dr. Rutenspitz, reappears as soon as Chapter 4 (numerically congruent with the rule of doubling) in the form of a lucid description of a dinner party. As this replication-strategy realizes only during one's second reading, "Golyadkin's monologue" may be regarded not as a source, but a sequel and, in fact, a condensation of the reiterated "description." This suggests a certain reversed procedure according to which a recourse to "the description" will precede one's reading of "the monologue."

In the description-part the discourse produces a novel character who is the narrator himself expressing his wish to be a poet "Homer or Pushkin," and confessing his present lack of eloquence, which amounts to his failure to "possess the secret of elevated and forceful style." As the latter hinders the fulfillment of the basic narrative task, to wit, depicting the "beautiful and modifying moments of mortal existence" (p. 53), the narrative code undergoes an essential transformation. The dramatized narration is supplanted by a pictorial code, foreign to the code of narrativization by definition. In this pictorial code, introduced by the formula "I will say nothing but will point out," the picture of "Vladimir Semyonovich, Andrey Filippovich's nephew," functions as a kernel unit, generating a series of other pictures: "the tearful eyes of the parents of the Queen of Festives, the proud eyes of Andrey Filippovich, the modest eyes of the Queen herself, the rapturous eyes of the guests and the decorously envious eyes of certain colleagues of this brilliant man" (p. 54). Presumably, the effect registered within the pictorial narrative ("tears," "pride," "ecstasy," "decorum," and so on) can very well compensate for the effect of the eloquent story-telling, which means that the figure of "Vladimir Semyonovich" can be viewed as one called for to supplant the narrator's figure in its basic task: verbalization. (The fact that "Vladimir Semyonovich" is the one whose function in the picture is to propose a toast, supports this point as well.)

As congruent with the pictorial code, furthermore, the nominal word-signs become ritualized with the effect of their suppressed semantic value: just as the notion of "young man" appears to mean the same as "old man," a relation of synonymy is to be established among such word-signs as "rank," "rosy cheeks," "lofty heights" and "good manners": "I will say nothing although I cannot help observing that everything about this young man--who,

let it be said in his favor, is more like an old man than
a young one--everything, from his rosy cheeks to the rank
of Assessor with which he is invested, speaks at this
triumphant moment of the lofty heights to which one may be
elevated by good manners!" (p. 54). And with a notable
persistence all these "ritualized synonyms" appear to be
the ones clarifying the reference to "Vladimir
Semyonovich, Andrey Filippovich's nephew," whose central
position in "the narrative description" is emphasized, as
he is the one to displace the narrator in his basic
function. The narrator not only annihilates his own ego,
just as his protagonist does later on prior to meeting his
own double,(5) but also dilapidates his style by a
disguised reference to the Gogolian code.

> How can I, the humble chronicler of the
> adventures of Mr. Golyadkin, which are, however,
> very curious in their way, depict this singular
> and seemly medley of beauty, brilliance,
> decorum, gaiety, amiable sobriety and sober
> amiability . . . depict all the daughters and
> wifes, who, I mean this as a compliment, are
> more like fairies thant ladies, with their pink
> and lily-white shoulders and faces . . . and--to
> use a grand word--homoeopathic feet? (p. 56).

This hidden indication of the Gogolian skaz-code concealed
behind an authentic object-language of the story, serves
not only to a narrator/character confusion, but also to an
entanglement between referential and meta-discursive
functions of the narrative language, especially in view of
the fact (the entree of which has been procured only by
the modern reader) that the recognition of the Gogol-code
cannot be acknowledged apart from an indication to a
Formalist reading of literary text. Indeed, the
Dostoevski dialogue with Gogol appears to be concurrent
with that of Eikhenbaum who held that Gogol uses the word
"hemorrhoidal," just as Dostoevski's narrator uses the
word "homeopathic," not as an authentic sign pertaining to
its object-language, but as a meta-discursive sign,
referring to another sign ("grandiose and fantastic"(6)).
    Apart from being a catalyst of narrator's
mortification the Gogol-code functions as a strategical
nucleus at which "the narrative description" can be
regarded as the one superimposed with the "Golyadkin
monologue" previously referred to as undecipherable.
Spacial limitations that had prevented me from quoting the
"narrative description" in full, force me to limit myself
to reference to a concluding segment of the "Golyadkin
monologue" as follows:

> Yes, a certain intimate acquaintance of mine was
> congratulating another very intimate
> acquaintance of mine, who was, moreover a close
> friend of mine, "a bosom friend" as the saying
> is, on his promotion to the rank of Assessor.
> The way he chanced to put it was: "I'm heartily
> glad of this opportunity of offering you my

congratulations, my sincere congratulations,
Vladimir Semyonovich, on your promotion--the
more so since nowadays, as all the world knows,
those who push their favorites(7) are no more."
. . . That's what he said, Doctor, and he
looked at Andrey Filippovich, the uncle of our
dear Vladimir Semyonovich. But what does it
matter to me his being made an Assessor? Is
this any business of mine? And there he is
wanting to get married and his mother's milk
still wet on his lips, if you'll pardon the
expression (p. 33).

It would be difficult if not impossible to persuade
the reader familiar exclusively with the fragment just
quoted that the narrator's reference to "a certain
intimate acquaintance of mine" is none other than a
self-reference semantically conflicting with its succeding
reference ("another very intimate acquaintance of mine")
the latter being in fact a reference to "Vladimir
Semyonovich, the nephew of Andrey Filippovich." Yet, an
inference as to a confusion between the two referents, the
"I" and "Vladimir Semyonovich," is not only a probable,
but rather a predictable narrative turn by which the theme
of the double is being executed. Indeed the retroactive
familiarity with the description-code where the "Vladimir
Semyonovich"-figure is realized to supersede the narrator,
prevents one from confusing identical signifiers and
dissociating the distinct ones. It follows that the
signifier "he" in "That's what he said, Doctor," and the
signifier "me" in "But what does it matter to me his being
made an Assessor?" would invariably point to a single
referent, precisely, the I/he of the narrator signified by
the name of "Golyadkin," the narrator and the acting
persona of the story.
    So far it can be said that my choice to juxtapose the
description-code with the monologue-code was justified
insofar as both codes deal with the notion of the
suppressed ego, be it an "I" of "the humble chronicler of
the adventures of Mr. Golyadkin," supplanted by the figure
of "Vladimir Semyonovich, Andrey Filippovich's nephew," or
a "he" of Golyadkin the character who buries his
monological first-person reference under the third-person
self-reference. But even though a discovery that the
referent behind the "I" of Golyadkin the narrator is the
same as that of the "he" of Golyadkin the character is
possible only retroactively, and only retroactively is one
to explain the subsequent transition for the initial "he"
into a generic, i.e., pertaining to the monologue-form,
"I," the key to the discursive meaning should be searched
by way of a reciprocal movement from description to
monologue and from monologue to description.
    This rule of reciprocity (a hermeneutical rule
indispensible for deciphering the theme of the double in
its modern execution) has various manifestations in modern
discourse from the slips of the tongue, pertaining to the
language of a character to what can be called a discursive
figure of anticipation.(8) I shall presently concentrate

my attention on the slips of the tongue which occur in the
concluding lines of the Golyadkin monologue to Dr.
Rutenspitz which I restrained from quoting so far for the
reason that the slips of the tongue make it possible not
to just witness the non-referential codification in modern
discourse, but also to interpret the very meaning of non-
-referents along with the narrative intention imbedded in
it. Let us recall the lines in question: "But to kill two
birds(9) with one stone, after I'd given the young man a
start with that bit about pushing favorites
[fortune-telling grandmothers] I turned to Klara
Olsufyevna, who'd just been singing a tender ballad--all
this was the day before yesterday, at her father's--and I
said: "Your singing is full of tenderness, but those who
listen haven't got pure hearts'" (p. 34).

What I interpret as the slip of the tongue in the
first place is the case of misusing the Russian idiom
"ubit' dvukh zaitsev odnim kamnem" (literally, "to kill
two hares with one stone"), in view of which an engimatic
substitution occurs of the word "hare" by the word
"sparrow." I am inclined to ascribe to this substitution
an important mental process, namely, the narrator's desire
to repress his sexual anxiety. It appears that in its
proverbial function the word-sign "sparrow" has an overt
erotic connotation(10) in the Russian language.

A tendency to neutralize the terminology pertaining
to the language of eroticism, futhermore, is not the only
interfering tendency capable of bringing itself to
expression in a perverted form. The twice reiterated
reference to the "fortune-telling grandmothers,"
interfering with the narrator's direct address to
"Vladimir Semyonovich, Andrey Filippovich's nephew,"
suggests the meddling of the allusion by omission that
betrays the complex of the Gogolian minor official,
manifested in a formula: "I should like to know why I'm a
Titular Councillor? Why especially a Titular Councillor?"
Consequently, a distinction in quality, an order or a rank
(of Assessor) achieved through (the) patronage (of Andrey
Filippovich, the departmental head) constitutes another
source of the narrator's anxiety, comparable with the
erotic drive and looming behind the foregoing allusion.

From both these sources of anxiety one can
reconstruct the interfering tendency which conditions the
appeerence of the narrator's first double, "Vladimir
Semyonovich, Andrey Filippovich's nephew," whose name is
especially suitable for the chosen role. Precisely,
"Vladimir" signifies one of the two Russian orders
established in 1782 for civil services and endowed all its
cavaliers, regardless of degree, with the inheritable
nobility; "Semyon" is derived from the root common to a
number of words, pertaining to the notion of "seed" of
"progeny," and, by extention, "sexuality."

Hence, in a search of support for a modern definition
of the non-referential reference, two narrative fragments
have been selected, one replicated by another, while
reproducing it in a condensed and undecipherable form,
existing as a substitute for its repressed self.(11)

Roughly speaking, the phenomena just described have already been detected under the name of mental process par excellence by Sigmund Freud(12) in view of which "Golyadkin's monologue" appears to be a repressed wishful impulse which continues to exist in "the narrative description": in the former case as the workings of subconsciousness (a dream, a joke, or a slip of the tongue), and in the latter case--as a conscious "facade behind which /the thinking process/ lies concealed."(13) A necessity for such detection can be now declared as an interpretative condition according to which a claim can be made that prior to the appearance of Golyadkin's double incarnate, i.e., Golyadkin junior, and even prior to the appearance of Golyadkin's double by unvoluntary desire ("Vladimir Semyonovich's" case), doubling becomes a meaning-generating mechanism. An in its executive strategy of selfunfolding the most authentic Golyadkin's double appears to be what Freud could have called a double by "transferrence," to wit, Dr. Rutenspitz(14) who functions as the one to subject the character to a psychoanalytic treatment (one should not forget that Golyadkin's first appearance in Dr. Rutenspitz's office is referred to in the narrative as his second appearence) resulted in what Francesco Orlando calls the "Freudian negation."(15) Golyadkin the patient negates all his repressed instincts and secret wishes ["I have no gift for fine phrases" (p. 25); "I am no great talker" (p. 26); "I don't like odd words here and there, miserable double-dealing I can't stand, slander and gossip I abominate" (p. 28)] that make their way to the surface only unvoluntarily: through his dreams, jokes, or slips of the tongue which in fact are no longer semantically segregated, insofar as they all are manifestations of the working of the unconscious, all constituting the forces seeking liberation from the repression. An even this semantic indifferentiation characteristic of the unconscious goes in accord with the Freudian understanding of the thinking process:

> Similarly, contraries are not kept apart from each other but are treated as though they were identical, so that in the manifest dream any element may also stand for its contrary.
> Certain philologists have found that the same holds good in the oldest languages, and that contraries such as "strong-weak," "light-dark," "high-deep" were originally expressed by the same roots, until two different modifications of the primitive word distinguished the two meanings. . . .(16)

At this point I wish to conclude that the nature of referentiality in The Double is the double itself detectable from the narrative strategy of deceptive replications. Yet, along with this conclusion I am tempted to resume the theme of the double by a recourse to the concept of the "two" viewed as a spacial versus temporal concept. I claim that the modern feature of temporality, in contradistinction to romantic speciality

derived from the notion of the "Doppelganger," does not
tolerate the polarized view of the world based on the
notion of perceptual evidence.(17)   And so does modern
discourse in general.
     As the last resort, I may say that the consequences
of not segregating romantic and modern codes would have
been only theoretically predictable were it not for the
fact that they are quite tangible already. Notably, the
two twentieth century interpreters of The Double, both
belonging to a category of distinguished contributors of
the Dostoevski scholarship, speak of the same "narrative
effects" in seemingly incompatible terms. Namely, what
for the formalist Vinogradov, presumably brought up in the
spirit of romanticism, appears to have a comic effect (an
effect of "ironic stylization"(18)), for the structuralist
Kramarenko, presumably prejudiced against romanticism as a
modern man, becomes a manifestation of tragedy. ("Thus,
the character's tragedy," he says, "is permanently
accompanied by noise, music, and festive guests."(19))
However, a recourse to Freud and after him to Kierkegaard
and a number of modern thinkers, will help us to observe
that modern mentality does not know any distinction
between comedy and tragedy, in view of which one of
Golyadkin's doubles, his servant Petrushka can be said to
be a predecessor of one of Stravinskij's doubles,
"Petrushka," the latter carrying comedy and tragedy of our
time.

NOTES

     1. I shall draw a few examples and leave the rest
for the reader to discover: "For two monutes or so he lay
motionless in bed," (p. 11); "he had encountered two of
his colleagues" (p. 17); "I have come to bother you a
second time and for a second time I venture to ask your
indulgence." (p. 24). Fyodor Dostoevski, The Double,
trans. George Bird (Bloomington: Indiana University
Press, 1966). Page references to this edition are given
parenthetically in the text.

     2. I call "spatial," as opposed to "temporal," any
reference that can be called authentic due to its being
verifiable by senses, such as, for example, a reference to
"one or to," "a word or two," "two or three people," taken
from E.T.A. Hoffman "Automata," in E. F. Bleiler, ed., The
Best Tales of E.T.A. Hoffman, (New York: Dover
Publications, 1967), p. 90:   "When he had heard one or two
of the Turk's answers, he took the exhibitor eside and
whispered a word or two in his ear. The man turned pale,
and shut up his exhibition as soon as the two or three
people who were in the room had gone away." Here all the
nominal word-signs and numbers point to a narrator's
attempt to reproduce an exact picture of what has
happened. The notion of exactitude is not only not
tottered by a reference to imprecise figures, but even
reinforced by them, for the narrative truth is assumed to
be ascertained via narrator's sincere effort to tell the
truth.

By contrast, the same signifiers can be said to lose their referentiality in modern discursive convention. In an example from Dostoevsky that follows: "He saw one or two people as well. Or rather he didn't. He was no longer aware of anybody. Propelled by the same spring that had brought him bounding into a ball to which he had not been invited, he continued to advance steadily." The Double, p. 61, the signifier "one or two people" refers to neither "one" or "two," but a great many with whom the "he" of the narrative is destined to communicate in a non-conventional way, so that "one or two" can be identified with no immediate signified, but with a number of syntagmatically conjoined signifiers that turn into synonyms. What makes them synonyms if the nature of discursive predication which cancels their referentiality by abolishing the means of sensual perception: "he saw ... or rather he didn't ... noticing none of this or, more accurately, noticing it, but not looking..."

3.   The meaning of simultaneity and a grammatical bond between the "double" and the "two" is supported by word etymology. DOPPELGANGER. "Das diesen Wortern zugrunde liegende lat. Adjectiv du-plus 'zwie- faltig' ist gebildet aus duo 'zwei' und dem Stamm *pel- 'falten' (wie dt. Zweifel; vgl. ferner duo und falten: s.a.Diplom) . . . Doppelganger m (1976 by Jean Paul 'we sich selbst an ainem andern Ort [gehen] sieght', heute varallgemeinert zu 'einem andern zum Verwechseln ahnlicher Mensch')." Duden ed' Paul Grebe (Dudenverlag: Bibliographisches Institut, Mahnheim), Band 7, p. 115.

4.   Todorov's attempt to identify Gogol's Nose as a "limited case" of the fantastic genre comprised exclusively of romantic texts has created unsurmountable difficulties. To incorporate a modern discourse into the body of romantic ones, Todorov was bound to loosen up his theoretical assumptions which still did not help him to avoid imprecision and even confusion in his reading of Gogol. Suggesting, as he did, that "the narrative does not observe the first condition of the fantastic, that hesitation between the real and the illusory or imaginary be present, and it is therefore situated from the start within the marvelous," The Fantastic, trans. Richard Howard (Ithaca, N.Y.: Cornell University Press, 1970), p. 72, Todorov permits himself to ignore the fact that such "hesitation" is linguistically present in the text yet maintained at the level of characters' perception. To still support his argument in favor of Gogol's place among the fantastic narratives Todorov is found to assume a non-semiological position from which he states that Gogol "describes the life of Saint Petersburg down to its most mundane details" (p. 72). Finally, he welcomes such contradictory notions as "alegorical" and "literal," (the latter being employed in both literal and figurative sense) in order to conclude: "What Gogol asserts is precisely, non-meaning" (p. 73), as if "meaning and non-meaning" were categories clarified by way of asserting or negating them.

5. The appearance of the "double" is gradually
prepared by the narrative Golyadkin either decides to
conceal his identity as a matter of his strategy of
behavior or he assumes a self-effacing philosophy
characteristic of his existential doubts: "'Shall I
pretend it's not me, but someone extraordinarily like me,
and just look as if nothing has happened? It really isn't
me, it isn't me, and that's all there is to it. . . .'"
(p. 19); "'I'm a simple man. There's no outward show
about me. On this point, Doctor, I lay down my arms--or
to continue the metaphor, I surrender.'" (p. 24); "He had
no more life in him. He was finished in the full sense of
the word, and if at that moment he was still able to run,
it was only by some incredible miracle." (p. 71); Mr.
Golyadkin wanted to annihilate himself completely, to
return to dust and cease to be" (p. 73).

6. B. M. Eikhenbaum, "How Gogol's 'Overcoat' Is
Made," in Gogol from the Twentieth Century, ed. by Robert
A. Maguire, (Princeton, N.J.: Princeton University Press,
1974), p. 279.

7. For the purposes which will become clear further
on I have to clarify the essentially correct translation
of this segment. The original version of it, to wit:
"vyvelis babuski kotorye vorozat," (literally: "the
fortune-telling grandmothers are no more") constitutes an
abbreviation of the idiomatic expression "khorosho tomu
zhit' u kogo babushka vorozhit" (literally, "with a
fortune-telling grandmother one can be doing fine"). The
sense of this idiom no longer immediately identified by
the modern reader, has been trasmitted by the translator
as "those who push their favorites."

8. There are two kinds of "anticipation"-figure in
Dostoevsky discourse: "anticipation" through a recourse
to the familiar: ["Everything looked back at him
familiarly" (p. 11); "he turned to look at Dr. R . . .
windows. It was as he thought! The doctor was standing
at one of them," (p. 37); "But he was now almost sure it
was someone he knew. He'd seen him often. He'd seen him
somewhere quite recently even." (p. 78); "Mr. Golyadkin,
we must add, knew this man perfectly well, knew his name
even." (p. 79)], and secondly, anticipation as a form of
knowing the future ["He had sensed that if he once
stumbled eveything would immediately go to the devil. And
so it did." (p. 62); "Mr. Golyadkin knew, felt and was
quite convinced, that some new evil would befall him on
the way, and that some fresh unpleasantness would burst
upon him: that there would be, for instance, another
meeting with the stranger." (p. 80); "'Still, I
anticipated all this,' thought our hero. 'And I've
anticipated what it'll say.'" (p. 159); "'This isn't the
way to the door,' flashed through his mind, and indeed, it
was not." (p. 245)"].
Quite congruent with its major function, the figure
of anticipation negates itself by the end of the
narrative, just as the narrator and protagonist did in

anticipation of their respective doubles, and it does it in a bifurcated fashion as well. This means that it deactivates both its figures, a "recourse to the familiar": ["But what our hero had apparently been fearing, did not happen" (p. 246)]and "knowing the future" one: ["At this point something unexpected occurred. The door flew open with a bang, and on the threshold stood a man whose very appearance made Mr. Golyadkin's blood run cold" (p. 250)].

9.   Literally, "two sparrows."

10.   Compare such idioms as "Sam s vorob'ja a serdtse s koshku" ("Himself as little as a sparrow, his heart as big as a cat"); "Za obedom solovej, a posle obeda vorobej" ("At dinner sings like a nightingale, after dinner--like a sparrow"); "Starogo vorob'ia na mjakine ne obmanesh'" ("An old sparrow is not caught with chaff") in Vladimir Dal', Tolkovyj slovar' zivogo velikorusskogo jazyka, Vol. 1,(Moscow: Akademiia Nank, 1955), p. 242.

11.   Replication patterns are hierarchical, as they comprise either a scope of the entire novel viewed as a replica of Golyadkin's dream (pp. 166-171), or a single symbol, say, a phallic symbolism of Golyadkin's "confession", i.e., "umejut podnesti koku s sokom--translated, unsuccessfully, I believe, as "know how to spring an old surprise" (p. 32)--replicated in narrator's comment on Anton Antonovich's toadyism--"an old man as grey as a badger, crows like a cock and speaks some jolly verses (pp. 54-55)."

12.   See A General Introduction to Psychoanalysis, trans. Joan Riviere (New York, New York: A Clarion Book, 1963); An Outline of Psychoanalysis, trans. James Strachey (New York: The Norton Library, 1963); Five Lectures on Psycho-Analysis, trans. James Strachey (New York: Norton Library, 1952); Jokes and Their Relation to the Unconscious, trans. James Strachey (New York: The Norton Library, 1960).

13.   Freud, Outline of Psychoanalysis, p. 47.

14.   The narrative choice for a doctor to be German as well as its choice of German names for all real and fantasized aphrodisiac objects of Golyadkin's desire: form a German landlady, Karolin Ivanovna, to a German waitress and German-sounding name for his imaginary fiancee suggests a hidden dialogue with romanticism always associated with Germany and understood as literary cliche to which modern discourse always responds.

15.   Towards a Freudian Theory of Literature With an Analysis of Rasine's Phedre, Trans. Ch. Lee (Baltimore: Johns Hopkins University Press, 1979), p. 10.

16.   Frend, Outline of Psychoanalysis, p. 53.

17. Hoffmann's title of The Doubles strikes me as hitting the essence of the distinction between romantic and modern discourse by its choice of plurality. Here, two distinctly real people both mistaken one for another are eventually "recognized" for what each of them should actually be. The idea is that from the concept of "mistake" and "recognition" one is to derive a concept of infalliable truth supported by a polarized mode of thinking: good versus bad, "Hohenflug" versus "Sonsitz," "Golden Ram" versus "Silver Lamb" and so on.

18. V. V. Vinogradov, "K morfologii natural'nogo stilja," Poetika russkoj literatury (Moscow: Nanka, 1976), p. 129.

19. M. Kramarenko, "Prostranstvo i vremja v povesti F. M. Dostoevskogo "˘Dvojnik,'" p. 19.

6.
The Idiot: A Feminist Reading
OLGA MATICH

Besides traditional women characters, who see their roles
as submissive wives and mothers, Russian literature is
also characterized by so-called strong women and to a
lesser degree femme fatale images, whose functions are
predicated on sex role inversion. In accordance with the
principle of complementary distribution, their male
counterparts are the superfluous man and the effete
decadent male, who are weak in the realm of action, both
in their private and public lives. The strong woman type
is emotionally stalwart and self-reliant which is not to
say that she rejects the notion of a male partner. On the
contrary, she has the need to make a commitment, and in
the context of nineteenth century values the commitment
commonly takes the form of providing emotional support for
a man weaker than herself. The definition of female
strength in nineteenth century Russian literature conjures
up the image of the nurturing female, loyal to her man and
to the patriarchal system he stands for in spite of his
particular weakness. On the nature/culture continuum the
strong Russian woman is clearly identified with nature.
Since all societies devalue nature, and treat it as
inferior to culture, women, who are everywhere more
closely identified with the natural processes, are seen as
inferior to men.(1) This is also true in Russia in spite
of the idealization of nature and the cult of moist mother
earth.
     While the strong woman is forceful in that she has a
commitment, the femme fatale is strong only in relation to
masochistic and impotent male partner. Aggressive and
cruel, she sucks away the man's traditional strength, but
she does so with his approval. The usurpation of male
power by the masculinized woman serves the inverted sexual
fantasy of the decadent male, which is characterized by
sex role reversal and an anti-nature world view. The
woman remains a sex object even though it is she who
wields the whip. If we were to evaluate the strength of
the two character types, that of the femme fatale would be
marked as destructive while the resilience and vigor of
the strong woman is at least potentially constructive.
But it is curious that Turgenev's various women, Pushkin's
Tatianas, and Goncharov's Olgas do not have an ultimately
salutary influence on their superfluous men counterparts.

Dostoevski's The Idiot is his most important sustained statement regarding women, their moral superiority yet inferior social position. In this chapter, the focus will be on the novel's images of women characters, sex roles, and sex role reversals. The most complex and moving woman character is, of course, Nastasya Filippovna whose image is determined by the interplay of the fallen, fatal and emancipated components of her behavior. The Epanchin women, Aglaya and her mother in particular, combine strong women characteristics with those of incipient fatal types. Aglaya is also influenced by emerging feminist ideas. Vera Lebedev and Mrs. Ivolgin represent traditional feminine domestic virtues which remain untouched by thoughts of female rebellion. Myshkin, the clearly marked counterpart of the strong woman, whether nurturing or devouring, is an interesting mixture of superfluous man, decadent male, and the savior of the fallen woman. General Ivolgin is also a feminized male, but his feminization, unlike Myshkin's, is the result of his failure to live up to the male role.

Nastasya Filippovna plays a femme fatale role in Myshkin and Rogozhin's lives and is destructive and sadistic in her behavior toward the men around her. Her sadistic tendencies are clearly manifest at her birthday party, where she is to choose a husband from among Ganya, Rogozhin, and Myshkin. There is, however, a deeper explanation for her seemingly vampiric conduct. Nastasya Filippovna is the classic female victim, ravished at a tender age by the worldly and powerful Totsky, who then attempts to sell her as a piece of property to avaricious Ganya. It is her treatment as a material object that provokes the spiteful scenes. Because he is unrefined, Rogozhin is most direct in his objectification of the woman he wants to possess. He literally bids for her as at an auction and brings his 100,000 ruble payment wrapped in the Financial News. He even treats her corpse as a possession which he does not want to relinquish. In spite of her anger and rebellion, Nastasya Fillippovna has internalized her fallen woman reputation, which is reflected in her psychological make-up.

Decadent sex role inversion focuses on nonprocreative sexuality. In compliance with the anti-nature orientation of decadence, the fatal woman rejects her reproductive function and exhibits life-negating behavior. A haughty beauty, Nastasya has no maternal traits while Myshkin is sexually impotent. The feminized Myshkin's loss of virility does not, however, lead to decadent self-indulgence. It is he who is associated with children, both in Switzerland and upon his return to Russia, although his impotence means the end of the Myshkin family line, a characteristic decadent touch. Nastasya Filippovna's first meeting with Myshkin points to a potentially "decadent" distribution of sex roles between a powerful woman and her social inferior in the manner of the French decadent novel Monsieur Venus.(2) Nastasya mistakes Myshkin for a servant, establishing for a moment a reversed hierarchical relationship between them.

When we look closely at the bond between Myshkin and

Nastasya Filippovna, we find additional traces of
decadence, especially in their death orientation. At the
same time Nastasya's suicidal behavior is the result of a
deep sense of shame for her fallen condition and not
simply a reflection of her morbidity. The last book which
she was reading and never completed was Madame Bovary,
whose title character's pathetic fate is reminiscent of
that of Dostoevski's heroine. Instead of reading the book
to the end, she replicates Emma's suicide in her own
actions. This intertextual allusion offers another subtle
touch of decadent aesthetics, according to which life
imitates art. Dostoevski reveals his eclecticism and
complexity in building the archetypal foundations for
male/female relationships. He offers us a reevaluated
relationship between the fallen woman and her redeemer, by
adding decadent touches. The fallen woman refuses to
accept her degraded status humbly and rebels both in the
manner of a femme fatale and an incipient feminist.(3)
     Like some emancipated women of the 1860s, Nastasya is
very well educated and even knows the legal sciences,
clearly a male domain at the time. She is better educated
than her male suitors Myshkin and Rogozhin and attempts to
influence Rogozhin's intellectual development by providing
him with a basic reading list, in yet another example of
sex role reversals. In fact, she is imitating her
experience with Totsky, who provided her with an excellent
education as compensation for her sexual favors. The
difference is that Nastasya's gesture is not part of any
payment or economic exchange. Yevgeny Pavlovich refers to
her as a blue stocking, an image which contradicts her
flamboyant reputation. The narrator speaks of Nastasya's
"billiant wit" and secluded bookish life before her
involvement with Rogozhin and Myshkin. In spite of her
talents, she remains idle and has no profession which
would make her economically independent. Her alternatives
are the streets or the lowly work of a washer-woman or
house servant. The humiliating realization regarding her
economic dependence on Totsky motivates her ambivalent
behavior as much as her fall from virtue.
     Nastasya's incipient and inconclusive revolt against
the female role also characterizes the behavior of her
rival Aglaya, whose portrayal is clearly influenced by
political considerations.(4) In one of her conversations
with Myshkin, the impetuous Aglaya tells him that she has
read all the banned books and wants to run away from home,
study in Paris, and become a teacher, thereby making a
radical change in her social position. She resents being
treated as a desirable and expensive commodity on the
marriage market and does not want to be continually
displayed to all eligible suitors. Aglaya wants a relationship with a man which will defy convention and
consequently chooses "the idiot" over Yevgeny Pavlovich.
Unlike her sisters whose proper upper-class hobbies are
music and painting, Aglaya has no pastime and does
nothing. She refuses the useless feminine activities of
her class, hoping to some day find something more
meaningful to do. Although Mrs. Epanchin empathizes with
her daughters' eccentricities and free-spirited attitudes,

as a mother she would like to see them married. She fears
in particular Aglaya's nihilist and feminist orientation
and is upset by her recent short hair cut in the manner of
the closecropped radical girls of the sixties. Aglaya
does reject a conventional marriage arrangement and
fulfills her desire for socio-political engagement by
marrying a radical Polish patriot and joining the
committee for the restoration of Poland. Although this
outcome clearly displeased the author and indicates his
disapproval of Aglaya, it does mark her emancipation from
the traditional woman's role.

Aglaya is not only repelled by the whole process of
courtship and securing a profitable marriage arrangement
imposed upon her and her sisters but is also envious of
the male role. It is she who is the aggressor in her
relationship with Myshkin and so-to-speak proposes
marriage to him. She insists on talking to Myshkin about
dueling, a well defined male ritual, and instructs him
about guns, their quality, and use. When discussing
public executions with Myshkin, Aglaya expresses her
indignation at society's repudiation of women who stay and
watch executions together with the men. An element of
caprice and decadent morbidity characterize her attraction
to male activities in some instances. There is also
something morbid and sadistic about her request that Ganya
stick his finger in a burning candle and hold it there.
It is, in fact, reminiscent of the money burning scene and
Nastasya's challenging Ganya to pull out the 100,000
rubles from the fire with his bare hands. In spite of her
vindictiveness and capricious behavior, we should not
forget the Amazonian physical description of Aglaya and
her sisters, which produces a curious masculinized com-
posite portrait. When Myshkin collapses during his coming
out party at the Epanchins, it is Aglaya who catches him
in her arms, a clear reversal of the stereotypical
fainting scene. In the end, however, Aglaya is deeply
hurt by Myshkin's inability to choose between her and
Nastasya Filippovna and behaves like a spiteful woman.
The ambiguity of Aglaya's behavior makes her marriage to
the Pole difficult to interpret. Was it a spiteful act or
a genuine expression of commitment to a new cause?

It is interesting that Dostoevski's image of the
"positively beautiful individual" is a man with female
attributes, and the two nascently masculinized women are
both attracted to him and vice versa. Based on
traditional psychological and mythological notions of
gender-typed behavior, Myshkin's character traits are pre-
dominantly feminine. He is intuitive rather than
analytical passive and not agressive or competitive. Thus
he is always willing to give Nastasya up to Rogozhin, his
rival for her affection. In his preoccupation with human
relationships and relatedness, Myshkin's concerns are in
opposition to masculine abstractions and binary thinking.
He is very different from Yevgeny Pavlovich, whose
analytical statements and occasionally supercilious social
posture reflect a superior male attitude. Myshkin's
supportive and nurturing behavior as well as his
extraordinary capacity for self-sacrifice reveal a

maternal nature, which has already been mentioned apropos his involvement with children. Except at the Epanchin soiree, he is not one to judge and punish in the manner of a patriarchal father.

It is perhaps Myshkin's feminization which makes him unacceptable to society and ineffective, and even destructive, in his mission to save the world and the Fallen Beauty? We have here an interesting example of the hypocrisy of traditional JudeoChristian morality. The Christian ethic teaches us the feminine values of selflessness and sacrificial love, while the qualities which are valued in practice by those in power are identified with masculine behavior.(5) Myshkin's feminine goodness is admired by all, but in reality it is unproductive and even destructive because it contradicts the dominant male ethic. Conversely, when sex roles are inverted in accordance with the decadent model, strength is devalued because the fatal woman represents a life negating point of view.

In spite of his ineffectiveness, Myshkin is the only developed positive adult male character in the novel and clearly the moral superior to everyone else. The narrator and Dostoevski himself are ambivalent about Yevgeny Pavlovich and his human values, even though he is the author's ideological spokesman. While his analysis of Ippolit's views carries Dostoevski's stamp of approval, his mocking tone and lack of sympathy for the dying youth indicate his insensitivity. One can conjecture that it is Myshkin's female traits that determine his moral preeminence, especially since the women characters surpass the males in dignity, strength, and intelligence.(6) The woman who embodies the feminie ideal of service and resembles Myshkin most closely is the submissive and generous Vera Lebedev, although Dostoevski describes her as "simple-hearted and blunt as a boy" (p. 483), in a curious example of inversion. She stands for the domestic ideal and her projected marriage to Yevgeny Pavlovich will be based on a traditional distribution of sex roles. It is impossible to envision Vera's success in the male realm of action, without which the admiration for the feminine ideal is merely an abstraction.

The men in The Idiot are weak and for the most part morally tainted. If we exclude Yevgeny Pavolovich and the nondescript stereotypical perfect husband and son-in-law Prince S., who does not even have a personalized name, the male characters are dominated by the women around them. Epanchin's social influence derives from his socio-economic role, but he is clearly inferior to his wife in intelligence and perceptiveness and has considerably less domestic power. In seeking husbands for he daughters, Lizaveta Petrovna never loses her sense of personal values. While the General is very happy to marry Alexandra to Totsky because he is rich and influential, his wife opposes the match on moral grounds. She also intuits that there is something disreputable about Yevgeny Pavlovich, a most eligible bachelor and seemingly brilliant partner for Aglaya. Later we learn that he has been involved in shady financial transactions.

Unlike the Epanchins, the Ivolgins are not prosperous and stable, which results in the breakdown of traditional sex roles in the family and the feminization of the unsuccessful male. General Ivolgin does not fulfill his male role as head of household on any level. He is a drunk, an inveterate liar, and a financial and emotional drain on the family, while his wife is the long-suffering Russian woman who retains her dignity and endures the very difficult familial circumstances. Their daughter Varya is also a pillar of strength as she becomes the support of her family after Ganya's demise. Her marriage to the moneylender Ptitsyn reflects her sense of responsibility toward the family. At the same time, General Ivolgin needs to retain a semblance of parental authority. When meeting new young people, he will invariably say that he knew them when they were very small in order to establish his superior role. This is, of course, a parody of the role since Ivolgin is a failure as a father and at the very bottom of the male dominated power structure. The function of his ridiculous fantasies, which he translates into blatantly fraudulent stories, can be compared to the romantic fantasies of young girls and women in patriarchal society. Nastasya Filippovna's escapist dreams about a "real man" and a savior indicate her helplessness and inactivity and point to the identity of Ivolgin's and Nastasya's social positions. Feminization has a dual and ambiguous meaning in The Idiot: it produces the morally superior Myshkin, yet it is also the result of male degradation. The two significations replicate in a curious way the Madonna/ whore vision of women.

Like Ferdyshchenko and Lebedev, Ivolgin is a buffoon who grovels before those in power. The buffoon is an emasculated or degraded feminized male, who is viewed as an object which amuses and can be bought and sold. His masochism and need to please and be rewarded are comparable to the behavior of an oppressed woman. Except for the captain's widow, who is not a buffoon, however, Dostoevski does not degrade women in this way. They do not lose their pride and sense of dignity so totally even when life becomes intolerable. But this is only a moral distinction since women and "fallen men" are equal socio-economically, meaning that they have no power in the public domain. The liars and cheats in the novel are men. The patriarchal lie of male superiority is told by those in power, who also establish the double standard in judging Nastasya's and Totsky's respective social positions. The "fallen man" lies compulsively and ineffectively in the manner of Ivolgin and Lebedev.

The treatment of sex roles in The Idiot indicates Dostoevski's belief in the moral superiority of women rather than a real concern with their socioeconomic status. While demonstrating his admiration for domestic virtue in women, their strength and nurturing capacities, the author makes amply clear his disapproval of feminist activism, most obvious in his polemical jibes at Chernyshevsky's What's to be Done? Dostoevski's feelings about women and their social behavior are also reflected in his essays on the woman question that appeared in The

Diary of a Writer and The Citizen: he supported the
higher education of women and their professional
development(7) but feared and opposed their concurrent
politicization.(8) In the manner of many a nineteenth
century Russian writer, Dostoevski celebrated the feminine
ideal and encouraged women's professional development but
rejected political activism in the defense of women's
rights.

NOTES

    1. Sherry B. Ortner, "Is Female to Male as Nature is
to Culture?" In Michelle Zimbalist Rosaldo and Louise
Lamphere, eds., Women, Culture and Society (Stanford,
Calif.: Stanford University Press, 1974), p. 72.

    2. In Rachilde, Monsieur Venus (1885) (author's real
name was Marguerite Vallette, nee Eymery), the femme
fatale/decadent male relationship follows the prescribed
pattern of sex role inversion to a "T."

    3. For a fuller discussion of the fallen woman
character and femme fatale in nineteenth century Russian
literature, see Olga Matich, "A Typology of Fallen Women
in Nineteenth Century Russian Literature," in Paul
Debreczeny, ed., American Contributions to the Ninth
International Congress of Slavists, vol. II Literature,
Poetics, History, (Columbis, Ohio: Slavica, 1983) pp.
325-343.

    4. Some commentators claim that Aglaya's prototype
was Anna Korvin-Krukovskaya, a young nihilist who
interested Dostoevski before his second marriage (Richard
Peace, Dostoevski: An Examination of the Major Novels
[Cambridge, England: Cambridge university Press, 1971],
p. 81, ff. 16. The debate on the "woman question" began
in Russia in the late 1850s and early 1860s. Influenced
by French cooperative experiments and Chernyshevsky's
What's to be Done?, young female nihilists left their
families to study and devote themelves to useful
activities in newly established cooperatives and communes.
This movement is the historical basis for some of Aglaya's
aspirations.

    5. Mary Daly, Beyond God the Father: Toward a
Philosophy of Women's Liberation (Boston: Beacon Press,
1973), pp. 100-101.

    6. From Fedor Dostoevski, The Diary of a Writer:
"Sincerity, persistence, seriousness and honor, the quest
for truth and sacrifice are more developed in our women
than in men; and it has always been so in the Russian
woman ... a woman is more persistent, patient in her
pursuits; she is more serious than the man, wants work for
its own sake and not for the sake of appearances." Polnoe
sobranie sochinenii F. M. Dostoevskogo. (Vol. 9, 4th ed.,
Petersburg; 1891), p. 315.

7.   "Can we continue to deny this woman, who has so
visibly revealed her valor, full equality of rights with
the male in fields of education, professions, tenure of
office . . . ! This would be shameful and unreasonable
. . . since the Russain woman of her own accord has
assumed a place to which she is entitled; of her own
accord, she strode over those steps which until now had
set the limit to her rights." F. M. Dostoevsky, The Diary
of a Writer, vol. II, trans. Boris Brasol, (New York:
Octagon, 1973), p. 845.

8.   "Learning is no longer the goal but has become
the occasion or the pretext to wage war against society in
the name of some kind of new rights and the eradication of
some kind of old prejudices regarding women," wrote
Dostoevski in 1873 (Grazhdanin, May 28, 1873, No. 22, p.
627). Quoted in N. F. Budanova, "Neizvestnye stat'i
Dostoevskogo po zhenskomy voprosu (Opyt atributsii)," In
G. M. Fridlender, ed., Dostoevskii: Materialy i
issledovaniia, vol. II, (Leningrad: Nanka, 1976), p. 241.

7.
Narcissus Inverted: Fantastic-Realism as a Way of Knowing in *The Idiot*
DENNIS PATRICK SLATTERY

In his essay, "What is a Traditional Society?" Allen Tate leads us to consider fantastic-realism when he suggests that "in ages which suffer the decay of manners, religion, morals, codes, our indestructible vitality demands expression in violence and chaos; it means that men who have lost both the higher myth of religion and the lower myth of historical dramatization have lost the forms of human action."(1) Dostoevski's own poetics would seem to capture those forms of human action by means of what may be called fantastic-realism.

Fantastic-realism is both a poetic disposition as well as an attitude of perception. The most inclusive record of Dostoevski's philosophical reflections on this double vision is in his Diary of a Writer. But his novel The Idiot best expresses the implications of seeing through a glass doubly. The fantastic-realism in The Idiot is also a way of knowing the world mythically through the metaphor of Narcissus, the pagan patron saint of doubling. The Idiot may be understood as a poetic mythologem in which the lost forms of the Petersburg community are revitalized.

That Dostoevski was continually engaged in understanding how one perceives by way of imagination is evident throughout The Diary. Responding to one writer on the subject of miracles, Dostoevski asks: "Do not true events, depicted with all the exclusiveness of their occurrence, nearly always assume a fantastic, almost incredible character? The aim of art is not to portray these or those events in the way of life but their general idea, sharp-sightedly divined and correctly removed from the whole multiplicity of analogous living phenomena."(2) He later adds that the act of the artist is to stare at reality until he "sees and arrests that moment in which the subject resembles himself most (already one can sense the presence of Narcissus). This ideal, he continues, "although almost fantastic, is as real and as necessary to art and man as current reality." Genre, then, he concludes, "is the art of portraying current reality which the artist has personally felt and seen with his own [imaginative] eyes" (The Diary, p. 83). To "see" the ideal embedded in the real is the act of perceiving the real fantastically. It is to uncover the myth in the

commonplace and to recognize the commonness of mythic
action.

Dostoevski's manner of seeing strikes at the heart of
the kind of knowledge myths offer. We might recall the
double-natured Pan who Socrates tells us in Cratylus
embodies the two originary ways of speaking,(3) or the
double-faced Janus, god of doors, thresholds, and
beginnings who was sacred to the start of any important
communal action such as sowing or feasting,(4) or of
Narcissus, who confronts the unfamiliar beauty of himself
through reflection, and through reflection learns of his
own nature.(5) Clearly, doubling is in some fundamental
way concerned with the origin of important knowledge. It
is an originary move of the psyche to reveal itself to
itself. The act of doubling promotes the act of
reflection. Doubling is then, revelatory; it reveals the
fantastic within the limits of the real.

What, then, can Narcissus teach us of Dostoevski's
double vision which accommodates both the ideal and the
real at once? And how does his epileptic Prince Lev
Myshkin, the product of Dostoevski's wish to create "a
perfectly good man,"(6) reenact the myth of Narcissus in
an inverted way through the reflection of Parfyon
Rogozhin, his diseased dark double? And what of the
Russian community, described in the novel so often as
"tired, yellow-skinned to match the fog" in the
streets?(7) Through the doubling of Myshkin and Rogozhin
the people are awakened to their own image; through
disease and disruption the psyche of the community begins
to re-vision itself. Dostoevski knows that his people
have lost its nourishing images of wholeness, proportion,
and harmony. For him, this image is the only perfectly
good man--Christ. In order to revitalize this dead image,
Dostoevski creates a fantastic parody of his perfect
image. In a letter to his friend, Nikolay Strakhov, he
asks: "But is not my fantastic 'Idiot' the very dailiest
truth? Precisely such characters must exist in those
strata of our society which have divorced themselves from
the soil--which actually are becoming fantastic" (Letters,
vol. 1, p. 167).

The myth of Narcissus presents the young man with a
fantastic image which reveals the truth to him
(Metamorphoses, Bk. 3, 11.463-64). Like The Idiot, it is
a story about love and justice, about paralysis in the
face of self-identity. There is something shared by
Prince Myshkin and Rogozhin in the figure of Narcissus,
just as Echo's suffering is embodied in Nastasya
Filippovna as she seeks forgiveness and repentance for her
former actions. She is denied contrition, however, by the
angelic force of Myshkin, who tries to convince her she
needs no pardon, for her actions are sinless. She is,
additionally, driven towards greater squalor by the lusty
pursuit of Rogozhin, that character who would have
instinct and passion dominate head and heart. Nastasya's
attraction to and revulsion of Myshkin's desire to reclaim
Eden, as well as her struggle with Rogozhin's desires,
leave her, like Echo, in a state of despondency and final
death. Like Echo, Nastasya's love for both men "clings to

her and increases / And grows on suffering"
(Metamorphoses, Bk. 3, 11.397-400).
     Moreover, while certain moments of awakening through
suffering described in the Narcissus myth operate in The
Idiot through fantastic-realism, one should recall that
the myth has been pathologized in the inverted doubling of
the prince and his chthonic brother. Offered in this
novel is a recognition closer to Golyadkin's new awareness
in The Double in which, through what Theodore Ziolkowski
has termed "an inverse mirror reflection,"(8) all of the
stuffy clerk's opposite characteristics assume both image
and action. And, like The Double's action, The Idiot
reveals a fascination for the other self. Myshkin and
Rogozhin alternately embrace and attempt to destroy one
another; they pursue each other throughout the text with
the same intensity to possess and to destroy that they
individually level at Nastasya. Myshkin desires to
consume Rogozhin with his forgiveness, his "rage of
goodness,"(9) as R. P. Blackmur has described it, as
intensely as Rogozhin's passion to destroy Myshkin's
innocent fantasy that pity alone is enough to save the
world. Their mutual obsession to engulf the other leads
to the destruction of beauty--Nastasya--for neither fully
understands the act of loving selflessly.
     The final scene in the novel, then, which has been
variously interpreted, may best be understood through the
double image of the Narcissus myth in which the young
Narcissus suddenly reflects his image and senses a
knowledge of his own nature by it. Before his death,
Narcissus gazes into the pond and sees there the image
which calls up love within him: "I know the truth at
last. He is myself! I feel it, I know my image now. I
burn with love. Of my own self; I start the fire I
suffer. What shall I do?... If I could only escape from
my own body!" (Metamorphoses, Bk. 3, 11.463-69).
     The love which Dostoevski depicts at novel's end,
however, is not clouded by a wish to escape human
embodiment, but is rather an act of Christian love in
which both men reach out to accept what has been
unrecognized in themselves. What was fantastic in the
other now metamorphoses into the most painful truth. The
price paid for such knowledge is the sacrifice of beauty.
The action ends in darkness, but I would call the work's
entire action infernally comic rather than tragic, for the
Petersburg community has been shocked back to the earth
once again, and is now able to hope. Jean Magretta's
observation that "it is only in the abnormal or diseased
state that man experiences reconciliation or synthesis" of
self(10) applies equally here as it does to her discussion
of Myshkin's disease.
     Thus far in my exploration I have been concerned with
the doubling of action. I wish now to reveal the doubling
of image, but a doubling by inversion. Recall for a
moment that Prince Lev Myshkin, a young man of nobel
birth, enters the action a victim of epilepsy, "the
falling sickness" (The Idiot, p. 3), as he returns from
the Swiss mountains to Petersburg on the speeding train
from Warsaw. He sits directly across from his inverted

double, Parfyon Rogozhin, who also reenters the city after
convalescing in the country where he has rested from acute
attacks of brain fever. One suffers the pathology of the
body, while the other suffers from the heat of the head.
Frenzied, passionate, Rogozhin returns as one possessed
with the young Nastasya's beauty. Dostoevski suggests
that she is an emblem of classical beauty by placing in
her apartment a large statue of Venus, which inspires in
all who visit her "an overwhelming sentiment of
respect--indeed almsot of fear" (The Idiot, p. 144).
Sharing Venus's disposition, Nastasya too can be "both
benign and malignant; she possesses that eternally
feminine capacity to hurl men into both fear and madness.
Yet without Venus, ad Edith Hamilton writes, there is
neither joy nor loveliness anywhere.(11)

The symmetrical doubling opening the novel's action
carries through to the last pages wherein the two men are
described lying next to one another; both are terrified
and immobilized by the corpse of the woman in the bed
above them. Moreover, initially both are described as
possessing contrary appearances, reflecting contrary moral
dispositions. Rogozhin is described as "a short man
. . . with almost black curly hair and small grey, but
fiery eyes. He had a broad, flat nose and high
cheekbones. His thin lips were continually curved in an
insolent, mocking, and even malicious smile" (The Idiot,
p. 3) His figure suggests a wild, instinctual power
seeking release.

By contrast, Prince Lev Myshkin (whose Russian name
includes both lion--lev--and mouse--mysh) embodies less
the passion of Rogozhin than the dreaminess of disease; he
appears "above average height, with very fair thick hair,
with sunken cheeks, and a thin, pointed, almost white
beard. His eyes were large, blue, and intense; there was
something gentle, though heavy in their expression,
something of that strange look which allows some people to
recognize at first glance a victim of the falling
sickness" (The Idiot, p. 3). Together these two figures
mingle instinct and dream, desire and humility. Their
dual natures, seemingly at odds, continually confront one
another over the nymph-like Nastasya. Though both images
are fantastic and diseased, they are nonetheless
reflections or doubles of the community. For together the
prince and Rogozhin reflect a love diseased, divorced from
the earth, and uninformed by beauty. Myshkin's love is
abstract, severed from the body and from time; Rogozhin's
love is of the loins alone, without the heart. But they
are both needed in a community which has lost its cultural
ground.

Shortly after entering Petersburg, then, Myshkin
seeks out the Epanchin family, to whom he claims relations
through some ambiguous connection in the past. During one
of his first conversations with the three Yepanchin
daughters, Aglaya asks him if he has ever loved. The
prince modestly replies that, owing to his disease, he has
not known woman. Moreover, in this early scene he
candidly admits that his separation from Russia has left
him ignorant of folkways and norms of behavior peculiar to

his people. He does, however, decide to relate his story
of Marie, a Swiss village girl, who runs off with a
commercial traveller, only to be deserted by him and
punished by the village to which she returns. We learn in
retrospect that this small tale is in fact a compressed
version of the entire central action of the story which
will follow. For Marie is of course the prototype, indeed
the double, of Nastasya; both women flee in terror from
the unconditional forgiveness of the prince. His words
and actions represent virtue absolutized, separated from
vice. His humility becomes terrible, his compassion
devastating.

Coupled with Myshkin's urge to forgive comes an
increase in his dreaminess, as if he is already, early in
the novel, beginning to retreat from the human order of
Petersburg. Shortly after he tells the Marie story, he
describes an image of Switzerland in the form of a
waterfall that speaks of his growing dissociation from
Russia and the finiteness of human existence. It is a
dream image of retreat: "There was a waterfall there, a
small one; it came down from a great height, such a thin
thread, almost perpendicular--foaming, white and
noisy . . ." (The Idiot, p. 57). Moving through the sound
of the waterfall and the loftiness of the mountains,
Myshkin feels that in such an isolated state he could find
"a life a thousand times richer and more turbulent than
ours" (The Idiot, p. 58).

But only after he muses on the double moment of his
epilepsy later in the story do we realize how the complete
description captures metaphorically the condition of
disease; yet his image is only half complete, for it
denies the reality of Rogozhin's presence which Myshkin
must later accept as the consequence of his illness.
Furthermore, his memory of isolation and dream in the
Swiss mountains captures best the original meaning of an
idiot, namely, a private person, one who creates his own
reality apart from the shared public world.

However, if Myshkin is a metaphor, or a double of
part of the community's psyche, then we must read his
image as one shared by his audience. I want to suggest,
therefore, that this epileptic prince is a daimon of the
people's psyche. He is one half of the Narcissus image, a
dreamy shadow in the clear pool of memory which reflects
the disposition of those in strata of society who have
lost touch with the earth and with their collective
memory. For when the myth of a people is forgotten, it
emerges in distorted forms. Prince Myshkin is the central
figure of this distortion through disease. Dostoevski
himself asked how this is true when he posed in the
Notebooks on The Idiot the question: "The Idiot's
character. How is all of Russia reflected?"(12)

Myshkin is not, as many critics understand him, a
holy fool, or even a "harlequin Christ"(13) who brings
play and festival back into the community; rather, he is a
figure who prompts first astonishment, then ridicule, and
finally rejection. He is closer to the Greek pharmakos
figure than he is to Dostoevski's image of Christ. He is
a fantastic reflection of a true condition; however, as a

figure who expresses what Lawrence Porter has called "the
archetype of inversion,"(14) he reflects what is
absent--the full image of Christ.(15) The prince's
waterfall image of reality promotes images not of a shared
mythic reality rooted in the earth and in Orthodoxy, but a
private eternity without the friction of temporality and
incarnation. Rogozhin's reality, no less forceful, rushes
in almost on cue to destroy, or at least to hold in check
the fantasies of eternity. Myshkin's dreams slowly defer
to Rogozhin's human nature, his passions, his embodiment,
and his mortality.

Part of Dostoevski's poetic intention in creating the
double nature of man in his two characters is to reveal
the often overlooked intimacy between violence and
innocence. For when the prince and Rogozhin join as
opposing tendencies in the "dirty green" gloom of
Rogozhin's home, their attention centers on the garden
knife resting on a table between them. The knife, which
will soon fail to kill Myshkin at The Balance Hotel, will
later find the heart of Nastasya with more deadly
accuracy; it returns us to the natural garden in which
Narcissus gazes dreamily at himself with self-destructive
consequences. It therefore unites innocence and passion,
passivity and violence. Divided, both are equally deadly
forces. The knife is as well a double image, for it
unites the garden as a space of retreat and innocence as
well as the space of murder and pathology.

From the doubleness of the knife we should look to
the doubleness of Myshkin's actual disease, an illness
that begins again to wash over him as he is continually
snagged by the temporal, embodied order of Petersburg.
For the metaphor of disease implicates Dostoevski's
understanding of fantastic-realism.

Myshkin's musings on his illness immediately prior to
confronting Rogozhin, who hides in the niche of the
winding staircase at the prince's hotel, reveal two
moments of epilepsy; it is a double disease because it
offers its victim, just prior to the actual seizure, a
moment of brilliant light and clarity (remember his
waterfall vision here) only to be followed suddenly by
darkness and stupefaction. Those moments of insight "were
only a premonition of that final second . . . with which
the fit began. The second was, of course, unendurable"
(The Idiot, p. 208). When he thinks of these brilliant
moments of clarity later, he concedes to himself that they
were only disease, "a violation of the normal state." As
such, they were not to be understood as the highest form
of being, but on the contrary must be the lowest.
"Stupefaction, spiritual darkness, idiocy stood before him
as the clear consequence of these 'supreme moments'" (The
Idiot, p. 208).

Reflecting on it later, Myshkin's understanding of
the doubleness of the human soul finally pierces his
fantasy of innocence: "No, it was not that 'the Russian
soul was a dark place,' but that in his own soul there was
darkness, since he could imagine such horrors" (The Idiot,
p. 212). The suffering of Nastasya for her sins, the
suffering over his lost faith, the suffering of Holbein's

grotesquely contorted Christ in the painting which hangs
over the doorway in Rogozhin's house--all these forms of
suffering terrify and threaten Myshkin's fantasy that
paradise can be reclaimed in a fallen world.

The prince climbs the winding staircase in his
hotel(16) and perceives a man hiding in the wall's recess.
He tries unsuccessfully to pass by the figure without
looking at him; suddenly Rogozhin lunges toward him:

> Rogozhin's eyes flashed and a furious grimace
> contorted his face. His right hand was raised
> and something gleamed in it; Myshkin did not
> think of arresting it. He only remembered that
> he thought he cried out, "Parfyon, I don't
> believe it!" Then suddenly something seemed to
> break open before him; intense _inner_ light
> flooded his soul. . . . Then his consciousness
> was instantly extinguished and complete darkness
> followed. It was an epileptic fit, the first he
> had had for a long time (_The Idiot_, p. 217).

Disease, suffering, murder's attempt, and darkness
all assault our senses as fantastic, but in its action the
doubleness of Rogozhin and Myshkin balance one another as
two fundamental realities of the soul. The reality of the
fantastic emerges from the fantasy of this encounter.

As the prince and his chthonic brother spread their
pathology through Petersburg, the people begin to see
themselves more clearly through the metaphor of dis-ease.
For theirs is a communal disease, articulated by a growing
number of characters who swirl around the two men. Their
pathology promotes a new perception in the folk through
the double reflection of absolute compassion and extreme
passion. But their new knowledge is gained at the expense
of beauty. The wish for paradise demands that one pay for
such fantasies. As Prince S. reminds Myshkin later in the
novel: "'It's not easy to reach paradise on earth, but
you reckon on finding it; paradise is a difficult matter,
prince, much more difficult than it seems to your good
heart'" (_The Idiot_, p. 312).

The novel's end is the community's beginning, for it
has seen itself in the insubstantial reflections of the
two daimons. Myshkin and Rogozhin join together over the
corpse of Nastasya. Both are paralyzed and feverish by
the horror of her death. The reality of mortality shocks
the prince out of his private dreams of innocence in order
that he might comfort Rogozhin, who has fallen victim once
again to brain fever.

Though short lived, Myshkin's active human love
replaces unconditional pity; his act is selfless. He
accepts man's fallenness through Rogozhin and is able to
love this imperfection. The prince's falling sickness has
brought the entire community back down to earth.

The myth of Narcissus carries to the end, for it is a
myth of the soul coming to know itself through its own
fantastic image. _The Idiot_, then, is a novel of awakening
and reflecting; it expresses the action of earth, not
paradise, regained. Dostoevski's double vision of

fantastic-realism situates anew the fantasy embedded in
the real and the reality of the fantastic. Unlike
Narcissus, however, here the Russian soul does succeed in
embracing its own image.

NOTES

1. Allen Tate, Essays of Four Decades (Chicago: The
Swallow Press, 1968), p. 554.

2. Fyodor Dostoevski, Diary of a Writer, trans.
Boris Brasol (New York: George Braziller, 1954), p. 90.

3. Cratylus, trans. H. N. Fowler, The Loeb Classical
Library, IV (Cambridge: Harvard University Press, 1953),
p. 87. In another article I have developed the figure of
Pan in The Idiot. "Pan, Embodiment and Epilepsy:
Dostoevski's The Idiot" in Dragonflies: Studies in
Imaginal Psychology, vol. 1 (Spring 1979), 39-45.

4. The Meridian Handbook of Classical Mythology, ed.
Edward Tripp (New York: New American Library, 1970), p.
328.

5. Ovid, Metamorphoses, trans. Rolfe Humphries
(Bloomington: Indiana University Press, 1964), pp. 67-73.

6. Fyodor Dostoevsky to his sister Vera, January 1,
1968. Letters of Fyodor Dostoevsky to His Family and
Friends, trans. Ethel Colburn-Mayne (New York: McGraw
Hill, 1964), p. 142. He goes on to explain in the same
letter that creating images of goodness and beauty is
almost impossible in the world, for "ideals have long been
wavering" (p. 142).

7. Fyodor Dostoevsky, The Idiot, trans. Constance
Garnett, revised Avrahm Yarmolinsky (New York: Heritage
Press, 1966), p. 3. All quotations from the novel will be
from this volume.

8. Theodore Ziolkowski, Disenchanted Images: A
Literary Iconology (Princeton: Princeton University
Press, 1977), p. 183.

9. R. P. Blackmur, "A Rage of Goodness: The Idiot
of Dostoevsky." The Critical Performance, ed. Stanley
Hyman (New York: Random House, 1956), p. 245.

10. Jean Magretta, "Radical Disunities: Models of
Mind and Madness in Pierre and The Idiot," Studies in the
Novel, 10(Summer 1978); 243.

11. Edith Hamilton, Mythology (New York: New
American Library, 1960), pp. 32-33. In Book 19 of
Metamorphoses Ovid describes how Venus is also the goodess
of love and charm as well as of marriage.

12. Fyodor Dostoevski, The Notebooks for The Idiot, trans. Katharine Strelsky, ed. Edward Wasiolek (Chicago: University of Chicago Press, 1967), p. 193.

13. Harvey Cox, The Feast of Fools: A Theological Essay on Festivity and Fantasy (New York: Harper and Row, 1969), p. 147ff. Myshkin is an even more originary figure than Christ, more of a daimon than a comic divinity.

14. Lawrence Porter, "Devil as Double in Nineteenth Century Literature: Goethe, Dostoevsky, and Flaubert." Comparative Literature Studies 15, (1978); 332. Porter rightly maintains, I believe, that "literary doubles may be represented by icons of the protoganist: shadows, portraits, reflections, statues, siblings, twins, etc." (p. 318).

15. "There is in the world only one figure of absolute beauty: Christ." Letters of Dostoevsky, vol. 1, p. 142.

16. While section of Elizabeth Dalton's recent study, Unconscious Structure in The Idiot (Princeton, N. J.: Princeton University Press, 1979), are informative, the heavy Freudian apparatus she brings to bear on the novel forces her interpretation to be more concerned with Freud than with Dostoevski.

8.
Notes from the Underground: One Hundred Years After the Author's Death

RADO PRIBIC

Ten decades have elapsed since Dostoevski's death, but many of the problems and ideas elucidated in his novels and novellas are still germane to the reality of our time. The same is true of Dostoevski's polyphonic style, which L. Grossman called "a truly brilliant page in the history of the European novel."(1)

Notes from the Underground(2) was written in 1864. It stands at the threshold of Dostoevski's post-Siberian period and includes in rudimentary form the fundamental ideas and aesthetic principles which underlie his subsequent major novels. The protagonist, the underground man, is the archetype of all underground men. His troubles are generated by the predicament of his generation, caught up in the toils of conflicting ideologies, none of which succeeded in fructifying and transforming real life. "Today we do not even know where real life is . . . we do not know what to join, what to keep up with, what to love, what to hate; what to respect, what to despise," says the underground man at the end of his confession (D, 244).

Assuming that creative literature constitutes a major expression of thought and response in a given period, the underground man may be considered a socio-historical phenomenon; yet Notes itself is, in the first place, a work of art, not an historical document. However, Dostoevski, who throughout the entire novel does not interfere with the underground man's stream of consciousness, adroitly closes the gap between fiction and reality in a footnote which reads: "people like the author of these notes may, and indeed must, exist in our society, if we think of the circumstances under which this society has been formed" (D, 133).

Let us now examine which of the underground man's problems and views are still applicable in our time.

The underground man's most conspicuous traits are acute intellect and heightened self-consciousness. These faculties make the protagonist extremely sensitive toward himself and critical of the surrounding world. They make him doubt and contradict everything, and, at the same time, they intensify his egocentrism and his vanity to such an extent that he loses the capacity to understand others objectively and begins to judge people only by his own consciousness. "Now, it is absolutely clear to me, because of an infinite vanity that caused me to set myself impossible standards, I regarded myself with furious disapproval, bordering on loathing, and then ascribed my own feelings to everyone I came across," confesses the underground man (D, 168).

The underground man's solipsism also corrodes his emotional life. He becomes unable to commit himself and can no longer reach out to and affirm the other's self.(3) Thus, from time to time, the underground man retreats into the world of dreams as a substitute for love and friendship. He plays this game so well that he takes it for reality; he sheds tears and suffers. But none of his dreams ever materialize, and the underground man remains an unfulfilled dreamer.

The underground man spends twenty years in self-imposed seclusion; he listens to his own consciousness and torments himself, to the brink of insanity. He indulges in self-destructive analysis; he engages in polemics with himself and other consciousnesses and draws the entire surrounding world into the process of self-awareness. Then he reveals himself and explains his views in a confessional utterance which, according to him, is mercilessly sincere, for the final truth about an individual can be given only by the individual himself. Since the confession is not intended for publication, the underground man does not embellish anything; neither is there a single flash of remorse in the entire work. "Doesn't it seem to you, ladies and gentlemen, that I am repenting of something before you, that I am asking for forgiveness for something? I am sure that seems so. . . . But I assure you that I do not care if it seems so to you," says the underground man (D, 135).

The first part of the Notes is a conglomeration of many views and ideas which never develop into a full narrative. Using interior dialogue, the underground man delves into his own consciousness, seeks assessments of himself and anticipates what others will think about him. In the next moment, he annihilates his own definition and shatters the final judgment of his fictitious discussant. He constantly strives to keep one step ahead of his interlocutor and creates loopholes for himself that enable him to continue the dispute as long as he wants and to cut it off whenever it pleases him. His entire train of thought is a vicious circle, consisting of thesis and antithesis without a synthesis.

The underground man begins his confession with a complaint about his poor health. He is aware of his illness but refuses to ask for medical help simply out of contrariness. "I know very well that I am harming myself and no one else. But, it is out of spite that I refuse to ask for the doctor's help. So my liver hurts? Well, let it hurt even more!" (D, 134). The protagonist continues to live in Petersburg, although he knows that he cannot afford it financially and that the climate is unhealthy. He annuls the ruthless sequence of cause and effect with inertia and opposes the mechanistic inevitability of the laws of nature with his whimsical will. "Where are the

primitive causes for any actions, the justification for
them? . . . I deliberate but the result is that every
primary cause drags along another cause that seems to be
truly primary, and so on and so forth, indefinitely. . ."
(D, 146). And he concludes his reasoning, "The best thing
is to do nothing at all, conscious inertia is the best. A
toast to the mousehole!" (D, 164). The underground man
dreams of a useful and worthwhile life, yet the first
thing he does after leaving school is to give up his
position and break all ties with the past (D, 190). He
longs for the sublime and the beautiful, but, just when he
is most conscious and capable of refinement, he behaves
abjectly (D, 137). In the office, the underground man is
rude and mean with people and makes them feel miserable,
yet he soon detects that there were many elements in his
nature that are just the opposite of wicked (D, 134).

The underground man painfully senses the disparity
between his character and its manifestation under given
circumstances, but he goes on destroying his emotions with
his intellect and annihilating his rational considerations
with his whimsical will. He cannot change, for only a
fool can make anything he wants of himself (D, 135).
Finally, the underground man reaches the point where he no
longer discerns what is right and what is wrong, whether
he believes what he is saying or is just telling a pack of
lies (D, 164). He begins to consider this as the normal
state; he even derives pleasure from it. And he draws the
conclusion that everything is all right as long as he is
aware of it. Thus, the underground man's self-awareness
absorbs all other features of his character, dissolves and
devastates all concrete traits of his image, until nothing
is left but utter inner alienation. But, at the same
time, he longs for at least one defining feature. He
would not mind if someone were to call him a sluggard.
"How awfully pleasant it would be to hear this about
myself. That would mean that I am clearly defined, that
there is something to be said about me" (D, 147).

The underground man's relationship with his fellowmen
is marred by the same contradictory elements that are
active in his personality. That brings him into conflict
with not only himself but the external world as well.
Aware of his keen intellect, the underground man considers
himself superior to his fellowmen, yet he immediately
develops an inferiority complex and retires into his
mousehole when he has to face normal men. In his hole, he
plunges into never ending hatred; he thinks up all kinds
of humiliation and prepares vengeance, knowing all the
time that there has been no humiliation; nor is there
anything to be avenged (D, 140-141). The vicious circle
of these polemics goes on and on, until the underground
man brings it to a sudden end.

In his self-absorbed reclusiveness, the underground
man rebuts the affirmation of another person's
consciousness. There is no "we" in the underground man's
thinking; there are only "I" and "the others." The
majority of these others is, according to the underground
man, stupid and narrow-minded; they resemble one another
like a flock of sheep, have no capacity for inventiveness,

and think and express themselves in prefabricated
patterns.

The others are repugnantly vicious and immoral. They
humiliate, hurt, and bully one another; they look down
upon others as if they were houseflies and use them as
doormats. They judge one another by their clothing and
professional success and not by their moral qualities.
But, no matter how arrogantly they behave, how deeply they
wallow in mud and vices, they will feel no pangs of
conscience, for they are not even aware of their depravity
(D, 137).

The others are also hypocrites. They pretend to be
honest and sincere, but all they have in mind is trying
not to lose sight of the useful. They rave about the
sublime and the beautiful but are rogues at the bottom of
their hearts. They speak of ideals but would not raise a
little finger to actualize these ideals, for they would
never jeopardize their careers by standing up against the
well-established order of society.

Now, how can an intelligent man function in a society
comprised of members who are corrupt, immoral, hostile,
and cruel? To this the underground man has three answers
to suggest. First, one may, against his better judgment,
accept the world, with its inanities and contradictions,
and become a spineless creature like the others (D, 135).
Yet, since an intelligent man cannot keep out his
conscience, he will loathe himself for this deliberate
self-deception (D, 103, 146). Secondly, one can continue
the struggle for truth, although that will entail never
ending clashes with the others and with society. Finally,
man may realize that there is no remedy to his situation
and, as a result, retire into abolute inertia (D, 142-143,
145).

Because of his critical and negative attitude toward
his fellowmen, the underground man is unable to establish
a close relationship with the others. Love, commitment,
and forgiveness are alien concepts to him. He hates his
distant relatives who had brought him up, because of their
nagging and because they had dumped him in a boarding
school He never communicates with his schoolmates, nor
does he make friends at work. Once, a nice, yielding boy
becomes his friend. But the underground man begins
immediately to rule his mind. He instills in him contempt
for the others and forces him to break with them. When he
finally has full possession of the boy, he hates and
rejects him. "It was as though I had only wanted his
total friendship for the sake of winning it and making him
submit to me," says the underground man (D, 190).

The only person who is capable, at least temporarily,
of standing up to the underground man's self-destructive
consciousness is the prostitute, Liza. The underground
man meets her after a disastrous evening with some former
schoolmates and begins to take out his own humiliation on
her. The short-lived relationship with Liza is a fine
example of the vicious circle in which the underground
man's diabolic consciousness spins. In order to
intimidate Liza, the underground man concocts a macabre
funeral story about a prostitute. Then, noticing that the

story does not touch Liza's heart, he shifts the center of
gravity to a more sentimental matter. He raves about the
beauty of family life, the mystery of love, the rosy
cheeks and miniature nails of babies (D, 214-215). This
time he succeeds. He gives Liza his address, immediately
regretting the move, since he is not sure whether he
really wants her to come. At home, the underground man
daydreams about rescuing Liza and turning her into a fine,
intelligent woman who would, of course, fall in love with
him (D, 227). When Liza finally and unexpectedly arrives,
she finds the underground man in a rather anti-heroic
situation, snapping like a vicious dog at his servant. In
a blind rage, the underground man shouts at Liza that he
has lied to her, that he wants only power and a role to
play. He reveals his perverse and selfish character and
then screams that he will never forgive her for having
witnessed his nervous breakdown and for having listened to
his confession.
    When the underground man finally realizes that,
despite all he has said, Liza intuitively understands that
he is a very unhappy creature, he is furiously drawn to
her. In order to shake off Liza's domination, he destroys
his image in her eyes with a devilish act. He makes love
to Liza and then, sending her away, slips a five ruble
bill into her hand (D, 233-243).
    The underground man explains his stupid and spiteful
conduct in a summarizing statement: "I could not fall in
love because, for me, loving meant bullying and morally
dominating. I have never been able to imagine any other
way of loving and have reached a point where I think that
love consists of a voluntary concession by the object of
my love and my right to bully it" (D, 240).
    Liza's departure signals the final break with the
outer world. It is symbolized in the squeaking and bang
of the heavy apartment door and the dead silence and
darkness of the street, which is covered with wet,
yellowish snow. The inner and outer alienation of the
underground man is now complete.(4)
    The underground man's polemics with himself and the
others are tightly interwoven with his ideological views.
One of the principal ideas set forth in the dispute with
socialist utopianism is that man is not a final quantity
upon which stable calculation may be made. The equation 2
X 2 = 4 is inapplicable to mankind. Man wants to be free
and will try to overturn any rules that are forced upon
him. He does not want to become a piano key or an organ
stop. He will reject the well-engineered crystal palace,
because the absolute order of it would destroy his
creative freedom. In a world in which everything is
planned, life will become extremely boring; there will be
no doubts, no suffering, no chaos, no destruction (D,
152).
    The underground man also argues with utilitarianism,
which was rather popular in the 1860s. It is
self-deceiving to assume that man will do only those
things that lie in his best interest. One may shower upon
man all earthly blessings, drown him in happiness, and
give him economic security. Still, he will give it all

up, just to inject his lethal fancies into all the
soundness (D, 154-158). Man will never stop doing nasty
things; he will not become good and virtuous only because
it is in his interest to do so (D, 148-149). And he will
send reason and all things useful and beautiful to hell,
just to establish his right to the most abstract wishes
(D, 153)

Another idea propounded by the underground man, on
various occasions, is that man has an aversion to seeing
his desires fulfilled. He likes to view his objectives
from a distance and enjoys the process of achieving more
than the goal itself. He is almost afraid of reaching the
goal toward which he is working. Achievement means
stagnation, the end of desires and wishes. Man is not an
ant, which considers the anthill its ultimate goal. His
life is an uninterrupted drive for new goals (D, 159-161).

The last idea advocated by the underground man is
that man does not mellow under the influence of
civilization, does not become less bloodthirsty or less
prone to war. Through the centuries, man only becomes
more vicious, more bloodthirsty, creating an ever greater
variety of sensations. In the past, man slaughtered,
without any pangs of conscience, those he felt had to be
slaughtered. Today, man considers bloodshed terrible, yet
he continues to practice it, on an even larger scale. The
tyrants of our time are so numerous and familiar to us
that they are not even conspicuous. Their methods are so
savage and horrifying that they push all the cruelties of
barbarous times into the background (D, 150-151). Men
"fight and fight; they are fighting now, they fought
before, and they will fight in the future" (D, 157).

The predicament of the underground man and the
problems and ideas he touches upon are all human and
universal; they transcend societies and time periods. One
has only to look around to find numerous glaring parallels
in our century. During the past hundred years, man's
intellect has performed miracles in technology and the
sciences, but the technical process has not really freed
man; it has only brought closer the era of the
well-engineered crystal palace. Most of all, man has
failed to match his scientific virtuosity with moral and
ethical understanding, and little has been done to improve
human relationships. As before, man is plagued by
divergent ideological, political, and social concepts.
The age-old question of good and evil is still a matter of
arbitrary interpretation, and the need for truth is not
strong enough to prevent man's imagination and train of
thought from being perverted into bias and prejudice. Men
are still vicious and cruel; they expose one another to
unjustifiable hardships and to the most incomprehensible
situations, far removed from ordinary life. Finally, if
one scrutinizes past historical developments, one might
draw the depressing conclusion that man learns nothing
from history; he is still fighting, fighting, fighting.
And yet, despite physical and spiritual imprisonment, man
continues to cherish his individual freedom and employs a
great part of his ingenuity to guard against interfering
elements. Thus, in conclusion, it can be said that the

three possibilities for survival given by the underground
man apply to our time as well: agree to everything and
become a spineless creature; fight for the truth and one's
own views and suffer; or withdraw and retire into the
underground.

NOTES

1.   Leonid Grossman, Poetika Dostoevskogo (Moscow;
1925), p. 165.

2.   Feodor Dostoevski, Sobranie sochinenii v desiati
tomakh (Moscow: Goslitizdat, 1956), IV, PP. 133-244.
Subsequent references to this edition will appear in the
text as D, followed by the page number. All quotes are
translations by the author of this chapter.

3.   Viacheslav Ivanov, Freedom and the Tragic Life.
A Study in Dostoevski (New York: Farrar, Strauss, and
Gironx, 1952), pp. 23-45;   Michail Bakhtin, Problems of
Dostoevsky's Poetics, trans. R. W. Rotsel, (Ann Arbor,
Mich.:   Ardis, 1973), pp. 7-8.

4.   About the nihilistic aspect in the Notes from the
Underground see Rado Pribic, Bonaventura's "Nachtwachen"
and Dostoevski's "Notes from the Underground". A
Comparison in Nihilism, Slavistische Beitrage, No. 79,
Munich, 1974.

9.
Kirillov, Stavrogin, and Suicide
ROGER L. COX

The question of suicide is crucial in The Possessed, and
it receives considerable attention in the rest of
Dostoevski's fiction as well. In The Brothers Karamazov,
Alyosha's manuscript on his elder's teachings records both
what is offered as the official church position and the
personal attitude of Zosima toward suicide:

> But woe to those who have slain themselves on
> earth, woe to the suicides! I believe that
> there can be none more miserable than they.
> They tell us that it is a sin to pray for them,
> and outwardly the Church, as it were, renounces
> them, but in my secret heart I believe that we
> may pray even for them. Love can never be an
> offence to Christ. For such as those I have
> prayed inwardly all my life, I confess it,
> fathers and teachers, and even now I pray for
> them every day.(1)

Thus, according to Alyosha Karamazov, the church regards
those who commit suicide as having separated themselves
voluntarily and eternally from the body of Christ; but the
man whom Alyosha takes as his model strives on the only
way he can to redeem them from that condition.
    In The Possessed, there are at least four actual
suicides if we include the chapter which contains
Stavrogin's confession; and the book's principal
theoretician of suicide is Alexei Nilitch Kirillov. At
the time of his first appearance, Kirillov is writing an
article on the subject; and in this respect he resembles
both Raskolnikov in Crime and Punishment and Ivan in The
Brothers Karamazov, who write on crime and on the relation
between church and state respectively. All three tend to
be philosophical and atheistic, and to attempt to
systematize their thinking on a subject that turns out to
be crucial to their own existence. In a conversation with
the narrator, Kirillov clarifies the subject of his
article, which had been misunderstood and misrepresented
by Liputin and others. "I only seek the causes why men
dare not kill themselves," says Kirillov, who goes on to
specify only two such causes, "one very little, the other
very big."(2) The first of these is "pain," and the
second is "the other world." As for the people who

actually commit suicide, "There are two sorts," Kirillov argues, "those who kill themselves either from great sorrow or from spite, or being mad, or no matter what . . . they do it suddenly. They think little about the pain, but kill themselves suddenly. But some do it from reason--they think a great deal" (p. 113).

It seems clear that for Kirillov, the two types of suicide correspond to the two impediments. Those who overcome the "very little" impediment, the dread of physical pain, "kill themselves suddenly." Their motive, which has its origin in sorrow, or spite, or madness, "or no matter what," is essentially irrational, and their action, within the framework of his analysis, is insignificant. But those who overcome the "very big" impediment, the philosophical fear of "the other world," are much more important. They are also few and far between--"He who dares kill himself is God. . . . But no one has once done it yet," says Kirillov (p. 115). The fundamental irrationality (the absurdity, if you will) of Kirillov's argument is apparent to the narrator, if not to Kirillov himself: "'Of course he's mad,' I decided," the narrator concludes as he takes his leave.

The contradiction implicit in Kirillov's philosophical theory parallels the one contained in Shigalyov's political theory set forth much later in the novel. But in Shigalyov's case the proponent of the theory, who is the butt of considerable humor and who is identified repeatedly as "the man with the long ears," at least recognizes the contradiction, though he clings to his theory no less tenaciously than Kirillov clings to his. Shigalyov is interrupted again and again by the laughter of his audience as he propounds his ridiculous theory to the ragtag group of "revolutionaries" headed by Pyotr Stepanovich Verkhovenski. "I am perplexed by my own data," says Shigalyov, "and my conclusion is a direct contradiction of the original idea with which I start. Starting from unlimited freedom, I arrive at unlimited despotism. I will add, however, that there can be no solution of the social problem but mine" (p. 409). Likewise, Kirillov starts with an emphasis upon pure rationality and ends with the obliteration of human consciousness; moreover, he implies that there can be no solution to the problem of God but his.

Despite this contradiction, Kirillov's theory has considerable appeal even for readers who do not share Dostoevski's religious concerns. The desire "not to be" is deeply rooted in human nature and probably comes to the surface of almost anyone's consciousness at least occasionally. For some people--especially those who, in the words of St. John the Divine, are "neither cold nor hot"--Kirillov's "other world" may be no impediment at all to suicide, whereas the fear of physical pain may be very real to them. Those who are utterly without hope so far as the "other world" is concerned tend, by the same token, also to be without fear. In such cases, Kirillov's theory could very well have some appeal as a basis for rationalization. It provides those who are in fact deterred from suicide by something which Kirillov regards

as insignificant an apparently profound philosophical
justification for doing what they are inclined to do
anyway and to remove, by concealment, what is for them the
most important actual impediment to such action.

For readers who do share Dostoevski's religious
concerns, Kirillov's theory is even more interesting.
Kirillov voices a number of thoughts and ideas which recur
frequently in the Dostoevski novels and which were
obviously dear to the author himself--Kirillov aspires to
"eternal life here" (p. 239); he asserts that all life is
good for those who know it is good (p. 240); and he is
able to specify the exact moment ("thirty-seven minutes
past two" of the preceding Wednesday, pp. 240-241) when he
became happy in such a manner that his life is utterly
changed from that moment on. To the extent that these
ideas are religious, they are related in Dostoevski's
thinking to passages in the Johannine writings of the New
Testament--particularly the Gospel of John and the Book of
Revelation. Both the story of Lazarus in Crime and
Punishment and the epigraph for The Brothers Karamazov
come from John's gospel; and the angel of the Apocalypse
who "swears that there will be no more time" (Rev. 10:5-6,
K.J.V.) is referred to specifically in both The Possessed
(p. 239) and The Idiot.(3) Likewise, the words "miracle,"
"mystery," and "authority," which figure prominently in
"The Grand Inquisitor" echo repeatedly through the Book of
Revelation. Clearly then, when Kirillov speaks of God, of
time standing still, and of knowing that "everything is
good," he is dealing with ideas that Dostoevski himself
cherished.

But the central contradiction of Kirillov's suicide
theory, the "madness" observed by the narrator, remains to
puzzle the reader. At what point does the reasoning go
astray? By what contortions of the intellect does the
ordinary and insignificant individual rise to the status
of a "man-god" by means of selfslaughter? The answer to
these questions comes closest to being explicit in the
conversation between Kirillov and Pyotr Stepanovich late
in the novel in the chapter called "A Busy Night" (esp.
pp. 625-630). Explaining his idea to the cynical Pyotr
Stepanovich, Kirillov says, "For three years I've been
seeking for the attribute of my godhead and I've found it;
the attribute of my godhead is self-will! . . . I am
killing myself to prove my independence and my new
terrible freedom" (p. 630). When Pyotr Stepanovich
suggests that killing someone else would be a better way
of showing one's self-will, Kirillov scornfully rejects
the idea--that, he says, would be "the lowest point of
self-will," not the highest (p. 628). Because he is no
longer a political person, what Kirillov desires is not a
practical assertion of power over someone else, but a
purely symbolic action, which would be not only
significant and irrevocable but also entirely
self-contained and perfectly harmonious--by "self-
contained" I mean "involving no one else's will but his
own" and by "harmonious" I mean "involving no conflict
whatever between the doer's will and the receiver's will,"
which is the case by definition since the action is

reflexive (unless of course the individual's will is
divided against itself). One cannot help thinking that
Kirillov's motive must be no less aesthetic than
philosophical and religious, since the theory does have an
almost classical symmetry and purity about it. Moreover,
the artist who executes such a design for action could
never be accused of repeating himself in his later works.

The theory has religious significance not simply
because it culminates in a violation of the commandment
"Thou shalt not kill," nor even because the Russian church
regarded the suicide as an utterly lost soul, but because
it involves--by design or by coincidence--a major point of
Pauline theology. St. Paul was of course the premier
theologian of the Western (Catholic) church, which
Dostoevski regarded with extreme distaste. In the seventh
chapter of Romans, Paul defines sin, at least indirectly,
as the disparity between willing and doing, as the failure
or bondage of the will. In Paul's words, "I do not
understand my own actions. . . . I can will what is right,
but I cannot do it. For I do not do the good I want, but
the evil I do not want is what I do. Now if I do what I
do not want, it is no longer I that do it, but sin which
dwells within me" (Romans 7:15-20, R.S.V.).

The converse is equally true; when I do not do what I
want to do, it is likewise indwelling sin which causes the
failure--hence the familiar distinction between sins of
commission and those of omission in the general
confession.

Kirillov succeeds in devising and carrying out an
action which perfectly embodies the intention behind it,
and which therefore gives the lie, as it were, to the
doctrine of the bondage of the will. In one grand gesture
he is able, perhaps for the first time in human history in
quite this way, to fuse willing and doing in one
"selfless" and "sinless" action. In so doing he "defeats
sin" and, in a manner of speaking, raises himself to the
level of a god. The classical beauty of that action is
somewhat marred, though, by Kirillov's ferociously biting
Pyotr Stepanovich's finger just before blowing his own
brains out. And the philosophical significance of the
suicide is probably not clear to Shatov's wife, who within
hours after giving birth to a child discovers Kirillov's
body while searching for her husband, who, though she does
not know it, already lies murdered by Pyotr Stepanovich's
"revolutionary quintet." One also wonders why Kirillov is
willing to write a note taking the blame for Shatov's
murder if his suicide must be "motiveless" in order to be
entirely successful. Such a note would tend to create the
impression that Kirillov's is just another suicide, done
"either from great sorrow or from spite."

Two of the suicides in The Possessed are intelligible
within Kirillov's analysis as being prompted by either
great sorrow or remorse. One of them--that of the young
man who shoots himself through the heart after squandering
his family's savings, which had been entrusted to him for
the purpose of buying articles for his sister's trousseau
(pp. 332-334)--is introduced into the story almost
gratuitously. A large party of the main characters are on

an expedition, a kind of holiday outing, the purpose of which is to visit the local saint and prophet (who is even more eccentric than most of Dostoevski's characters), when they get word of what has happened. They stop at the hotel to investigate, and the occasion provides the opportunity for a number of them to comment upon the suicide of a complete stranger. One of the ladies, in seconding the suggestion that they go in to see the body, says, "Everything is so boring, one can't be squeamish over one's amusements, as long as they're interesting." After everyone has stared at the body 'with greedy curiosity,' the narrator prefaces comments made by members of the party with the suggestion that 'in every misfortune of one's neighbor there is always something cheering for an onlooker—whoever he may be' (p. 334). The comments which follow seem heartless and inane at best: "One observed that his was the best way out of it, and that the boy could not have hit upon anything more sensible; another observed that he had had a good time if only for a moment." The reader cannot help thinking that the attitude from which these comments spring may itself be one of the most effective encouragements to suicide.

The other self-murder, besides those of Kirillov and Stavrogin, comes in by way of Stavrogin's confession in the suppressed chapter, "At Tihon's." Matryosha, the child who hangs herself presumably as a result of her encounters with Stavrogin, is a more enigmatic figure than the other three suicides in the book. All that we know about her is the information provided by Stavrogin himself, and the manuscript page giving details of the decisive encounter is withheld from the reader, though Stavrogin assures Tihon that "Nothing happened. Nothing" (p. 706). Matryosha's suicide is certainly the most pathetic of the four—she is a very young child who apparently deals in a completely open and trusting fashion with an adult that is incapable of responding appropriately to such openness and trust. Stavrogin's only comment on the contents of the missing page is very brief and evasive: "It would take too long to explain . . . it was . . . simply a psychological misunderstanding" (p. 706). At any rate, after several days of feverish illness and delirious murmuring—during which "she kept saying, 'I killed God'" (p. 709)—she hangs herself in a dark closet; and her image haunts Stavrogin for the rest of his life. "But what is intolerable to me," he writes toward the end of his confession, "is only this image, namely, the little girl on the threshold with her little fist lifted threatening me, only the way she looked then, only that moment, neither before nor after, only that shaking of the head" (p. 716).

The fourth suicide, that of Stavrogin himself, is the final and climactic event of the book, which ends with the discovery of his body. Unlike Kirillov, Stavrogin is not concerned to articulate a theory of suicide, though he thinks about it a good deal if we may judge by his conversations with Kirillov and his own testimony in the confession. When he does finally kill himself (by hanging, as Matryosha had done), it comes as a surprise to

the reader partly, I suppose, because he does not fit
neatly into Kirillov's analysis--he "thinks a great deal,"
but when he acts, he does so "suddenly"; and his immediate
motive seems more likely (when we recall the "image" of
Matryosha) to have been "great sorrow or spite" than
whatever Kirillov means by "reason." I leave aside the
phrase "being mad" in Kirillov's description of the sudden
suicide--the last sentence of the book, which seems to me
to be dripping with irony, tells us that "At the inquest
our doctors absolutely and emphatically rejected all idea
of insanity." The word "madness" and its synonyms echo
endlessly through the book, but I do not think it would be
particularly useful to pursue the question of Stavrogin's
sanity. To be sure, in certain quarters he has "the
reputation of being a madman" (p. 714); and some of his
behavior is wildly eccentric at best. His mother is
partly right in likening him to Hamlet and regretting that
he has no Horatio, or even Ophelia, in whom to confide (p.
190); but I suspect that the question "Is Stavrogin's
Insanity Real or Feigned?" would yield nothing more
substantial than the corresponding question about Hamlet
has done.(4) Whatever the word "mad" means in The
Possessed--and at times (in epithets, for example) it
seems to mean very little--I can only understand it as a
reference to one of the "devils" which provide the book's
Russian title (Besy).
     Stavrogin's thinking is sometimes akin to Kirillov's,
but it is far less analytical and systematic--he seems, in
short, to put less trust in "reason." He says to
Kirillov, for instance, "I understand shooting oneself, of
course. . . . I sometimes have thought of it myself, and
then there always came a new idea. . . ." (p. 238). He
sounds even more like Kirillov in the confession: "I
clearly formulated the following for myself: I have
neither the feeling nor the knowledge of good and evil,
and not only have I lost the sense of good and evil, but
good and evil really do not exist (and this pleased me)
and are but a prejudice; I can be free of all prejudice,
but at the very moment when I achieve that freedom, I
shall perish" (p. 712). What recalls Kirillov is not only
the thought that ultimate "freedom" brings with it the
dissolution of consciousness,(5) but even the attitude
reflected in the words "I clearly formulated the following
for myself." Kirillov, however, has been in some vague
way a political activist; and the reader remains fairly
sure that he will finally act upon his decision to end his
own life. Stavrogin, on the other hand, holds himself
aloof and seems unwilling to act in any reasoned or
deliberate way. For him, as for Hamlet, "the native hue
of resolution / Is sicklied o'er with the pale cast of
thought"; and the reader is both surprised and shocked
when he hangs himself.
     Another Dostoevski character whom Stavrogin resembles
in many ways appears six years later as the narrator in
"The Dream of a Ridiculous Man" (1877).(6) Like that
narrator, Stavrogin is intensely conscious at times of
being ridiculous; like him, he contemplates suicide; like
him, he has a significant encounter with a little girl;

and like him, he has a vision or dream of the earthly
paradise as represented in the Claude Lorraine painting
"Acis and Galatea." But it is with Kirillov that the
"ridiculous man" shares the experience of the timeless
moment, precisely identified on clock and calendar, during
which he becomes aware that "all is good." Unlike both
Kirillov and Stavrogin, however, this narrator is finally
able to respond to the encounter with the child and to the
vision of the earthly paradise. In Dostoevski the crucial
experience often takes the form of such an encounter
between child and adult. If the child is lucky, he or she
may run into a confident and loving adult, like the
peasant Marey or Alyosha Karamazov. If not so lucky, then
someone like Svidrigailov or Stavrogin. In the latter
cases the results are disastrous--not only for the child,
but for the adult as well.

Because the circumstances of his death are so
ambiguous, one cannot help wondering why Stavrogin takes
his own life. The manner of his doing so--by hanging,
"behind a door"--is so clearly parallel to the manner of
Matryosha's suicide that one is inclined to regard the
child's death as the cause, as well as the model, for
Stavrogin's desperate action. Dostoevski obviously does
all he can to make this final suicide as surprising and
shocking as possible--no more than two pages from the end
of the story we read Stavrogin's claim, contained in a
letter to Darya Pavlovna, "I can never, never shoot
myself" and his admission that "I am afraid of suicide."
The net result of this emphasis upon "suddenness" in
Stavrogin's case, upon confusion and grotesqueness in
Kirillov's, and upon the insignificance (from Kirillov's
point of view) of the other two suicides is to suggest
that Kirillov's theory--like Raskolnikov's, which
culminates in murder, and Shigalyov's, which ends in
"unlimited despotism"--is simply an attempt to rationalize
a thoroughly primitive impulse, to dignify one of man's
darkest desires, and to give meaning to something which
threatens constantly to rob human life of any meaning
whatever. Unfortunately, however, the attempt is
invariably self-defeating; its enactment is at best deeply
pathetic and at worst merely absurd. Like Ivan Karamazov,
Kirillov rejects the human condition and hastens to
"return the ticket." Unlike Ivan, he proposes to do it
with a grand, theatrical flourish.

NOTES

1. Fyodor Dostoevski, The Brothers Karamazov, trans.
Constance Garnett (New York: Modern Library-Random House,
1950), p. 388.

2. Fyodor Dostoevski, The Possessed, trans.
Constance Garnett (New York: Modern Library-Random House,
1936), pp. 112-114.

3. Fyodor Dostoevski, The Idiot, trans. Constance
Garnett (New York: Modern Library--Random House, 1935),
p. 365.

4. The nineteenth-century Variorum edition of <u>Hamlet</u> (1877) gives forty pages to the question "Is Hamlet's Insanity Real or Feigned?" The twentieth century has of course been even more prolific on the subject. The question remains open even though certain critics appear to have settled it at least to their own satisfaction. <u>The Oxford Companion to English Literature</u>, for instance, asserts (as if it were stating an obvious fact) that Hamlet "counterfeits madness to escape the suspicion that he is threatening danger to the king" (Fourth Edition Revised, p. 366). Needless to say, there is no clear consensus on the matter since the evidence provided by the play's text is itself contradictory.

5. An attentive reader of Dostoevski's novels can hardly help thinking that the association Kirillov makes between a supreme feeling of freedom and a nearly simultaneous loss of consciousness has its origin, at least for Dostoevski, in the epileptic seizure, as described in <u>The Idiot</u> (part II', chapter 5). At that moment, according to the narrator, all feelings merge "in a lofty calm, full of serene, harmonious joy and hope"--all in "that final second (it was never more than a second) with which the fit began" (<u>The Idiot</u>, pp. 213-214). As I have argued elsewhere, the same kind of experience is represented, in <u>The Idiot</u>, in connection with the feelings of persons about to be executed. The difference between the two types of experience is that the feelings of the person led out to be executed are a one-time occurrence, apprehended thereafter (if the person survives) only through memory, whereas for the epileptic the experience is constantly renewed. (See "Myshkin's Apocalyptic Vision," Chapter VIII of <u>Between Earth and Heaven</u> [New York: Holt, Rinehart and Winston, 1969].)

6. Contained in <u>The Best Short Stories of Dostoevski</u>, trans. and intro. David Magarshack (New York: Modern Library-Random House, n.d.), pp. 297-322.

10.
The Demon of Irony: Stavrogin
the Adversary at Tihon's
REED MERRILL

Fedor Dostoevski's The Possessed is a compendium of
conflicting opposites: of belief and nihilism, tradition
and revolution, conservatism and anarchism. These
antitheses represent what Mikhail Bakhtin, in his profound
study Problems of Dostevsky's Poetics, calls the
"plurality of independent and unmerged voices and
consciousnesses and the genuine polyphony of full valued
voices which are in fact characteristic of Dostoevski's
novels." This plurality of attitudes and actions is
manifested in Dostoevski's works as a "great dialog . . .
artistically organized as the unclosed entirety of life
itself, of life on the brink,"(1) according to Bakhtin.
Of all Dostoevski's works, perhaps The Possessed best
illustrates the dualism, if not the pluralism, to which
ideas and actions are submitted and that is largely
because of the negative reverberator of those
ideas--Nikolai Stavrogin. Although his relationships are
constantly governed by seeming indifference, neutrality,
and silence, at best by disinterest--the most notable
exception being his "confession" to Father Tihon--in the
minds of others he nevertheless epitomizes a mysterious
potential for lofty projects and heroic actions. Although
he is remarkably consistent and predictable in his
unrelenting nihilism, the paradox of his nature lies in
what others conceive to be his dormant dynamic capacity to
move mountains if mountains need to be moved. Ironically,
in spite of his past Stavrogin is an ideal, the idol of
others' obsessions and desires, a man of seemingly
limitless potential. Like so many of Dostoevski's heroes
(Ivan, Dmitri, Alyosha Karamazov, Myshkin, and Zosima, to
name a few), Stavrogin knows the arguments and he is
intellectually capable of comprehending the nature of the
"important questions." As Bakhtin puts it, "there is not
a single idea which does not find a dialogical response in
Stavrogin's consciousness."(2) To his friends, all
Stavrogin requires is the impetus and motivation for
action--his potential and his charisma are givens. He is
a man whose heroic capacity could transcend good and evil
(paradoxically, something he has already accomplished in
the darkest and most sadistic possible ways). However, to
himself Stavrogin remains in a state of static
indifference throughout the novel. He is passive,

inauthentic, empty of belief and commitment, possessed by
what his old mentor Stepan Trofimovitch refers to as the
"demon of irony." It is only in the episode where
Stavrogin visits the holy Father Tihon that Stavrogin's
debased and empty life is exposed, and where it becomes
obvious why his life reflects nothing but the most
desolate kind of nihilism. Irony is one thing, nihilism
another. Irony occupies a borderline position between
aesthetic indifference and ethical commitment to universal
values. Nihilism suggests indiscriminate relativity and
meaninglessness, a world in which, according to Ivan
Karamazov and Friedrich Nietzsche as well, "everything is
permitted," and, by extension, nothing has measure. The
Tihon episode provides proof of the important difference
between an ironic situation, which can be resolved through
action and ethical decisions, and nihilism, which--at
least in the world of Dostoevski--cannot. This crucial
episode dialectically demonstrates why Stavrogin is no
longer capable of moving from the no-man's land of
nihilism to belief in anything.
    Stavrogin is a nihilist who has methodically
neutralized his positive sensibility and tragic capacity
through perversity and depravity. Like his famous
predecessor, the Marquis de Sade, his life of aesthetic
degradation is self-willed. Good and evil in Stavrogin's
view are essentially synonymous concepts. It should be no
mystery what Stavrogin is. Although he has been
characterized as a man of masks who is hiding behind a
series of personas which disguise his real self, such is
not the case. Stavrogin's friends themselves manufacture
the masks and personas to mirror their own egotistical
illusions: Stavrogin can have no illusions. In the face
of their various offers of love, friendship, complicity,
political power, Stavrogin remains essentially sceptical,
largely silent, always indifferent. Yet this ironic
position seems to others strangely compelling and
provocative; his pessimism paradoxically reinforces their
beliefs. However, in spite of these efforts (the Tihon
episode being the exception), Stavrogin consistently
maintains the position of devil's advocate, nihilistic
adversary, a negative sounding-board for people's
obsessions. In addition, because of his staticism, he
seems to suggest a kind of stability and reliability which
his friends lack, while in actuality he is in a constant
state of inertia and entropy. Stavrogin has no
anticipations and no affirmation, but stands a solitary
consciousness confronting his self-made abyss.
Nevertheless, it is his seemingly latent dynamic capacity
for heroic action that sustains the tension in The
Possessed, for it is assumed that if only Stavrogin could
find something to believe in the result would be dramatic
and positive. However, as the Tihon episode demonstrates,
it is not possible for Stavrogin to transcend his
nihilism; his only position, in the interim of his
remaining days, is rejection of hope or despair in a
neutral zone of silence mediated only by unrelenting
ironies.

Without "At Tihon's" ("Stavrogin's Confession"), the chapter which lies at the center of the novel, it would be impossible to comprehend the nature of Stavrogin's depraved "fall," and the cumulative reasons for his rejection of human relationships and ethical values. This chapter is the central focus of The Possessed just as "The Grand Inquisitor" eqisode is the structural and ideational center of The Brothers Karamazov. As a matter of fact, the two episodes compared display, in the confrontations of the characters of Stavrogin and Tihon, and Ivan-Christ-The Grand Inquisitor, the greatest depth of insight into the subject of nihilism in conflict with Dostoevski's particular kind of Christianity in all his works. Stavrogin in the nihilist in extremis, while Tihon is either a Kierkegaardian "knight of resignation," or a "knight of faith," equally in extremis, whose despair of knowing is paralleled either by his absurdist faith or his despair of knowing. Ivan is Dostoevski's most persuasive intellectual who is motivated by humanistic belief, but who "falls" by questioning God and His works, while the silent Christ and The Grand Inquisitor personify respectively Christianity as opposed to nihilistic Christianity.

"At Tihon's" is the most dramatic and dialectically informative episode in the novel. Whether or not one would agree with Konstantin Mochulsky that it is the "culmination of Stavrogin's tragedy and Dostoevski's loftiest artistic creation,"(3) it seems difficult not to agree with Bakhtin's statement that "it is possible to represent the inner man, as Dostoevski understood him, only by representing his communication with another person. . . . It is quite understandable that the dialog must lie at the center of Dostoevski's artistic world, and the dialog not as a means but as an end in itself."(4) Without the Tihon chapter it would be impossible to understand the nature of Stavrogin's dialectic of nihilism or, for that matter, Tihon's problematical faith. The Tihon chapter concerns Stavrogin's visit to the controversial "saint" Father Tihon. During his visit, Stavrogin reads a narrative of a past event from his student days concerning his rape of the child Matryosha, and of her subsequent suicide.(5) It is an episode the absence of which would deny the direct and literal exposure to those events which have culminated in Stavrogin's parodistic "confession" to the priest. The chapter is additionally crucial to the plot, as Mochulsky points out, because it marks the climax of the novel after which the action falls off into a fragmented and prolonged series of catastrophes(6) which are demonstrative of the apocalyptic thematics from Revelations so frequently referred to in the novel. In addition to the explicit information derived from the confessional are the ideational and dialectical implications of the chapter. Bakhtin has suggested that as a genre the confessional narrative best accommodates dialectics and certainly this would be the case in Dostoevski ("Notes from Underground," "The Dream of Ridiculous Man," and, among many others, the confessions of Ivan, Versilov, and Ippolit). These

confessions exemplify Dostoevski's genius in depicting the
paradoxical and ironic "dual thoughts characteristic of
all Dostoevski's heroes. . . . One thought is the obvious
one, which determines the <u>content</u> of their speech, and the
other is the hidden one, which nonetheless determines the
<u>structure</u> of their speech, on which it casts a shadow."(7)
It is only through this confession and the dialectic which
it unfolds that Stavrogin's true self becomes apparent.

In the Tihon chapter, the contrapuntal distinctions
between Stavrogin's radical irony and Tihon's desperate
faith result in a dialectical confrontation which has the
most important philosophical consequences in the novel
because of the two dramatically opposite positions of the
"disputants." Although Bakhtin analyzes the formal
structural and rhetorical devices of this narrative, all
of which tend to make it unresolved and argumentatively
circular, he does not concern himself with the dialectical
importance of the dialogue.

> Stavrogin's confession . . . is a confession
> intensely oriented toward the other person, who
> is indispensable to the hero, but whom he at the
> same time despises and whose judgment he does
> not accept. Therefore, Stavrogin's confession,
> like the other confessions which we have
> discussed, is devoid of the power to finalize
> and tends toward the same vicious circle to
> which the "underground man's" speech so clearly
> tended. Without recognition and affirmation by
> the other person Stavrogin is incapable of
> accepting himself, but at the same time he does
> not want to accept the other person's judgement
> of him.(8)

Although the meeting results in a standoff, that is not to
say that it serves no purpose, only that Tihon and
Stavrogin are antitheses and that because their positions
are polarities they would obviously reject each other's
ideas. It must be added that neither of them could
<u>finalize</u> his position if he wanted to because of the
totally ambivalent and inherently unresolvable nature of
his beliefs. In Kierkegaardian terms, before the dialogue
Stavrogin would seem to inhabit the ironic mode of
existence (the zone of paradox between the aesthetic and
ethic modes of existence), the Father Tihon the border-
category of "humor" (the zone of unmediated silence
between the ethical and religious modes of existence).

Stavrogin's life is given to aesthetic indifference
occasionally modified by nagging ethical dilemmas. In the
Tihon episode, there seems to be the possibility that
Stavrogin's pessimism has been challenged by matters of
conscience or even by possible religious contrition. In
other words, it seems that Stavrogin is moving from a
standoff position of "closed" irony which is reductive and
circular, to open, "philosophical" irony which at least
will permit him to reach out to other choices in a world
of relativity. In contrast, Tihon personifies the agony
of Kierkegaardian Christianity which can only be

comprehended on an individual, subjective basis, through
unreason as a principle, and in a state of "infinite
subjectivity" --commitments which humanism and reason
would reject out of hand. Although in the beginning
neither man seems cognizant of the other's beliefs, at the
end of their exchange they are fully aware of the relative
strengths and weakness of the other's position. Each
recognizes the essentially untenable philosophical
position of the other. Their dialogue indicates that
there are no "final truths," and that any attempt to
accept absolutes of any kind would of necessity come from
a position which would be further from the truth than
their own: for instance, acceptance of universal reason.
Bakhtin refers to this dilemma of subjectivism and
relativism in Dostoevski's works as the absence of
"impersonal truth": "His form-determining Weltanschauung
recognizes no impersonal truth, and in his works there are
no detached, impersonal verities. There are only
integral, indivisible idea-voices or viewpoint voices, but
they, too cannot be detached from the dialogical fabric of
the work without distorting their nature."(9)
     Nikolai Stavrogin is the "leader" of an anarchic
retinue of young friends who have returned from
universities and separate travels abroad to their
hometown. As a group they collectively reject the
bourgeois standards of their elders, and as individuals
they exhibit their contempt in varying degrees of nihilism
ranging from Nechaevian violence and destruction (Pyotr
Verhovensky), to the nihilism of the man-God (Alexey
Kirillov), or the fascistic social utopianism of
Shigalyov. In the absence of their leader, the group is
led by Pyotr, whose passion for destruction for violence's
sake is the direct cause of most of the disasters which
occur throughout the novel (Stavrogin's indifference being
the indirect cause). Stavrogin exerts an equally
pervasive influence on the women in the novel, from his
mother to Shatov's wife and Liza, as well as to his own
wife Marya, and the young Dasha. He is a Don Juan, a
fatal force whose mysterious and enigmatic qualities and
negative sensibility fire the imaginations of men and
women who are drawn to him even at the risk of their own
destruction. Throughout the novel, he is compared to
Shakespeare's young profligate Prince Hal, more ominously
to Pechorin, Lermontov's negative and destructive hero of
A Hero of Our Time, and as well to the Prince of Darkness
himself. Virtually everything Stavrogin confronts turns
to ashes.
     The "intellectual" leader of the philistine town to
which Stavrogin and his friends have returned is a
sentimental idealist, his former teacher Stepan
Trofimovitch Verhovensky. Immediately upon their return,
Stavrogin and his negative herd create scandal after
scandal, turning the complacent and self-satisfied town
into a tumultuous holocaust filled with horror and death.
It is in the midst of these events that Stavrogin breaks
his silence with the visit to Father Tihon in his
monastery. The "confession" which Stavrogin reads to
Tihon concerns his dissolute student days when the rape of

Matryosha occurred. The confession has been written
assumedly as an act of penance and contrition for which
Stavrogin is visiting the priest for absolution.
However, during the course of their discussion which
frames the reading of the confession, it becomes obvious
that Stavrogin's unrepentant pride and his "satanic
impertinence" have motivated the meeting. The confession
resolves the mysterious enigma of Stavrogin's strange
recent behavior because it exposes him literally for what
he is--the basest sort of nihilist and immoralist.
Without this crucial chapter, Stavrogin would appear to be
but one more fascinatingly romantic anti-hero in the dark
and brooding tradition of Byron and his more satanic and
believable Russian disciples. However, Stavrogin's
corruption of the innocent is beyond humanity, echoing in
a terrible ironic way Ivan's condemnation of a God who
would allow little children to suffer. Stavrogin is
beyond redemption.
     Stavrogin's visit to Tihon occurs the morning after
he has spent a sleepless night staring at a corner of his
room ruminating the consequences of a previous evening's
conversation with Pyotr, who has stated that he will lead
a revolution after which Stavrogin will be installed as
Czar of Russia. Pyotr tells Stavrogin that he will be the
aristocratic genius, the "imperial democrat," who will
initiate a new democratic paradise on earth.

     "Nobody would slap you on the shoulder. You are
     an awful aristocrat. An aristocrat is
     irresistible when he goes in for democracy! To
     sacrifice life, your own or another's, is
     nothing to you. You are just the man that's
     needed. It's just such a man as you that I
     need. I know no one but you. You are the
     leader, you are the sun and I am your worm."
          He suddenly kissed his hand. A shiver ran
     down Stavrogin's spine, and he pulled his hand
     away in dismay. They stood still.
          "Madman!" whispered Stavrogin.(10)

This conversation and the impetus for Stavrogin's visit to
Tihon seem to be the direct result of Pyotr's crazed
hypothesis and Stavrogin's belief that he is somehow
responsible for it.
     The first thing Stavrogin notices upon meeting Tihon
is his "sickly, vague smile and a strange, rather shy
expression" (588). Tihon's appearance is strangely
paradoxical, expressing the same incongruous behavior that
Stavrogin has heard about him. Stavrogin knows that many
come from as far away as Petersburg to visit Tihon, but
that others consider him "half crazy," even a possible
drunkard. Stavrogin's reputation has also preceded him.
However, Stavrogin's doubts about Tihon's authenticity as
a man of faith are mysteriously resolved when he
insightfully feels that Tihon somehow knows the real
purpose of his visit and that he is attempting to spare
Stavrogin's feelings with his ambiguous expression.
Immediately, Stavrogin tell the priest that he has been

hallucinating, seeing devils. The subject then turns to
faith in God and atheism. Neither Tihon nor Stavrogin is
fully aware of the nature of the other's real beliefs.
Stavrogin has assumed that Tihon is a kind of stereotype,
plaster saint whose faith will be ideologically correct,
condescending, and selfrighteous; instead he is surprised
to find a man filled with self-doubt and trepidation. On
the other hand, Tihon's assessment of Stravrogin seems
remarkably consistent from beginning to end; his insight
and instinct seem to provide him with a lucid view of
Stavrogin's bad faith in coming to see him.
     Their first verbal exchange is an example of
Stavrogin's attempt to force Tihon to make orthodox
statements about unorthodox problems in theodicy.
Tihon responds, much to Stavrogin's surprise, with his own
kind of ambivalence based upon his despair of knowing and
his acknowledgment of the "insanity of faith," to use
Kierkegaard's term.

          "It is written, isn't it, that if you have
     faith and bid a mountain remove itself hence, it
     will do so. . . . However, pardon this nonsense.
     Still, I am curious to know: can you remove a
     mountain or can't you?"
          "If God commands, I will remove it," said
     Tihon in a low, restraining voice, dropping his
     eyes again.
          "Well, but that would be the same as if God
     Himself removed it. No, you--you--will you be
     able to do it, as a reward for your faith in
     God?"
          "Perhaps I shall not."
          "'Perhaps'! That's not bad. Ha! ha! You
     are still a doubter, then?"
          "I doubt because my faith is imperfect."
          "What! Even your faith is imperfect?
     Well, I wouldn't have supposed it, to look at
     you." He suddenly stared at Tihon with wholly
     naive amazement, which did not at all harmonize
     with the derisive tone of the previous question
     (593).

It is paradoxical that Stavrogin is the interrogator while
Tihon is the defendant and it is immediately clear that
Stavrogin's cynicism pays no homage to contrition. On the
subject of atheism, Stavrogin is again surprised when
Tihon condemns the lukewarm indifference of the agnostic
view of God more than that of the ardent atheist. At the
same time, Tihon has exposed Stavrogin's essential
flaw--his inertia and indifference--in a statement so
close to the bone that Stavrogin becomes irritated, and
angry, and consequently even more sarcastic than before:
"Say what you may, but the complete atheist stands on the
penultimate step to most perfect faith (he may or he may
not take a further step), but the indifferent person has
no faith whatever except a bad fear, and that but rarely
and only if he is sensitive" (593-94). Throughout the
episode, and in spite of Stavrogin's vicious cynicism and

his imperious contempt for Tihon's faith (a manner
remarkably similar to Raskolnikov's treatment of Sonya in
Crime and Punishment, and to The underground man's verbal
attacks on Liza in Notes From Underground), Stavrogin is
nevertheless in awe of Tihon's humility. Stavrogin
resolutely continues his merciless assault on Tihon at the
same time bemusedly, if sardonically, admiring his
passionate faith when he says, "And still you are an odd
fellow and a saintly fool" (595).

Stavrogin begins the reading of his tract, "From
Stavrogin," after denying that he has anything to hide or
that there are ulterior motives for his having come to
Tihon's cell. The confession itself is a dehumanized and
arrogant chronicle of "dissipation in which I found no
pleasure" (597). During his college years, Stavrogin's
bouts of boredom were countered by various amusements--an
affair with a lady and her maid, the study of
theology--all of which resulted in an even more acute
sense of world-weariness. To pique his interest,
Stavrogin rented a room for an assignation with the maid,
discovered the landlady's young daughter Matryosha there,
whom he gratuitously accused of stealing his pen-knife,
then enjoyed seeing her wrongfully punished. Finally, he
raped her; several days after she hanged herself. His
reaction was all too typical: at first self-hatred and
disgust, then hatred of Matryosha, followed by guilt and
fear, resolved in ironic indifference.

As a consequence of his guilt and seemingly to
accentuate his pleasure in suffering, Stavorgin married
the cripple Mary Timofeevna Lebyadkin and finally left
Petersburg leaving behind him "the reputation of being a
madman--" (605). In his travels abroad, he was on a tour
of the gallery at Dresden where he experienced an ecstatic
epiphany of the Golden Age while viewing the painting of
Acis and Galatea which appeared to him "in a dream, yet
not as a picture but as though it were an actual scene"
(606). It is not clear whether or not Stavrogin views
this scene in the Christian sense of Earthly Paradise or
of the "pagan" Greek tragic Age described by Nietzsche in
The Birth of Tragedy. However, based upon Dostoevski's
own predilections, one must assume that the scene is meant
to be an earthly Eden. In either instance the scene is
symbolic of Stavrogin's knowledge of what ideally could
have been and of the brutally incongruous result his
decisions and actions have brought about. It is a vision
of paradise and totality which could, in either a
Christian or tragic sense, provide the impetus for
positive belief and action in an ethical world guided by
choices between good and evil. Stavrogin is aware of his
denial of responsibility ("wanting a burden") and of the
empty result. He knows that if his doubts about the
efficacy of ethical choices could be rejected that he
would achieve a kind of freedom which at the same time
would be a denial of morality. He says to Tihon: "I have
neither the feeling nor the knowledge of good and evil,
and not only have I lost the sense of good and evil, but
good and evil really do not exist . . . and are but a
prejudice; I can be free of all prejudices, but at the

very moment when I achieve that freedom I shall perish"
(604). The dream persists and reappears in Stavrogin's
imagination every day after its first appearance. Without
this scene it would not be clear whether or not Stavrogin
had knowledge of humanistic values, ethical choices, and
tragic capacity, but his awareness of the vision of
totality and its meaning gives him a dimension lacking in
an often predictable gallery of aesthetic types like
Dorian Gray or Des Esseintes, Baudelaire or Rimbaud.
Stavrogin is aware that without belief in some
transcendent value life will remain desolate and
meaningless.

     Stavrogin has tragic capacity because he is fully
aware of his abnegation of responsibility toward himself
and others. However, instead of following the path of
affirmation and ethical action he has chosen negation,
pessimism, and meaninglessness. His "confession" mirrors
his mind. Where initially it seems his dialogue with
Tihon might lead to affirmation, it rather regresses into
algolagnia, sado-masochism, exhibitionism, and perverse
aesthetic gratification through suffering. In a certain
sense it would be difficult to detect differences between
the two men; they have both withdrawn from life and they
ruminate the "essential secrets" in their private worlds.
Their verbal statements are equally indirect, ambivalent,
and paradoxical. The dialogue ends with Tihon imploring
Stavrogin to become a novice of the Chruch to which
Stavrogin derisively responds: "Quit it, Father Tihon"
(618). Tihon suddenly, and in "intense grief" prophesies
that Stavrogin will commit an even "more terrible crime
than at this moment" (619) (seemingly a reference to
Stavrogin's threat to publish his confession, but also
possibly a presentiment of Stavrogin's future suicide).

     In The Myth of Sisyphus, Albert Camus states that
"the absurd is born of this confrontation between the
human need and the unreasonable silence of the world.(11)
Individual response to this condition is obviously varied
but it is fundamentally three-fold: aesthetic
indifference governed by nihilistic relativism and
negation of "values"; ethical acceptance of a tragic world
in which humanistic universal concepts of value must be
individually created; religious hope based upon despair of
knowing but also by "passionate certitude" in divine
benevolence. Stavrogin's selfishness and Tihon's
selflessness, though polar, are at the same time denials
of humanistic affirmation of the finite world. Either
position denies the necessity of individually derived
concepts of value. Stavrogin embodies cosmic despair--a
negation; Tihon personifies cosmic hope--also a negation.
Both positions are rejections of life and are consequently
untenable, in Camus's mind, because they lack the equally
paradoxical but necessary requirement: the affirmative
principle of humanism. For Nietzsche, both Stavrogin and
Tihon would fall into the realm of nihilism because they
deny the efficacy of Dionysian "yea-saying" perspectivism.
In their negations of the life principle for metaphysical
speculative concepts, they reflect the same paradoxical

dead-ends. Vaclav Cerny refers to this reciprocity of
viewpoint by calling Stavrogin a "saint in reverse."

> In the instant in which Stavrogin rushes to
> saint Tihon seeking relief and expressing a
> willingness to confess his shame in public, to
> accept humbly the punishment of human hatred and
> disgust, the elder realizes with horror that the
> highest Christian virtue, humility, is in
> Stavrogin the crowning form of his pride. What
> Stavrogin wants to demonstrate is precisely his
> readiness to stand the most terrible trial,
> namely human disgust, mockery, and pity. The
> lightning of triumph and of unbending, scornful
> strength first whips through his ardor for
> martyrdom and self-sacrifice. And the elder
> sees that before him stands a saint in reverse,
> a demon incarnate for whom there is no human or
> divine help. And as such Nikolai Stavrogin
> meets his end in an act of despair that is a
> satanic parady of Christ's salvation: a devil
> of pride who finally sneaked into Golgotha
> itself, intending, out of ironic and derisive
> arrogance, to slyly set himself on the cross in
> the place of the humble Christ.(12)

It must be added that despite Tihon's acceptance of divine
absurdity as an article of faith, his life is dedicated to
serving others, and his faith is driven by love and pity.
Stavrogin's mode of existence is dedicated to
self-love/hate and an almost as great hatred of mankind as
for himself. He is aware of his destructiveness and
perhaps the final irony of his life is his almost
altruistic act of suicide which at least saves his
betrothed, Darya Shatov, from his fatal grasp. He does
not want her to "be his nurse." "One may argue about
everything endlessly, but from me nothing has come but
negation, with no greatness of soul, no force. Even
negation has not come from me. Everything has always been
petty and spiritless . . . I can never lose my reason, and
I can never believe in an idea to such a degree as he
[Kirillov] did (581-82). Stavrogin's suicide note reveals
the same emptiness as before but with the addition of a
theme which has increasingly consumed modern thought--the
nihilistic destructiveness of reason as a substitute for
belief. As Nietzsche puts it, "to grasp the limits of
reason--only this is truly philosophy."(13)

NOTES

1. Mikhail Bakhtin, Problems of Dostoevsky's
Poetics, trans. R. W. Rostel (Ann Arbor: Ardis
Publishers, 1973), pp. 4, 51.

2. Ibid., p. 60.

3. Konstantin Mochulsky, Dostoevsky: His Life and
Work, trans. Michael Minihan (Princeton, N.J.: Princeton

University Press, 1967), p. 459. Certainly Bakhtin's
Problems of Dostoevski's Poetics and Mochulsky's book are
two of the most important works of Dostoevski criticism,
and both authors concur that the value of "At Tihon's" is
of the highest order. It is therefore unusual and
perplexing that another of the important commentators on
Dostoevski, Edward Wasiolek, should maintain his low
opinion of this chapter: "The Stavrogin that appears in
the expurgated confession chapter is unnecessary, and
Dostoevski wisely did not include it in editions of the
novel after he was free of Katkov's [one of his
publishers] objections. . . . The portrait of Stavrogin in
the confession chapter is morally consistent, but
dramatically inconsistent. Throughout the novel we have a
Stavrogin of silence and self-containment, a portrait that
accords powerfully with the silent wasteland that his
inner strength makes for him. The analytic Stavrogin of
the confessional chapter mars this impassive, unattached
air." Dostoevski: The Major Fiction (Cambridge, Mass.:
MIT Press, 1964), p. 132.

4. Bakhtin, p. 213.

5. It is difficult not to think of the ethical
implications of Ivan Karamazov's condemnation of a world
in which innocent children suffer (the "Pro and Contra"
section of The Brothers Karamazov), and Stavrogin's
awareness of his heinous, evil act for which there can be
no redemption.

6. Mochulsky, p. 438.

7. Bakhtin, p. 209.

8. Ibid., p. 206.

9. Ibid., p. 79.

10. Fyodor Dostoevsky, The Possessed, trans.
Constance Garnett (New York: The Heritage Press, 1959),
p. 357. Future references to The Possessed are from this
text.

11. Albert Camus, The Myth of Sisyphus and Other
Essays, trans. Justin O'Brien (New York: Vintage Books,
1961), p. 21.

12. Vaclav Cerny, Dostoevsky and His Devils, trans.
F. G. Galan (Ann Arbor: Ardis Pulbications, 1975), pp.
56-57.

13. Friedrich Nietzsche, The Anti-Christ, trans. R.
J. Hollingdale (Baltimore: Penguin Books, 1971), p. 174.

11.
The Concept of Beauty in
The Possessed

VALIJA K. OZOLINS

In an article printed in the journal Vremya in February, 1861 under the heading Mr. -bov and the Question on Art, Dostoevski criticizes the utilitarian view of art according to which art must have a purpose and an aim, while artistry, the formal aspect of art, is at best of secondary importance. Dostoevski's opinion is that art has its own organic life and therefore its own immutable laws. This, however, does not mean that art is entirely unrelated to life. On the contrary, Dostoevski considers art a necessity, a need of man which is just as urgent as his need to eat and drink. In his opinion, the desire for beauty, and thus man's creativity, has its origin in the fact that man's wishes and desires are normally greater than their fulfillment in reality. Therefore, his desire for beauty develops most intensely in conflict with reality, when he is fighting to bridge the gap between expectation and fulfillment, namely, when he is living most intensely, for in those moments there develops in him a desire for all that is harmonious and peaceful; and this harmony and peace he finds in the experience of beauty and its creation. On the other hand, when man finds what he has been striving for and the tension between expectations and fulfillment has been reduced, there will begin a lull in the course of his life, and a sense of melancholy will develop, which will result in the search for another ideal. This process will continue until, in the end, he is satiated completely with what he has been able to attain, and in disgust, he develops and nurtures by-tastes, which are sickish, exciting, and disharmonious; he loses his tact and his aesthetic sense of healthy beauty. True art, Dostoevski continues, is always contemporary and real; it cannot exist without reality, contemporary reality.(1)

To sum up, art has its origin in man's life and its expectations, conflicts, and frustrations. It is a manifestation of man's freedom and his ability to transform his concrete observations into an aesthetic form which is essentially different from life--yet which has its origin in life and has its appeasing and ennobling effect upon life. It is part of man's life, which means that it is neither utilitarian surrender to life, nor a purist's escape from life into "art for art's sake."

These views of Dostoevski on art, which were written

about ten years before the appearance of his novel The
Possessed, serve as a foreshadowing of the aesthetic views
developed in this work. My methodology in this analysis
follows an approach suggested by Dostoevski in the
introduction. An omniscient narrator is placed between
the author and the reader, a device which forces the
reader gradually to form his own opinion about the major
characters of the novel, and in this way participate in
the author's creative process. Dostoevski somewhat blurs
the image of his characters and thus invites his reader to
correct his first impressions. However, the narrator's
account of the major characters is not blurred to an
extent which would be completely misleading. For
instance, he introduces Stepan Trofimovich Verkhovensky
with an irony which may be regarded as a kind of prelude
to the description of the other characters, namely,
Varvara Petrovna Stavrogina and Juliya Mikhailovna von
Lembke.
     In the first chapter he speaks about Stepan
Trofimovich's university career, emphasizing the
importance of his lectures about the Arabs. He also
mentions "a billiant dissertation on the rising civic and
Hanseatic significance of the little German town of Hanau
in the epoch between 1413-1428 and, simultaneously, also
on the special and rather obscure reasons why this
significance was never fulfilled."(2) To appreciate the
irony of this account, one has to consider that Hanau is a
small town in Central Germany, and that the "epoch"
consists of no more than fifteen years which are of no
significance in the course of history. The narrator thus
first exaggerates the importance of some of Stepan
Trofimovich's achievements and then reduces them to almost
nothing by the statement itself. In the same paragraph
the narrator also speaks about Stepan Trofimovich's "most
profound research,--it seems, about the causes of the
extraordinary moral nobility of certain knights at a
certain epoch or something in this manner."(3) The
investigation itself alredy sounds very trifling, but the
narrator's irony reaches its climax when he begins the
explanation of its discontinuation with possible political
censorship and ends with the probability "that the author
himself was too lazy to conclude his research."(4)
     The contrast inherent in such an ironical treatment
is characteristic of the entire relationship between
Stepan Trofimovich and Varvara Petrovna. It belongs in
the category of Dostoevski's view that genuine art is
comtemporary and not an escape into an imagined,
insignificant past. When the narrator describes in fairly
elaborate detail Stepan Trofimovich's "some kind of an
allegory in lyrical-dramatic form, calling to mind the
second part of 'Faust',"(5) he attributes to him at least
some immediate contact with and interest in art. When
Stepan Trofimovich studied at the University of Berlin, he
came under the influence of German Romanticism. But his
poetic experiment has neither order nor plan; only the
rather irrelevant fact that all kinds of natural objects
and animals appear and converse; they simply celebrate the
"Festival of Life"; development is replaced by a static

picture, <u>Werden</u> by <u>Sein</u>. Instead of leading to ever
higher spheres of life and beauty--to the most beautiful
woman and the union of Greek and Northern forms, whose
offspring is Euphorion, the personification of
romanticism, there suddenly appears a beautiful youth,
personifying <u>Death</u>! A truly romantic combination of
extremes!

The place at which Stepan Trofimovich's poetic
experiment is described, namely the beginning of the
introductory chapter, is significant also, insofar as it
characterizes Stepan Trofimovich as a romantic individual,
who like Euphorion, tries to escape from all serious
contact with practical life, meets only failure and death.
Euphorion's fate remains the leitmotif of the novel:
failure and death because of his aesthetic escape from the
concrete responsibilities of life. To this Dostoevski
adds another aspect, characteristic of his great novels:
the idea that aloofness from practical life involves in
guilt as much as participation in it.

The loss of contact with reality, typical of a
deteriorating romanticism, finds its expression in Stepan
Trofimovich's life when Varvara Petrovna invites him to
stay with her: here he begins to play at cards and loses
ever more money in his games, as long as Varvara Petrovna
pays his debts--yet he blames Russia for his weakness:
"Who has shattered my activity and turned it into whist?
Eh, perish, Russia!"(6) he exclaims. His occasional
conscientiousness causes a "civic grief" regularly three
or four times a year - which later degenerates into a
"champagne grief."(7)

Show, illusion, and self-delusion are outwardly
manifest in the apparel a la Kukol'nik, an inferior
romantic poet and playwright, which Varvara Petrovna had
designed for Stepan Trofimovich, with hair flowing on his
shoulders, and a hat with a wide brim; for this costume is
practically all that has remained of the former would-be
poet. In the beginning of his stay at Varvara Petrovna's
estate, he still was preparing a book--and forgot about
it. Nevertheless, he wants to be considered a martyr and
complains about being forgotten and being of no use to
anyone--the typical self-pity of idle and inefficient
people, who always blame others for their failure.
However, when by some chance he is mentioned as an "exiled
martyr," or as a "former star in a famous galaxy," he
immediately assumes "an air of great importance"(8) and
becomes condescending and patronizing to Varvara Petrovna,
without whose support and adulation he could not exist,
although his martryrdom exists only in his own
imagination, and temporarily in the mind of those who try
to exploit the idea for their personal aspirations or for
revolutionary purposes. This fact is borne out on Stepan
Trofimovich's trip with Varvara Petrovna to Petersburg
where he is received and applauded in the highest circles
of the movement because he "represents an idea"(9)
although with the sensitivity of an aesthete he remembers
after nine years "with tears in his eyes" that no one in
the audience knew anything about him.(10)

The clash between reality and aesthetic escape from
the world of action is being highlighted for the first
time at the end of Stepan Trofimovich's and Varvara
Petrovna's Petersburg journey, when Stepan Trofimovich
"agreed without an argument in the uselessness and absurdity of the word 'fatherland'; he even accepted the
thought about the harmfulness of religion, but he loudly
and firmly declared that boots were of less value than
Pushkin, and very much so."(11) This is obviously
intended as an invective against any utilitarian
conception and exploitation of the arts and the artists,
for just that is the purpose of his audience: to exploit
Varvara Petrovna's idea of founding a magazine for their
own profit, concealed under the pretense of "the cause."
In this connection we may refer to Dostoevski's article
which appeared in the journal Epokha in 1864, under the
title Mr. Shchedrin or Schism Among the Nihilists, a
fierce attack against the nihilists and those who insist
that art be useful. In this satirical article Dostoevski
presents a few chapters of a novel by a young novelist.
In Chapter One of this novel Shchedrodarov becomes co-
editor of the journal Svoevremennoe (The Opportune One)
and is told to defend all those who claim to be
progressive. He should do so "even if they are not worth
it, if they came from the second grade of high school, but
as soon as they have presented to the public, be it only
four progressive lines, or if they have for two successive
years toiled for their livelihood and composed two little
verses like the following:

        Vek and Vek and Lev Kambek
        Lev Kambek and Vek and Vek,(12)

then you must know that they are sacred for you."(13)
Exactly these same monotonous, nonsensical lines are put
into the mouth of Stepan Trofimovich after his failure to
impress his exalted views about art upon his nihilistic
audience. They also express his "sadness and wrath" which
overcame him because "a great idea which you have long
cherished as holy, is snatched up by the ignorant and
dragged forth before the fools. . . ."(14) Stepan
Trofimovich's great idea, of course, is the incomparable
dignity of art when compared with the exigencies of
reality.
    In spite of his disappointment, however, he makes a
"supreme effort" to return to Berlin, in order "to set to
work," to that city "where everything reminded me of my
old past, first raptures and first tortures,"(15) the city
where he lost his "old self, strong as steel, firm as a
rock,"(16) as the narrator ironically reports; for all his
most serious resolutions are no more than day-dreams, and
an aesthetic escape into the realm of imagination,
emotional exaggerations which have hardly any roots in
reality, neither as their source nor their aim and end.
In the letters which he sends from Berlin to Varvara
Petrovna, he claims to be working twelve hours a day at
his literary pursuits--in addition to spending the nights
until dawn with friends where "everything is noble: much

music, Spanish tunes, dreams of the regeneration of all
humanity, the idea of the eternal beauty, the Sistine
Madonna...."(17) Apart from the preposterous account of
his daily (and nightly!) activities, the topics of
discussion he mentions, with the single exception of the
Sistine Madonna, are so general and vague that they would
do little more than stimulate the emotions without
contributing anything to the personal growth of the
participants--if they have any existence outside of his
imagination. "Nonsense," is Varvara Petrovna's reaction
to this exaggerated report and the reader is inclined to
agree with her at least to a considerable extent.

     The following nine years in Stepan Trofimovich's life
hold a further decline of his aesthetic pattern of life;
hysterical outbreaks, "majestic" losses at card games, and
champagne at Varvara Petrovna's expense. The conviction
that he has spent years "fulfilling the loftiest duty of
disseminating ideas,"(18) is nothing but a highsounding
cliche and an increasing conceit and an almost pathetic
self-delusion about his own importance. A passage in Part
One, Ch. I-9 is perhaps the strongest expression of the
sickness which Dostoevski ascribes to the romantic mind:
"For twenty years already I have been sounding the alarm
and calling to work! I have given my life to that call
and, fool that I am, I believed it! Now I do not believe
any more, but I am sounding the alarm and shall sound it
to the end, until death; I shall pull at the bell-rope
until they toll for my own requiem!"(19) And these words
are spoken by a man who is so afraid that something would
happen on the day of the Emancipation that he suggests to
Varvara Petrovna to go abroad for safety! To understand
passages like this, one always has to remember that his
"great idea" represents an aesthetic escape from active
life, as Stepan Trofimovich says: "I shall give away all
the Russian peasants for one Rachel,"(20) that is, the
material source of his existence, and the centre of his
country's existence in Dostoevski's mind.

     With such extreme conceit and exaggerations and a
corresponding disregard for all reality, the reader is
prepared for the climax of Stepan Trofimovich's escapism
and for the resulting catastrophe at the literary Fete,
arranged by the Governor's wife, Juliya Mikhailovna von
Lembke. At this occasion he begins his speech with an
extreme statement about political manifestoes. This
political part of his speech ends with the shocking
paradox "that, en parenthese, stupidity as well as the
loftiest genius are equally useful in the destiny of
mankind,"(21) a statement which contains a grain of truth,
of which however the speaker does not seem to be aware at
all. He continues with a complete disregard and contempt
for all reality by reducing the whole existing unrest to
the one question: "which is more beautiful: Shakespeare
or boots, Raphael or petroleum?"(22) And then Stepan
Trofimovich, being "in the last stage of passion
screamed"(23) words which must be studied in detail to be
fully appreciated:

But I declare . . . I declare that Shakespeare
and Raphael are--
higher than the emancipation of the peasants,
higher than nationalism,
higher than socialism,
higher than the young generation,
higher than chemistry,
higher than almost all humanity,
because they are already the fruit,
the real fruit of all humanity, and perhaps,
the highest fruit that can possibly be!
The form of beauty has already been attained,
Without the attainment of which I, perhaps,
will not consent to live . . .   Oh, God!(24)

The growing excitement with which these words are spoken
and the importance which Stepan Trofimovich attributes to
them, are emphasized not only by the use of anaphora but
also by juxtaposing key values with the works of
Shakespeare and Raphael at first without recognizable
order, yet reaching its climax in the most universal
ideal, "all humanity;" the whole is once more generalized
and made absolute by his rhetorical readiness to die in
the service of beauty.

Comparing Dostoevski's notebook entries with the
final version of Stepan Trofimovich's speech at the Fete,
one can see that the author did not only preserve the main
idea of the speaker's conception of beauty, but elaborated
on it and achieved a marvelous emotional ascent which then
suddenly collapses and degenerates into a fit, for the
narrator says that at the end of his speech Stepan
Trofimovich "suddenly began to sob hysterically."(25)

While there can be no doubt that Stepan Trofimovich
has some genuine aesthetic interests and even talents,
they gradually deteriorate in his isolation from the
practical world on Varvara Petrovna's estate. Petrovna's
own attitude concerning the world of beauty cannot be so
clearly defined. She considers herself as Stepan
Trofimovich's "Maecenas," a protectress of the arts and
the artists. Stepan Trofimovich, whom she hired as a
tutor for her son, is largely her own invention as far as
the artist is concerned. He must have a poetic nature and
be a poet because she willed him to be one, since she
needs an emotional stimulus in her loneliness on her large
estate as a widow, as well as an ornament for her social
gatherings. As the narrator remarks, "she would not have
slept for whole nights because of her worry, should the
matter concern his reputation as a poet, a scholar, a
public official."(26)

In aesthetic matters she is mainly receptive without
convictions of her own. For her too, as for Stepan
Trofimovich, though to a much lesser and more passive
degree, the emotional experience relieving her boredom, is
more important than any personal gain she might derive
from it. Characteristic is her reaction to Stepan
Trofimovich's excessive letter writing. Whereas for
Stepan Trofimovich they are a residue of a creative
effort, Varvara Petrovna never answers them. She has read

the tragedies of Shakespeare's Kings' Cycle not for their
aesthetic value, but in order to find some hope for a
change and improvement of her son Nikolai's social and
moral behavior. In this case her interest in literature
is understandable.

In general, however, Varvara Petrovna's aesthetic
interests must be classified as utilitarian, although they
are on a more refined social level than those of Juliya
Mikhailovna von Lembke. They are on the same level with
her growing interests in newspapers, magazines, prohibited
publications, and revolutionary manifestoes, when the
rumors of the Emancipation begin to disturb her. In spite
of her violent reaction to Stepan Trofimovich's "Hurrah,"
when the visiting baron calls on her,(27) her feminine
curiosity and desire to exploit the political ferment for
her social prestige prevail over any concern for her
possessions. When she goes to Petersburg with Stepan
Trofimovich, her idea is to join the movement, to found a
progressive magazine, and, in her exaggerated expression,
"devote from now on her whole life to it."(28) In
reality, all her plans are not designed to help the cause
of oppressed people; there never is any talk about
humanitarian aims. Self-enhancement is Varvara Petrovna's
major motivation, for in Petersburg she hopes to play her
role among the literati and at the same time to
"re-establish the highest connections."(29)

It is disappointed social ambition which finally
drives Varvara Petrovna, a proud woman, to make up to
Juliya Mikhailovna and to decide upon a separate Fete
which should surpass in taste and luxury everything her
rival had to offer. With such a plan her former aesthetic
interests are revealed as an outgrowth of vanity. Shortly
before the literary Fete of her rival she realizes the
futility of her pseudo-romantic relationship to Stepan
Trofimovich. She accuses him now of not having taken care
of her intellectual education; that he had given her only
Kapfig (a French writer of no literary merit) to read and
books which he did not give to her, but which she had
ordered for him, who did not even bother to cut the pages.
Now everything was "twenty years of mutual egoism, and
nothing else. Every letter written to me was not for me,
but for posterity."(30) Varvara Petrovna further says
that Stepan Trofimovich is a stylist and that their
friendship is a mutual outpouring of dish-water.(31) It
is interesting to note that Varvara Petrovna has now
identified herself with Pyotr Stepanovich Verkhovensky and
is repeating his words. But the crowning symbol of this
break with Stepan Trofimovich is not the fact that Varvara
Petrovna reduces his allowance and stipulates a fixed
pension for him, but the reproach about the Sistine
Madonna, which I quote in full:

"When you came back from abroad you looked down
upon me and did not let me utter a word, but
when I myself went there and began to talk to
you later of my impression of the Madonna, you
did not listen to the end, you began to smile
condescendingly into your cravat, as if I could

not have exactly the same feelings as you."
"It wasn't that--probably not that . . .
J'ai oublie."
"No, it was the same, but anyway, there was
nothing to boast about before me because it is
all nonsense, and just one of your inventions.
Nowadays nobody, nobody is getting excited over
the Madonna or is wasting time on it, except
inveterate old men. It has been proved."
"So, it has been proved too?"
"She is completely of no use. This jug is
useful, because one can pour water into it; this
pencil is useful, because one can write down
everything with it, but here is a woman's face
that is worse than all other faces in nature.
Try to draw an apple and put beside it a real
apple--which one will you take? Surely you
wouldn't make an error. This is what all your
theories boil down to now as soon as the first
ray of free investigation has illuminated
it."(32)

To understand the complete intellectual bankruptcy
displayed by these remarks, however, one has to remember
what the narrator has to report about the earlier meeting
of the two ladies. During their chatter Juliya
Mikhailovna says that she had never heard anything about
the activity and erudition of Stepan Trofimovich,
whereupon Varvara Petrovna replies that Stepan Trofimovich
"had never been a critic, but had, on the contrary, spent
all his life in her house. He is famous through the
circumstances of his earlier career that is too well known
to the whole world,' and very lately for his works on
Spanish history; he also wants to write about the
situation of the present German universities, and it
seems, something about the Dresden Madonna."(33) In other
words, she is still bragging about her protege, her "own
creation" and defending his immensely exaggerated and
non-existent merits. However, when Varvara Petrovna
mentions the Madonna, Juliya Mikhailovna cannot withhold
her nasty criticism, which at the same time exposes her
lack of aesthetic taste:
"About the Dresden Madonna? You mean the
Sistine Madonna? Chere Varvara Petrovna, I sat
for two hours before this picture and left
disillusioned. I did not understand anything
and was in great amazement. Karmazinov too says
that it is difficult to understand. Nobody
finds anything in it now, neither the Russians
nor the English. All this glory has been spread
by old men."
"Does it mean that it's the new fashion,
then?"(34)

At the beginning of this meeting Varvara Petrovna had
already made a socail concession to Juliya Mikhailovna's
vulgar taste, saying: "I did not understand that
woman!"(35) Afterwards, when speaking to Stepan

Trofimovich, she repeats Juliya Mikhailovna's criticism,
and even uses the words she had used in deference to the
governor's wife: "I must admit, that I have always (!)
considered you only a critic; you are a literary critic;
and nothing more."(36) It is under her influence too that
she now proclaims the utilitarian views about art, because
this is the "new fashion" now. A jug, a pencil, a real
apple, and a real face are for Varvara Petrovna more
useful than the Madonna, for she wants to be now as
fasionable and up-to-date as Juliya Mikhailovna. And did
the latter not quote the opinion on art held by "the
great" Karmazinov whose visit Varvara Petrovna was
expecting with a trembling heart, Bukhara rug, Chinese
vase, and a painting by Teniers? Juliya Mikhailovna likes
generalizations and so does Varvara Petrovna after her
"conversion" to aesthetic utilitarianism. For Juliya
Mikhailovna the world and its opinion on art consist of no
one else but the English and the Russians; this for her is
"vse"--all. Moreover, in her pretended "desperate desire"
to understand the Sistine Madonna (as she pedantically
corrected Varvara Petrovna), she had surpassed in patience
the maximum length of time attributed to dilettantes by
Chernyshevsky, who wrote this disparaging remark about
beauty in art: "The beautiful in art is deadly static in
its beauty. One can look at a live face for several
hours; a picture bores one after fifteen minutes and rare
are the examples of dilettantes who would have the
patience to stand before a picture for an hour."(37) But
Juliya Mikhailovna claims to have been sitting before
Raphael's Madonna for two hours--as if the length of time
she spent sitting before that picture could possibly
awaken in such a prosaic character any aesthetic feeling
and understanding at all! Since Varvara Petrovna does not
wish to stay behind the times, she has no use for
Raphael's Madonna any longer.

     As indicated before, the Sistine Madonna functions in
The Possessed as the touchstone of our three characters
with regard to their understanding of beauty as well as of
the intrinsic value of their characters.

     While Stepan Trofimovich's sublimation of beauty in
general, and Raphael's masterpiece in particular, goes to
an extreme which would deprive aesthetic experience and
creation of its necessary foundation in reality, Varvara
Petrovna's change to utilitarian views about art
characterizes her as a person who may be capable of a
certain aesthetic appreciation, but no socially or
intellectually independent enough to have a firm
conviction and taste of her own. Juliya Mikhailovna lacks
even that mental and spiritual refinement which would
enable her to have any genuine aesthetic reaction--and so
the Sistine Madonna does not make any impression upon her.
In accordance with such a frame of mind, she is not
introduced as a person in her own right, but as Governor
von Lembke's wife, that is, as somebody who is nothing
except what others think of her. In the beginning she was
praised for bringing the local society of the provincial
town together and of bringing some life into it. However,
in her social affairs she soon displays the same

coarseness as in her aesthetic taste. The circle which
meets in her drawing room is not a selected group of
persons with some nobler ideas or aims. Her main object
is to gain social recognition and personal admiration and
flattery at any price. Therefore she caters particularly
to young people and tolerates all kinds of adventures,
scandals, and mischief of a most revolting kind. One
example will suffice to describe her lack of both social
and aesthetic refinement. When Lyamshin placed obscene
photos in the bag of a gospel woman, who was locked up
when they were found in her possession, Juliya
Mikhailovna's first reaction was to forbid him her house;
but then she yielded because of an amusing composition for
the piano, called "The FrancoPrussian War" in which the
melody of the French national hymn, "La Marseillaise"
gradually "passes somehow in the most foolish way" into
the German beer-song "Mein lieber Augustin," and ends in a
vulgar waltz describing "Jules Favre sobbing on Bismarck's
bosom and surrendering everything, everything...."(38)
Upon the same Juliya Mikhailovna, who claimed to have been
sitting for two hours before Raphael's Madonna without
being able to discover anything extraordinary in it, a
vulgarization of patriotic emotions makes such a powerful
impression that she pardons an almost criminal deed. She
shows similarly vulgar taste and discrimination when she
criticizes and ridicules a relatively harmless person like
Stepan Trofimovich and yields to the flatteries of his
corrupt and criminal son Pyotr, whom she chooses as her
adviser for the literary Fete "for the governesses of the
Provinces." The whole description of the Fete too is a
satire against the utilitarian conception of art. The
alleged purpose of collecting money for charity is a
fraud. The principal lecturer, Karmazinov (in whom
Dostoevski intended to caricature Turgenev, whom he
disliked as a Westerner), almost ruins the literary
matinee with his endlessly boring poem "Merci," which only
the ladies accept with the politeness customary in good
society, and which Juliya Mikhailovna rewards with a
laurel wreath--which the disappointed "poet" declares to
be better handed over to the cook. And he is right, for
it would be more useful there as a spice! This remark is
obviously meant as another satirical dart aimed at the
utterly superficial and dishonest utilitarianism of Juliya
Mikhailovna. The mixed audience and the combination of
the so-called art, a degenerate art, to be sure, and the
serving of food and drink at the same time further ruin
even the semblance of a decent presentation of poetry; it
makes it all-too obvious that the purpose of the Fete is
nothing but an attempt to cater to all sections of society
by appealing to both the aesthetic or pseudo-aesthetic
taste of the higher stratum and vulgar instincts of the
lowest. Although the matinee has disgusted Juliya
Mikhailovna so that she would like to omit the "literary
quadrille" and a dance entertainment of the evening, she
is so anxious to be deceived again about her influence in
society that she listens to Pyotr's treacherous flattery
again and personally appears at the ball--which is
interrupted by the murder and arson on the other side of

the river, made easier by the distraction of the Fete.
The paradoxical result of the abuse and desecration of the
arts for Juliya Mikhailovna personally is that she, who
wanted to strengthen her social and political position as
the wife of the governor, should become the cause of his
mental collapse and the end of his career.

In general, the influence of all three characters
upon one another follows a negative, downward course. The
reason is that none of them is his _authentic self_, or, to
use Sartre's expression (which is very appropriate in this
case), no one tries to _create_ himself. They are either
egocentric aesthetes, such as Stepan Trofimovich--
(although with the admixture of the other type), or they
are that which they would like to be in the eyes of
others, and thus make themselves dependent upon the
opinion of others, like Varvara Petrovna, and on a much
lower level, Juliya Mikhailovna. The want to create an
image of themselves in others, whose function then is to
serve as a mirror in which they can admire themselves;
they belong to the average types of human beings which
Heidegger in _Sein und Zeit_ calls _das Man_. They must
finally be disappointed because their "mirror" constantly
changes its surface and, the image is further distorted by
the fact that it is dependent upon two incompatible
factors, namely, the _haute volee_, the higher stratum of
society, consisting mainly of superficial and vain people,
and the mob, which is devoid of any taste and not
interested in anything except the most material things.

The three characters depicted here represent three
types of possible aesthetic attitudes which Dostoevski
obviously intended to examine and criticize, and which
therefore may permit some conclusions concerning
Dostoevski's mature aesthetic views. They may be
tentatively formulated as follows: art must be integrated
with life, since life provides the material which may be
transformed into aesthetic forms, culminating in beauty.
This is the guiding principle which in The Possessed is
substantiated mainly in a negative way, namely, by
demonstrating that the "aesthetic way" of life (Stepan
Trofimovich--Varvara Petrovna) is an escape from life in
which even some initial talent deteriorates to cliches and
may even further deteriorate to a utilitarian conception
of the arts.(39)

Art and life are inseparable from one another, if
life is to fulfill the higher purpose of peace and
harmony. To assign the works of art a place on a level
which deprives all human endeavors and ideals of their
intrinsic value, as Stepan Trofimovich does in his lecture
at the Fete, is almost as futile and disruptive as the
opposite extreme--the exploitation of the arts for social
and political reasons.

From all this follows that the artist has a
responsibility toward life from which he cannot escape;
the mere fact that he is capable of creating ideas and
ideals which may enhance the value and meaning of life
already imposes a serious obligation upon us. The fact
that Stepan Trofimovich has never taken this duty upon
himself and tried to escape into a life of leisure and

pseudo-aestheticism is the guilt which makes him one of
the "Possessed."

NOTES

1.   This is an almost verbatim paraphrase of
Dostoevski's article in Vremya (Time) as found in Dnevnik
pisatelya za 1873. god, vol. X (Sankt Peterburg; 1906), 44
ff. Translation is by the author of this chapter.

2.   Fyoder Dostoevski, Sobranie sochinenii, vol. 7
Besy, (Moskva: Gos./zdat. Khud. Lit., 1957), Pt. I, Ch.
I-1,9. All translations from this volume are by the
author of this chapter.

3.   Ibid., 9.

4.   Ibid., 10.

5.   Ibid.

6.   Ibid., Ch. I-2, 14.

7.   Ibid., 14.

8.   Ibid., Ch. I-5, 23.

9.   Ibid., Ch. I-6, 24.

10.   Ibid., 24.

11.   Ibid., 26.

12.   Ibid., 27.   Mikhail Yevgrafovich Saltykov
(1826-1889), the important satirist of the nineteenth
century was associated with the radical journal, The
Contemporary (Sovremennik), the target of Dostoevski's
fierce attacks.   Saltykov wrote under the pen-name of
Shchedrin. Vek was a weekly journal published in
Petersburg between 1861 and 1862; Lev Kambek was a
jounalist and publisher of The Family Circle, (1859-1860)
and St. Petersburg Messenger (1861-1862).

13.   Epokha, Zhurnal literaturnyi i politicheskii,
Peterburg, 1864-1865, No. 5, p. 280 (quoted from Microfilm
made in Tumba, Sweden, International Documentation Centre
AB, 1964).

14.   Fyodor Dostoevski, Sobranie, Pt. I, Ch. I-6, 27.

15.   Ibid., Ch. I-7, 28.

16.   Ibid., 28.

17.   Ibid., 29.

18.   Ibid., Ch. I-9, 36.

19. Ibid., 40.

20. Ibid., 38. Elisa Rachel-Felix (1821-1858) was the French tragic actress who gave very successful guest performances in Russia from 1853 to 1854.

21. Ibid., Pt. III, Ch. I-4, 506.

22. Ibid., 506.

23. Ibid., 507.

24. Ibid.

25. Ibid., 508.

26. Ibid., Pt. I, Ch. I-3, 17.

27. Ibid., 17.

28. Ibid., Pt. I, Ch. I-5, 23.

29. Ibid., 23.

30. Ibid., Pt. II, Ch. V-3, 355.

31. Ibid., 355.

32. Ibid., 356-357.

33. Ibid., Pt. II, Ch. IV-1, 316.

34. Ibid., 317.

35. Ibid., 316.

36. Ibid., Pt. II, Ch. V-3, 356.

37. N. G. Chernyshevsky, Estetika, Gosizdat (Moskva-Leningrad; 1939), 53.

38. Dostoevski, op. cit., Pt. II, Ch. V-1, 340.

39. The extreme case is Karmazinov.

Part II

Keynote Essay

12.
The French Face of Dostoevski
HENRI PEYRE

It is a noble undertaking of Hofstra University to have
gathered scholars from all over this country and abroad in
order to mark the centenary of the death of Dostoevski.
It was generous and courageous to invite, among a host of
Slavic scholars, one who reads Russian authors only in
translation and who lays no claim to being a specialist on
the subject. I happen to have read and admired Dostoevski
from my adolescent years on, which means that I am in a
position to appraise the immense progress effected in our
knowledge of the Russian novelist in the last sixty years,
The increased precision of our research on a writer who
has become a classic does not, however, imply that his
influence has become correspondingly stronger. Some of
the zest of discovery and of the enthusiasm which carried
away a few in the 1920s has probably flagged by now.
Still, my native country, France, from the pioneering book
by E. M. de Vogue on the Russian novel to Gide, Claudel,
Proust, Malraux, counted heavily in the spread of
Dostoevski's appreciation in Western Europe. Within the
dozen years which preceded the hundredth anniversary of
Dostoevski's death, important volumes by French Slavic
scholars have appeared, some of them voluminous ones:
Pierre Pascal, the Dean of Dostoevski studies in Western
Europe published in quick succession in 1969 and 1970 a
balanced and perceptive appraisal of the novelist's
religious attitudes (often very diversely interpreted),
Dostoevsky devant Dieu (Paris, Desclee, 1969) and an
elegant synthesis Dostoevsky, l'Homme et l'Oeuvre in
Switzerland (L'Age d'Homme, 1970). Jacques Catteau
followed with a thorough study, La Creation litteraire
chez Dostoevsky (Paris, Institute d'Etudes Slaves, 1978);
he had already organized and edited a very rich "Cahier de
l'Herne," gathering significant texts recently revealed
and including Russian as well as French contributors.
Important "theses de doctorat" are due to appear in print;
by Gustave Aucouturier and by Jean-Louis Backes. All pay
tribute to the French diplomat who, only four years after
Dostoevski's death, had been the first to reveal him,
guardedly but intelligently, to what is called "the West":
Vogue.
  Other countries had resisted the invasion of "the
Scythian," as Vogue had called him, more stubbornly. In

England, a very young man, John Middleton Murry (later
Katherine Mansfield's husband), a versatile critic who was
to champion the most varied causes, had brought out in
1916 (he was then eighteen) a delirious eulogy of the
Russian novelist whom he had just discovered. He praised
him as a thinker and as a prophet, one year before the
Russian revolution: "The Russian thought which shall
renew humanity found its most perfect expression in
Dostoevsky's novels." Richard Garnett, husband of the
translator of Dostoevski's novels, who had close relations
with the outstanding English men of letters in the years
preceding World War I, endeavored to spread the fame of
the new idol. His success was scant. Henry James's
aversion for "those loose baggy monsters" was stubborn.
He blamed both Tolstoy and Dostoevski for "their lack of
composition, their defiance of economy and architecture";
he could hardly have been farther from what appears to us
today as the chief virtue of Crime and Punishment and of
The Idiot. But it is notoriously difficult for a creative
artist to praise, or even to tolerate, another creator
whose technique brings his into question. In a private
letter to Hugh Walpole on May 18, 1912, he reiterated his
unwillingness to find any worth in The Brothers Karamazov,
for the novel was deficient in form: and form is the one
safeguard "from the welter of helpless verbiage that we
swim in as in a sea of tasteless tepid pudding." John
Galsworthy did read that novel twice, but with little
relish. He wrote on April 15, 1914 to Richard Garnett:
"It's a mark of these cubistic, blood-bespattered-poster
times that Dostoevsky should rule the roost."   The Slav
Joseph Conrad was even more outspoken in his exasperation
and decreed the novels of Dostoevski "terrifically bad."
D. H. Lawrence who had no reason to share the prejudices
of the Oxbridge alumni and of the men of property, was
just as scornful of The Idiot and of The Demons: he found
their author's "mixing God and sadism, foul, worse than
Petronius who, at least, was 'straight and above
board'".(1)
     Indeed for a long time, and not necessarily for
political reasons, it was in his own country or among
Russians living abroad that Dostoevski was least
appreciated. Henri Troyat, a French Academician of
Russian birth (his name was originally Lew Tarassow), the
author of a bulky biography of Dostoevski, fought against
the comforting Western belief that the epileptic and
hysterical and crazy characters in those novels were
typical Russians. He quotes contemporaries of the
novelist, in particular Count Kuchelew-Bezborodko who,
commenting on one of the strange characters in The
Insulted and the Injured, remarked that he could not
possibly be taken for a Russian: he would be more
convincing if he were a Frenchman, a Belgian, an
Englishman. Vladimir Pozner, a Russian born French
writer, was the author of a widely spread history of
modern Russian literature from 1885 to 1929 (Paris, Kra,
1929) which granted little influence to Dostoevski. He
mocked the naivety of the French admirers of that writer

who considered Raskolnikov, Stavrogin, and Ivan Karamazov
as typical Russians. They were indeed no more Russian
than Hamlet is Danish, Romeo Italian, Racine's Phedre
Cretan. The Russian novelist gave bodies of prostitutes
to chaste hearts and inversely. A spirit of corruption
and of negation emerges from Zosima and his stinking
corpse, and even from Alyosha, who resembles his
father.(2) Other Russian writers who lived in France in
the 1920s and gained a wide audience there (Nikolai
Berdiaev, Andre Levinson) were no less sarcastic in making
fun of the French view of the Russians. Periodically,
according to them, the French like to take a holiday from
their Cartesian rationalism and their classical wisdom and
revel in the antics of Russian buffoons, tolerant
cuckolds, and irascible and unpredictable women. They are
full of wonderment, but also relieved that those strange
monsters are Russian. Prince D. S. Mirsky, whose History
of Russian Literature (New York, Alfred Knopf, 1949) was
long the standard one in English, questioned the more than
doubtful Christianity of Dostoevski; he distrusted his
"partiality for sensationalism and elaborate intrigue"
which makes him a true disciple of Balzac; he warned that
his most cruel book Notes from Underground, "is a strong
poison, which is most safely left untouched" (p. 286).
Vladimir Nabokov's vituperations against the Westerners'
preposterous rating of Dostoevski as a great novelist were
notorious. To him, Dostoevski is not an artist, but "a
prophet, a clap-trap journalist and a splashdash
comedian." The creator of Lolita (to whom he gave not a
few Dostoevskyan features) vented his scornful impatience
with Dostoevski's "sensitive murderers and soulful
prostitutes." He considered Balzac no less grossly
overestimated. Many a Russian, annoyed at being called
"an Oriental," and therefore an Asiatic barbarian, likes
to contend that their best poets (from Pushkin and
Tiutchev to Ivanov and Maria Tsvetaeva), their novelists,
their musicians from Glinka to the twentieth century ones,
are far more sensible, orderly, and "classical," and are
truer descendants of the ancient Greeks, than the crazy
geniuses of Germany, England, or France. Still, it would
be regrettable if, in Western eyes, Dostoevski were
deprived of all exotic strangeness, if some of his
characters were no longer being seen as monsters and if
they lost all power of disturbing us. Francois Mauriac
recalled how, a timorous youth in Bordeaux, clinging to
his Catholic training, tormented by his anxiety as an
adolescent, he started reading Dostoevski's Raw Youth
(L'Adolescent, in French). He was soon seized with
embarrassment and shame, threw the book into the fireplace
and watched it burn. "I was the Grand Inquisitor, setting
a match to that pyre." Later, having realized that he
should recapture that adolescent anguish even in his old
age (his last novel, in 1969, when he was 84 years old,
was entitled Un Adolescent d'Autrefois), he generously
forgave the Russian novelist his anti-Catholicism, even
more virulent than his anti-Semitism, and hailed him as
"the most passionate Christian of the nineteenth century".

     Andre Gide was close to forty when, in 1908, he gave
his first article, hesitant and embarrassed, on
"Dostoevsky and his Correspondence." He had recently
discovered him, decided at once that he preferred him to
Tolstoy and to all French novelists, even to Flaubert
whose letters had for a time been his favorite reading.
He had published two admirable novels, which he chose
later to call "recits" rather than novels: :L'Immoraliste
and La Porte etroite. Both were intensely personal, woven
out of the conflicts which had disturbed him since his
adolescence. He felt the need of broadening himself
through the stimulation afforded by foreign authors:
Nietzsche first, then Dostoevski. He wanted to escape
from the rich but cramping tradition of the psychological
novel and from the first person narrative; he would try to
conjure up a host of diverse characters, often acting in
disregard of logic, and to multiply plots with an
appearance of studied incoherence. But it was the man in
him, and not only the technician of the art of fiction,
who was rapturously discovering the strange husbands and
lovers of Dostoevski's world, their outpouring of their
inmost secrets, their disregard of "pudeur" and their
scorn for conventional behavior.
     Some fifteen years previously, on October 8, 1895,
Gide had married his cousin; a few months earlier, he had
met Oscar Wilde in Algiers; and in 1894, in Tunisia, he
had accepted himself as a pederast, and as a born again
man who would cease to struggle against what he admitted
as the law of his own nature. His was to be an "amazing
marriage" in a sense different from Meredith's title: it
was never to be consummated. Yet he maintained to the end
that his wife, Madeleine, was the only being whom he ever
truly loved. He was, just at the time of his first
Dostoevski essay, putting the finishing touches to his
most moving novel, in which he lent to Alissa, tragically
and at the same time ironically, or at least critically,
several of the features of his pious Protestant
cousin-wife. Except for a brief piece, in 1911, on The
Brothers Karamazov, which his friend Jacques Copeau was
then dramatizing for the stage, Gide only returned to
Dostoevski after World War I, to give a lecture in 1921 at
Theater of the Vieux-Colombier, then six more in 1922:
those form the bulk of his book. Gide's Dostoevsky
appeared in English translation in 1925, presented to the
British public by the novelist Arnold Bennett: it has
been reprinted since and widely read in American colleges.
     Much had happened in the world, plunged into tragedy,
between 1908 and 1922. Gide had been moved by the deaths
of several of his friends in the trenches, and by the
conversion of others to Catholicism. He himself had for a
time been close to shifting from his Protestant education
to the acceptation of a rigid discipline which a Catholic
priest and confessor might have imposed upon him. He was
even tempted, briefly, by the Royalist doctrine of
Maurras, which was to impress T. E. Hulme and T. S. Eliot
across the Channel. Between 1916 and 1919, he put down a
series of notes, later incorporated into his voluminous

Journal, and dedicated them to a friend recently
converted, Charles du Bos. He entitled them "Numquid et
Tu?": the Latin words are, as translated from Luke (xxii,
29) and John (vii, 52), those which are addressed to Peter
by a woman in Jerusalem when, as had been predicted to him
and much to his own humiliation, the disciple, thrice
before the cock crew, denied being, he too, a Galilean.
Vacillations, or studied reversals, then marked Gide's
spiritual life, fully worthy of any Dostoevskian
character. In 1914, he had published an entertaining and
blasphemous novel, Les Caves du Vatican, which had
distressed his Catholic friends, especially Claudel, who
had hoped to convert him. In 1919, simultaneous with the
fervent "Numquid et Tu?," appeared La Symphonie pastorale,
which alienated Protestants and Catholics alike. Still,
Gide always insisted that he was the one writer in France
who felt, and understood, Christianity, and therefore
could approach the truest Christian novelist, Dostoevski.
    Meanwhile, crises had rocked his private life. His
wife had ignored, or pretended to ignore, the true nature
of her husband's sexuality until a homosexual friend of
Gide, the medical doctor Henri Gheon (also a critic of
talent and later the author of pious plays, now
forgotten), with whom Gide had exchanged many a letter on
their expeditions in search of adolescent "friends,"
having been seized with remorse and turned to religion,
enlightened her. Then in 1918, Gide took off for
Cambridge, England, with a young lover, Marc Allegret, the
son of a pastor who had been a friend of the Gide family.
When he returned, he discovered that his wife had burned
all his letters to her. It was a hard blow to his strange
and complex affection for her: for he needed her as a
suffering presence, a witness (the word in Greek is "a
martyr") to his idiosyncrasies. "The spiritual force of
my love for her inhibited all carnal desire," he will
confess in a pathetic and cruel book on her published in
1951 after her death, Et nunc Manet in Te (Madeleine, in
the English version). He could have given her a child, he
avowed, "provided there had been no admixture of the
intellectual or of the sentimental." Instead, he
consented to father one to the daughter of close friends
of his, the Van Rysselberghe: Catherine Gide was born in
1923. His wife must have suspected what happened. In
that posthumous little book, whose Latin title is taken
from a pseudo-Virgilian poem, "Culex," Gide portrayed the
silent degradation of Madeleine and her sinking into self-
sacrifice and premature aging. Callously, in his pages on
his deceased wife, he slipped the admission: "As for
pleasing me, there was no longer any point for her to
think of it. Thenceforth what did culture, poetry matter?
She sank into devotion". His grief was over the loss of
his letters: "to them I had entrusted my heart, my
joy. . . . She suppressed the only ark in which my memory,
later on, could hope to find refuge.... It was the best of
me that disappeared."
    Little wonder that Gide found himself in sympathy
with characters in The Eternal Husband and in the naked

and complacent confessions of The Idiot and The Demons.
He could enjoy being humiliated, incriminating himself,
convincing himself that he was most sincere, hence
triumphing as an artist and a psychologist, when he laid
bare what appeared to the others as his own abjection; at
the same time feeling proud of a humility which he could
believe to be genuinely Christian. Dostoevski's
underground man may well have struck Gide as anticipating
his ever renewed and proud confession of his lowliness:
"To be a hero or to be mud: nothing in between. . . .
That was my own ruin, for in the mud I found comfort in
the notion that, at another time, I was a hero and the
hero concealed the mud." His French admirer indulged an
even more sophisticated dialectics between his two
favorite terms: "Humility opens the gates of heaven;
humiliation, the gates of hell."(3)
       Gide was a self-diffident and often disconnected
lecturer, who interspersed his remarks with lengthy
quotations. He did not wish to organize his lecture notes
into a polished volume. He left in the published text a
number of summary remarks on Balzac, several of them
excessively dogmatic and controversial. Scholars have
since laid bare Dostoevski's debt to Balzac, to Hugo's
Dernier Jour d'un Condamne, to George Sand, and his loudly
proclaimed affinities with them and with Eugene Sue.
Gide's discovery of the Russian novelist, and of himself
through that intermediary, had taken on the appearance of
a revelation. With the enthusiasm of a neophyte, he
railed, often unfairly, at his chief predecessor in
France, Count Eugene Melchior de Vogue. To be sure, that
diplomat, later academician, the author of novels of some
merit and an official figure of the Third Republic, had
only partially understood Dostoevski. His volume, Le
Roman russe, had come out in 1886; it nevertheless remains
an excellent introduction to the subject. The author had
spent some time as an attaché to the French Embassy in St.
Petersburg. He learned Russian, associated with Russian
men of letters, met Dostoevski several times between 1878
and 1881, and was present at his funeral. He begins the
penultimate chapter of his book (the chapter on
Dostoevski) with the oft quoted and in truth neither
ridiculing nor ridiculous words: "Here comes the
Scythian, the true Scythian, who is going to revolutionize
all our intellectual habits." He entitled his
seventy-five page chapter on him "The Religion of
Suffering," a facile formula which incurred the sarcasm of
Gide, and he concluded it with his reflections while
attending the funeral of the novelist on a windy February
day: the words which came to his lips then were the very
ones Raskolnikov told Sonia: "It is not before you that I
bow, it is before all the suffering of mankind." Recent
Dostoevski scholars, on the contrary, have praised the
shrewd anticipations in Vogue's criticism.
       The remarks, desultory at times, unsystematic and
highly personal, which make up Gide's volume may be
grouped under three convenient headings and appraised from
the perspective which, sixty years later, appears to be
that of our contemporaries. They touch on the Russian

novelist's philosophical and religious attitude first. Through one side, and an essential one of his personality, Gide was and remained a moralist. "La morale" (ethical and moral issues and behavior; the French term is comprehensive) "is the stuff of which my books are made," he said at times. The second broad domain is the portrayal of character and the conflicting directions toward illogic and relentless demonstration, the Devil's snares and angelic humility, in human beings. Least original and convincing, partly because Gide did not know Russian and was not closely familiar with the Russian literary tradition and environment from 1860 to 1880, is his discussion of the artistry and craft of the novelist.

Like a majority of powerful creators (Balzac, Dickens, Tolstoy, Mann, Proust), Dostoevski is strikingly didactic: he overflows with ideas felt with passionate intensity and yields to the urge of "propagating" them through their incarnation in fictional creatures. Balzac, carried away by his theorizing on almost every subject, from cosmology to gambling, dress and journalism, once proclaimed: "It is not enough to be a man; one must be a system." If system there be, neither with Balzac nor with Dostoevski nor any other imaginative creator, is it characterized by an impeccable rigor or sclerosed into inflexible propositions. Even with professional philosophers, as Renan hinted with a smile, "a system is but an epic poem on the nature of things."

The phrase "a philosophical novelist" in no way implies that the teller of tales has an orderly set of answers to the questions discussed by philosophers and hides them behind allegories or poetizes them through symbols. Very tersely, Sartre put it in one sentence in the first volume of his Situations: "A fictional technique always refers us to the metaphysics of the novelist." Dostoevski overflows with ideas on God and man, suffering, social and political problems, "et de omne re scibili et quibusdam aliis." Those ideas may be debated pro and con; often they meet with their refutation in the same chapter. But the personality which informs those ideas cannot be confuted so easily. In the bulky number of L'Herne, in 1973, a well known Russian participant, Alexis Remizov (1877-1957) was quoted as asserting: "His heroes are ideas, his world is a world of ideas." Another Russian, a professor at the Leningrad University, Boris Bursov, submits that dialectical oppositions are inherent in Dostoevski's thought; he calls in question a certain passion soon after he has depicted it; he steeps every one of his ideas into anguish. All in all, he remains "the greatest philosopher of Russia," but a philosopher within the compass of his imaginative creations. Fortunate are the cultures, like those of Russia and Spain, perhaps even that of modern France, in which philosophy is best expressed through literature, remains subordinate to it and thus trebles its radiating power.

Gide, in a sweeping and simplifying generalization, contends that, with Russian fiction in general and that of Dostoevski more particularly, an altogether new slant was

given to the art of fiction. It ceased being concerned
with wordliness: social relations, a man rushing to
conquer society, ambition, the clinging to property,
nostalgia for the past. It no longer put inevitably at
its core the relations between man and woman, or even sex.
Instead, man's relationship to God became the central
issue. If God does not exist, everything is allowed, as
the oft quoted and oft refuted assertion puts it in The
Brothers Karamazov. Conflicting interpretations of
Dostoevski's shifting religious attitudes had been offered
before Gide lectured on him, and many times since. It was
tempting to many to present the novelist in mystical
terms. Some readers remarked that the arguments put
forward by Ivan against the revolting injustice in the
world are never confuted and that the novelist appears to
tolerate the blasphemies, perhaps even at certain moments
to approve of them. Did he not confess himself that he
would remain in doubt until his dying day? He does not
seem to accept the divinity of Christ or to hail him as
the Son of God. He is more than vague on the possibility
of personal immortality; he is averse to subscribing to
the Augustinina, Calvinist, and Jansenist belief in the
universality of original sin inherited through generation.
But he clings to Christ and would rather err with him even
if it were proved to him that his belief is groundless.
He spurns the prospect of improving the world materially,
as he does the building up of utopias, whose inevitable
outcome is more regimentation. Verkhovensky (the murderer
of Shatov in The Demons) agrees with another intellectual,
Shigalyov, that "starting from unlimited freedom, one
arrives at unlimited despotism." For freedom and equality
can only exist along with despotism. Gide, some ten years
after his volume on Dostoevski, acclaimed for a time the
Bolshevik regime under Stalin as the fulfillment of a
utopia. He altered his views soon after being officially
welcomed in Russia at the very time (1935-1936) when the
Moscow trials were taking place and innocents forced, or
persuaded, to incriminate themselves in abject
humiliation. But in his Dostoevsky he evinced admiration
for the novelist's praise of the Tsar whose police had
sentenced him to death and whose magnanimous mercy saved
him in extremis. Dostoevski's own forgiveness did not
extend to those Russian intellectuals who had lost touch
with their native soil and traditions. He was living
abroad himself, away from creditors and close to gambling
resorts; The Idiot was composed in Switzerland, The Demons
in Dresden. Yet he compared those compatriots of his to
the Gadarene swine in whose bodies Christ expelled "the
possessed of the devils," in St. Matthew's phrase (viii,
26). To his contemporary Nikolai Chernyshevsky, born the
same year as Tolstoy (1828), who spent nineteen years in
forced labor in Siberia and before that, 1862-1863, was
writing his Utopian novel, What Is To Be Done?; imprisoned
in the Peter and Paul fortress, Dostoevski, the former
reader of Fourier, remained impervious to pity.
     If Gide, torn by his own inner contradictions and
seeking receptive ears into which to whisper his
occasional avowals of repentance, felt temporarily drawn

to Catholicism in 1917 and 1918 while he was rediscovering
Dostoevski, he was even more embarrassed by the self-
righteousness of those of his friends who had joined the
Roman faith: Claudel, the indefatigable converter of
others, Francis Jammes, Henri Gheon, and Charles du Bos.
They had turned complacent and self assured in their new
faith. What amazed Gide, who had lived in the constant
company of his Bible until his first liberating voyage to
North Africa, was their lack of all acquaintance with the
Scriptures. The same ignorance surprised him in his young
friend Jacques Riviere when the latter, under Claudel's
influence, wanted to return to the faith in which he had
grown, Catholicism with no knowledge of the two
Testaments. Gide delighted in stressing Dostoevski's
abhorrence for the Catholic faith. To no other than to
Prince Myshkin, of all his characters the closest to their
creator, did Dostoevski attribute his most outright
condemnation of Catholicism, pronounced by "the idiot" to
be worse than atheism. For the Roman Church bowed before
earthly powers, joyfully grasped the kingdoms proffered
(according to St. Matthew, iv, 10) by the Tempter to
Christ but spurned by the Savior. There ran a saying in
Geneva in Rousseau's time to the effect that one
Protestant, armed with his Bible, was worth ten Catholics.
Gide, the one important Protestant writer in France in his
century, would probably, though discreetly, have
subscribed to that boast.
     On March 2, 1918, Gide addressed a curious letter to
a Belgian friend, Andre Ruyters (1876-1952) in which he
blandly declared that Dostoevski's influence on him was
one with that of the Gospels, and that the lack of
familiarity with the New Testament in his correspondent
kept him from understanding the Russian novelist in depth.
He pursued: "He is . . . the one Christian author known
to me, or recognized by me as such. Others are Catholic,
or Protestant, before they are Christian. For the Gospel
often is opposed to the Churches. Soon after I discovered
Dostoevski . . . I merged myself into his works, saying to
myself: 'At last! That one did understand.'" Later, in
the mid 1930s Gide astonished some of his devotees when he
declared that it was the Gospel that had brought him to
Communism. If so, the influence of the Scriptures failed
in this case to prove lasting. It must be confessed that
the waning of that influence, and the fading of the
author's passion for Dostoevski, went hand in hand with a
progessive despiritualization in his writings.
     In the realm of character creation, Gide singled out
a few features which, in his judgment, sharply separated
Dostoevski from other novelists. The fundamental absence
of unity in human creatures is basic. It would be
caricaturing the writers of France or her rulers, to
assert that they were ever the heroes, or the slaves, of
consistency. Contradictions abound in Alceste, even in
Chimene, certainly in Racinian heroines, in Phedre or
Hermione in their disarray exclaiming: "Ah! Ne puis-je
savoir si j'aime our si je hais?" French school children
have all, at some stage in their literary training, had to
dissert on the tenuous separation, or even on the

identity, between love and hatred. Still there often
lingered some logic in the passionate exasperation of
those characters. The tragic soliloquies and the
analytical avowals of French personal novels delighted in
neatly distinguishing between the two groups of feelings
which alternated in their disturbed souls. In Dostoevski,
according to Gide, the ambivalence of the coexisting moods
is a constant feature. The female personages in The Idiot
certainly contrast with Balzacian and even Proustian
women, and with the dolorous, submissive, resigned female
martyrs who held the preference of Gide the man and the
novelist.

In his revolt against the French classical tradition
(which, at other times, he exalted as the most valuable
one in the West), Gide hailed in Dostoevski the broadening
of literary psychology. In the Russians, rashly
generalizing from fiction to reality, he celebrated the
near-disappearance of the "point of honor" which prompts
Westerners (Spaniards and French in particular, but also
gentlemen from across the Channel) to feel, not as they
actually and spontaneously do, but as their training has
instructed them that they should. "Amour-propre," that
typical French word, spite, jealousy of a rival in love,
are stifled, or only faintly present, in the characters of
The Eternal Husband or The Idiot. We know from occasional
jottings in his Journal and other indirect confessions
(from the figure of Passavant, alias Cocteau) how beside
himself with jealousy of his young male friends Gide could
be in actual life. He repeatedly proclaimed that all his
works were, after a fashion, "ironical works" and that
satires, "soties," picaresque adventures were congenial to
him. But at other times, and in his occasional attempts
to rival Dostoevski in the portrayal of humility, he
repudiated the role of will power in Corneille's and
Balzac's characters. Those strove hard to become what
they deliberately aimed at becoming, straining every nerve
to reach their self-appointed goal. If they sensed the
presence of contradictions in themselves, they hastened to
obliterate them, or to merge them in the pursuit of some
goal set outside themselves: money, power, a woman,
social success, or merely self-mastery. In Dostoevski,
characters did not claim to be or to become heroes in the
traditional sense. To be logical, or all of a piece, or
merely consistent, and to offer to others the facet of
ourselves which they expect, is the sin par excellence.
"To become the one that we are", as the Greek formula
borrowed by Gide from Nietzsche and by the latter from
Pindar, is to lay bare all our inner contradictions and
not to attempt any conciliation among them. Claudel, who
may well have displayed more insight into Dostoevski's art
than Gide, called those moods and passions abruptly
supplanted by contrary ones in the Russian novelist,
"rapid mutations," analogous to those that a biologist,
Hugo de Vries, had identified in natural evolution.

It need hardly be added that Gide's interpretation of
Dostoevski is a simplification. Irony is far from lacking
in the dialogues and narratives of The Idiot. The humor
and the burlesque are part and parcel of those buffoons

whom Camus admired in The Demons and elsewhere. The
Russian critic Bakhtin termed that element in Dostoevski
(which he grossly magnified) "carnivalesque" or
"Menippean." Relentlessly, for a time Gide strove hard to
become the high-priest of humility. Some element of that
supreme virtue--"the only wisdom we can hope to acquire",
T. S. Eliot calls it in "East Coker"--has not been
wanting, even among those paragons of vanity, the French
(Napoleon dixit), in Pascal and a number of female saints.
Dostoevski's friend and first biographer, Strakhov,
perceived few traces of humility in the novelist's
behavior to women and to servants. Myshkin's humility
fails to help Nastasia Filippovna whom Rogozhin eventually
murders. Alyosha's humility does not save his father or
his brothers. Father Zosima himself holds out scant hope
of brotherhood ever coming to pass in this world. Gide's
own author's conceit and his pride at being for a time
idolized by the younger generations and cursed as Satan's
Henchman by his enemies, always kept him from becoming a
rival to those russian saints. Still, he never ceased
quoting the verse from Luke (xvii, 33) which he had seen
illustrated in the novels of Dostoevski: "Whosoever shall
seek to save his life shall lose it, and whosoever shall
lose his life shall preserve it." In more senses than
one, he had attempted to "lose his life" and, though he
spurned all transcendence in the metaphysical sense, he
became convinced that he had outstripped all his
contemporaries of the French literary world in humility.
He prided himself of having crushed his personality in the
hope of an ultimate gain in this world. He clung to the
hope that he would be judged, and fully vindicated, "on
appeal."

The process of influence in matters pertaining to the
intellect is naturally widely different from that of mere
imitation. Victor Hugo, at the very time when he and
other young romantics in France were raving over
Shakespearean drama, wisely warned his fellow-dramatists:
"One does not imitate Shakespeare." Proust has likewise
counted few followers in his own country. Gide, who has
repeatedly and guardedly written on the nature of literary
influences(4) knew better than to attempt to write fiction
in the manner of the Russian. But his prolonged study of
Dostoevski spurred him to adopt a new conception of the
art of the novel and, temporarily at least, to depart from
the type of rectilinear "recit," often told in the first
person singular, that he had composed until his Pastoral
Symphony (1919). He called The Counterfeiters (1925),
published two years after his Dostoevsky, "my first
novel."

That ambitious work has generally not been judged a
success. The juxtaposition of plots smacks of artifice:
the symbol of counterfeit money around which they are
woven is unconvincing. The adolescents who wander around
the Sorbonne and the Luxembourg Gardens, flee from their
families, fall under the sway of pallid would-be
corruptors, at no time strike us as endowed with life.
Inevitably, as in all Gide's narratives, we are served
with lengthy extracts of the private diary of one ubiq-

uitous character: he is striving to compose a novel which
never takes shape and never stimulates our curiosity; that
brings in elaborate and arid discussions on the technique
of fiction and the point of view from which the plot might
most fruitfully be told. The traditional paraphernalia of
the French novel are purposely left out: a progressive
evolution, characters retaining some unity amid their
contradictions and some mystery even in their confessions
or in their introspective diaries. In long epistolary
exchanges with a fellow-novelist, Roger Martin du Gard, to
whom his "first novel" is dedicated, Gide claimed to
repudiate the Tolstoyan type of novel in which an equal
amount of lighting is spread on several episodes; he
advocated rather what he presents as the Dostoevski model,
a glaring focus of light occasionally thrown on a certain
scene or on a certain feature of a character, followed by
zones of darkness. Analogies are hardly in order. The
author of The Thibault is as remote in his technique from
Tolstoy as Gide is from Dostoevski. Gide, it should be
added, could not in 1922-1925 reach the complex view of
Dostoevski's art which the publication of the fuller
Correspondence, then of the Notebooks of the novelist has
since made possible for us. The word "realism" was looked
askance at in the era of Proust and Giraudoux, of
Surrealism and of Cocteau, in the 1920s; it was only
tolerated if qualified with the adjective "magical." In
fact, Dostoevski, while spurning the deterministic and
mechanistic psychology prevailing in the 1860s and 1870s
in Western Europe, did not object to being called a
realist. The word is hardly more precise than "romantic"
or "modern." In his Notebooks, he refused to be termed a
psychologist and he added: "I am but a realist in the
best sense of the word, that is to say, I express all the
depths of the human soul." Elsewhere, in one of his
letters, Dostoevski recurred to the use of the term: "I
have a personal vision of reality and what most people
call fantastic and exceptional constitutes for me the very
essence of reality."

     It would be cruel to prolong the sketch of a parallel
between two novelists so widely different in genius and
temperament. Gide provided us with revealing insights in
his Diary of the Counterfeiters which followed the novel
in 1927: he took us there into the penetralia of his mind
as a technician laboriously composing a work of fiction
which clearly was not the fruit of an irresistible
creative urge. He lacked the supreme heroism which would
have been needed for him to point out the deficiencies of
his "first novel." Simply, he never repeated the
attempt.(5) It was not in his nature to emulate the
ferociously comic and tragic scenes or the passionate
ideological confrontations of Dostoevski's novels. The
latter could successively or alternately identify himself
with each of his characters, even with those whom he
inwardly found the preys to "demons." Gide, try hard as
he might to forget himself when creating the
schoolmasterish Edouard, the fumbling teenagers in revolt
against their families and even more the pale and unreal
female characters, always remained in the tradition of

Stendhal: ironically, through numerous asides and occasional defensive remarks addressed directly to the reader, he endeavors to disarm in advance the objections of imaginary interlocutors. He gently mocks his heroes, just as Stendhal affectionately smiled at the amiable ridicules of Julien Sorel or Lucien Leuwen. The sophisticated reader feels flattered at thus being taken into the novelist's confidence. But he cannot be blamed for being unable to suspend his disbelief when confronted with the angel approaching Bernard at the Sorbonne and the night long wrestling between the schoolboy and his winged visitor. Nor does he take very seriously the Devil that visits Vincent before the latter, a prey to insanity, takes himself for the Devil. "The more we deny him (the Devil), the more reality we endow him with," Gide asserts in the Diary of the Counterfeiters. We do not have to deny Satan in this case or to bid him step back: he simply does not convince us that he is real. But we did not dissent from Ivan Karamazov's retort to his Devil: "You're I . . . with another face." One of Gide's favorite assertions, in the aesthetic realm, was that "there exists no work of art without the collaboration of the demon" (the French language distinguishes between the two adjectives demoniaque and the more Goethean demonique). Regrettably the Devil failed to cooperate wholeheartedly with Gide's only half-Dostoevskian novel.

Recent French students of his Dostoevski volume have faulted him for railing a little too readily at his predecessor, Vogue, instead of following up the most incisive remarks of that early admirer of "the Scythian."(6) Vogue had indeed bestowed his warmest praise on the admirable structure of Dostoevski's novels: "The materials are so simple and so expertly sacrificed to the impression of the whole that a severed fragment loses all value; it becomes no more meaningful than the stone torn from a Greek temple, in which all the beauty rests in the broad lines. The pages add to each other, silently, drops of water slow and digging deep; suddenly the reader is lost in a deep lake." Far from objecting to the length of those novels, as an impatient French reader might have done, Vogue had submitted: "The author is especially effective through what he leaves unsaid; we are grateful to him for all that he allows us to guess." Indeed, such and other remarks anticipated the Russian poet and critic, Viatcheslav Ivanov who, in 1911, in a lecture delivered in Saint Petersburg, praised the symphonic composition of Dostoevski's novels, corresponding to the counterpoint in music. Bakhtin, whose book on Dostoevsky's Poetics first appeared in 1929 (and in French in 1970, Paris, Seuil) acknowledges that Vogue and Ivanov had anticipated him in that respect. He, resorting to a more pretentious terminology, defines that technique as that of the "polyphonic novel." He aligned it insistently with the Satyricon of Petronius and to a tradition traced back to the Carnival. Adverse ideologies exhaust each other in their confrontation. The composer Glinka, whom Dostoevski had admired, had repeated "All in life is counterpoint, that is, opposition." In a letter of July 29, 1923,

written from Tokyo, where he was then the French
Ambassador, Paul Claudel proposed a few corrections to
Gide's presentation of Dostoevski: he regretted that Gide
had not taken the time to discuss the art of the Russian
novelist, the extraordinary skill of his composition "with
its ample crescendos in the manner of Beethoven."(7)
Again, in his conversations with an interviewer, when he
was eighty-three years old, Claudel declared his great
debt to Dostoevski as to "the inventor of the polymorphous
character" and repeated that he considered the first two
hundred pages of The Idiot as "a masterpiece of
composition equal to Beethoven's masterpieces."

Gide could not help realizing that his book on
Dostoevski was (as he called it) "a volume of confessions
. . . or rather a profession of faith" even more than a
work of criticism. He prepared the lectures in which the
book had originated with great emotional difficulty,
feeling that his deepest self was involved in them. He
realized that many of his assertions might arouse dissent,
and not solely among scholars who would find his
information imperfect. In one of the lectures, the third,
he alluded to a recent article by a friend and admirer of
his, Jacques Riviere, who, on returning from a prisoners
of war camp in 1919, had been placed, through Gide's
advice, at the post of editor of La Nouvelle Revue
Francaise. Riviere's article, "De Dostoevsky et de
l'insondable" was indeed noteworthy.(8) The author was
neither a conservative critic whom Russian novelists might
have frightened nor a nationalist (there were many such
then in France), arguing that Asia began at the Rhine and
that the Russian writers were Asiatic barbarians out to
wreck Western values. Warily, after having been
enraptured by Dostoevski, he wondered whether it was not
lazy on the part of Dostoevski's admirers to fall on their
knees before psychological contradictions and to gape
uncritically at "unfathomable abysses." Were Balzac and
even Corneille to blame, as Gide was arguing, if they
searched for some continuity behind the vacillations of
the characters? And are not truest, in psychological
matters, those depths which one fathoms, instead of gazing
at them with awe and a voluptuous giddiness?

The friend (and brother-in-law) of Riviere was Alain
Fournier, whose Le Grand Meaulnes proved one of the
lastingly popular novels of the century. He was killed in
1914 at the battle of the Marne. In part owing to Gide's
influence, he developed in the last four or five years of
his life a passion for Dostoevski, and particularly for
The Idiot. Strongly tempted by a return to his Catholic
faith, he found in that novel, despite its marked
anti-Catholicism, a mystical model. By a curious stroke
of chance, it is through Alain Fournier that T. S. Eliot
discovered Dostoevski, in a French translation as he
himself specified, and not through Mrs. Garnett's. The
unambiguous allusions to Dostoevski, or reminiscences from
his novels, in "The Lovesong of J. F. Prufrock," were due
to Eliot's tutor, Alain Fournier who, in 1910, steeped his
American student into The Idiot, Crime and Punishment, and
The Brothers Karamazov. "Prufrock" was composed between

1911 and 1913. It was turned down in London by every
magazine, despite Conrad Aiken's attempt to place it there
and, after much trying on the part of Ezra Pound, it
finally appeared in 1915 in Harriet Monroe's Poetry
Magazine in Chicago.(9)
    Gide never reneged the enthusiasm of his fiftieth
year for Dostoevski. But he never cherished any of his
several "masters" long without wanting to outgrow them.
"Nathanael, throw my book away" remained his motto, as he
wanted it, coquettishly, to be that of his own disciples.
About the same time as he hailed Dostoevski as one of the
stars in his firmament, leaving his early Nietzscheism
behind, he adopted Blake, then more surprisingly,
Browning. The latter, unconcerned with the Devil's inter-
ventions in our inner lives, advocated faith in the future
and eventual victory for the forces of progress and of
good. "I say that man was made to grow, not stop": that
line in a poem by Browning which hardly counts among his
best, "A Death in the Desert", became for a time Gide's
motto. Then he returned to Goethe, celebrated him as did
the rest of the literary world on the centenary of his
death in 1932. He indulged rapturous though somewhat
hollow sounding eulogies of the life of the senses in his
New Fruits of the Earth, and composed intellectual,
analytical, arid "recits", such as L'Ecole des Femmes,
which stand at the opposite pole of Dostoevski's symphonic
profusion. Malraux, Bernanos, Camus, and other lesser
luminaries were, in part thanks to the impact of Gide's
crusade, to attempt novels in French not altogether
unworthy of the great Russian who had found a second home
in France. In the 1950s and 1960s, Dostoevski continued
to impress and to inspire the French Existentialists.
Technical experimentation with the form of the novel has
since taken on different paths. But, through Dostoevski,
for several decades, French literature was emboldened to
ask some of the fundamental questions of our time and had
become invested with a passionate meaningfulness.

NOTES

    1. The reaction of those English novelists to
Dostoevski's fiction was intelligently studied in a Bryn
Mawr thesis by Helen Muchnic, subsequently published in
Smith College Studies in Modern Languages (1939);
Dostoevsky's English Reputation, 1881-1936.

    2. Vladimir Pozner, "L'Ame slave et l'esprit
gaulois," Les Nouvelles Litteraires, June 26, 1926. See
Melvin Seiden, "Nabokov and Dostoevsky," Contemporary
Literature Vol. 13 (Autumn 1972). Maxim Gorky was also
incensed, as was Nabokov, by the preference given by
Western Europeans to Dostoevski over Gogol and Pushkin.
He consoled himself with the hope that Dostoevski's
influence would act like a poison on Western countries and
upset the psychic balance of their middle classes.

3. Gide's Dostoevsky is quoted here in the edition of the "New Directions" paperbook 1961: page 81, second 1922 lecture.

4. I have presented Gide's position on the subject of influences in an essay "Gide and Literary Influences," collected in my volume: French Literary Imagination and Dostoevsky (University of Alabama Press, 1975).

5. Searching, and more favorably inclined, critical analyses of The Counterfeiters have been given, in English, by Wolfgang Holdheim, in Theory and Practice of the Novel: A Study of Gide (Geneva; Droz, 1968) and by Irving Stock, Fiction as Wisdom (University Park, Pa.: Pennsylvania State University Press, 1980).

6. Jean-Louis Backes, a Slavic scholar of note, praises Vogue's "very subtle remarks on Dostoevsky's narrative technique" and his "very suggestive hints on the religious dimension of his work" in Le Magazine litteraire, (March 1978):134. Jacques Catteau hails Vogue as having anticipated Russian critics, especially Bakhtin, in perceiving the musical and polyphonic character of The Insulted and the Injured. See La Creation litteraire chez Dostoevsky, 1978, pp. 385, 389.

7. Claudel-Gide Correspondance (Gallimard, 1949), p. 238. Caludel, Memoires improvises (Gallimard, 1954), pp. 37, 39.

8. Riviere's brief and pregnant essay came out in the February 1922 number of La Nouvelle Revue Francaise. It was reprinted after the critic's premature death in a posthumous volume, Nouvelles Etudes (Gallimard, 1947), pp. 176-179 and translated in America as "On Dostoevsky and the Creation of Character," in Riviere, The Ideal Reader, (New York; Meridian Books, 1960), pp. 245-248.

9. This information was provided by T. S. Eliot himself to Professor John C. Pope. See American Literature 18, (January 1947): 319-321.

Part III

Comparative and Interdisciplinary Studies

13.

The Russian Iconic Representation of the Christian Madonna: A Feminine Archetype in *Notes from Underground*

PATRICIA FLANAGAN BEHRENDT

In 1876, Dostoevski recorded his observations on women and womanhood in The Diary of a Writer. He claimed that the letters from women which he received while writing the Diary gave him an opportunity to behold "the Russian woman at closer range."(1) He states that her principal fault is her "extraordinary dependency upon several masculine ideas; her inclination to accept them credulously and to believe them without scrutiny." Although Dostoevski does not specifically define "masculine ideas," he contrasts woman's acceptance of them with what he calls her "excellent qualities of the heart: women value most a fresh feeling, a live word; but what they treasure even more is sincerity, and once they believe in sincerity, even if it be a false one, they are inspired. . . ." Lastly, he observes that it is a woman's capacity to "assuage . . . sorrow by self-sacrifice and love."(2)

These lines, written five years before Dostoevski's death and after all of the major novels except The Brothers Karamazov, characterize the relationship between Liza and the underground man from the Notes from Underground,(3) written twelve years earlier in 1864. The underground man's tyrannical manipulations of Liza depend upon her naive belief in his knowledgeability and sincere interest in her. But, it is Liza who ultimately perceives the underground man's personal torment and reveals her own capacity for love and self-sacrifice. This suggestion of consistency in Dostoevski's view of women from the Notes from Underground, a pivotal work with characters which prefigure many of those from the later novels, to The Writer's Diary indicates that the observations in the Diary were well formed embryos in Dostoevski's thought before the writing of his major novels. What, then, were the sources of Dostoevski's images of women and womanhood in the major fiction? "Image" refers to the physical and thematic attributes conveyed to the reader through the text.

Clearly, Dostoevski was eclectic in the types of women which he portrayed. Robert Louis Jackson has noted what he called "the cult of the Madonna" in the works of Dostoevski.(4) Jackson's observation derived from the fact that Dostoevski himself described certain characters as having the physical beauty of certain Western Madonna

portraits. His Madame M. in <u>The Little Hero</u> (1849) was
compared physically to the Sistine Madonna which was
regarded by Dostoevski as a painting representing "the
most lofty manifestation of human genius." Anna Snitkina
Dostoevskaia's diary supports the idea that, as Western
works of art, the Italian Madonnas represented ideal
female beauty for Dostoevski.(5)

As the same time, Richard Peace has noted that the
image of Nastasya Filippovna in <u>The Idiot</u> possesses the
kind of beauty generally associated with the female form
as portrayed in the Eastern artistic tradition of the
Russian religious icons. He interprets the figure of
Nastasya as a Mary Magdalene type or fallen woman.(6)
Jackson's observation reminds us that Dostoevski focuses
our perceptions of the beauty of certain characters by
specifically invoking the title of a Western Madonna
portrait. Peace, however, bases his perception of an
iconic figure in the text on impressions conveyed through
Dostoevski's verbal descriptions alone. Is Russian
Orthodox iconic art, then, as well as Western Madonna
portraiture, a source of female imagery in the works of
Dostoevski? And secondly, does the possible appearance of
an iconic image necessarily invoke other aspects or themes
from religious myth as well?

The following chapter focuses on a characteristic
Russian iconic portrait of the Madonna, (the central
female figure in iconic art) The Virgin of the Don (1392),
and the portrait of Liza in Dostoevski's <u>Notes from
Underground</u>. It procedes from important factors
concerning Dostoevski's religious and cultural
perspectives which stand apart from his acknowledged
appreciation of much in Western art, especially the
Italian madonnas.

The Virgin of the Don (1392).   Tretyakov Gallery,
Moscow(7)

Dostoevski was educated in Russian Orthodox thought
and remained dedicated to Russian Orthodoxy throughout his
life.   Eastern Russian Orthodoxy--with aesthetic values
which shaped Dostoevski's novels--and Western
Christianity, most notably Roman Catholicism--with
aesthetic values from which the Italian Madonnas
sprang--treat the figure of the Madonna differently in
doctrine as well as in visual art.   In brief, Western
Christianity stresses the themes of virginity and the
Immaculate Conception as proof of the divinity of Christ.
The Russian conception of the Madonna stresses the theme
of motherhood rather than virginity.   In Russian religious
thought, Christ derives His humanity from His mother.   For
the Russian Orthodox Christian, Western emphasis upon the
themes of virginity and the Immaculate Conception inhibits
a comprehension of the Incarnation of Christ, thereby
limiting man's ability to identify with him.
Identification with the humanity of the man-god Christ,
rather than with the vengeful God the Father, was an
organizational principle of Dostoevski's religious thought
as well.
Likewise in Russia the word virgin is not used in
reference to the madonna.   She is the Bogoroditsa or
Mother of God.   The word virgin appears in certain psalms
where the full name, Holy Virgin Mary, appears.
Hence, the visual art of Eastern Russian Orthodoxy,
as part of Dostoevski's religious heritage, diverges from
the visual art of the West in the treatment of the Madonna
through stress upon the themes of motherhood, protection,
and intercession rather than virgin motherhood as proof of
Christ's divinity.   The Western representation of the
Madonna can be traced to the worldly, sensuous adoration
of the human form stemming from Hellenic and Hellenistic
art which in time "led to investing the Virgin with the
tunic, the coiffure, and sometimes even the earrings of
the great ladies of Alexandria."(8)   This trend, which
sought to glorify the Virgin through a form of physical
perfection linked to the natural world, persisted beyond
the Renaissance in the West to become what the historian
Bulgakov calls the chivalric, "belle dame cult of the
Madonna, entirely unknown to the sober spirit of
Orthodoxy."(9)   A corollary of the Russian devotional
emphasis on motherhood is that in Russia, in contrast with
the West, "beauty was not the main feature" of the
Virgin's image.(10)
The icon of the Mother of God of the Don is a clear
statement of the Russian conception of the Christian
Madonna.   The icon is prototypical of icons of the
"tenderness type" accentuating the theme of motherhood and
which were the most popular icons of the Madonna
historically in Russia.   Icons of the tenderness type
share a symbolic language dictated by the canons governing
icon painting.   This language determines a consistency
among paintings of this type which in turn projects a
distinct conception of the Madonna throughout an entire
body of Madonna portraiture.
In both the Mother of God of the Don and the portrait
of Liza, physical characteristics and themes suggesting

aspects of religious myth are revealed through the
relationships of the Madonna and Liza with a second
individual. In the case of the Madonna, in general, Andre
Grabar notes that "the topology of functional portraits of
the Virigin derives entirely from her relationship to
Christ." Or, "what serves to define Mary in her
relationship to God and to man is the exceptional
character of the ties that bind her to Christ."(11)
     The ties that bind the Madonna and Child in Russian
iconic art are the theme of motherhood and the protective
embrace which prefigures the theme of intercession. In
order to determine whether Dostoevski draws upon this
imagery, it is necessary to consider exactly how an icon,
such as the Mother of God of the Don, emphasizes
particular physical and thematic characteristics.
     In the icon of the Mother of God of the Don, the
Madonna and child gaze toward each other with expressions
of mutual concern. The physical posture of the child as
he presses toward his mother, with his head held back and
his neck exposed, conveys the impression of childlike
vulnerability. The figure of the child is not exactly
that of an infant, but that of the Christ Emmanuel. The
scroll symbolizes the teachings of his life on earth.
Together, the scroll and the clothing invoke the image of
the risen Christ. But in the icon, he presses toward his
mother, his delicate head protected under the curve of her
cheek in a posture suggesting not the autonomy of Christ
but the vulnerability and helplessness of a child. This
vulnerability and helplessness suggests the humanity of
the Christ figure, which he received through his mother.
In addition, the delicate quality of the child's legs and
feet transmitted by their thinness and pale coloring, is
contrasted with the Madonna's massive, supportive hands.
These contrasts emphasize her maternal strength.
     The Madonna and child are united also through the use
of color. The child's robes, although striped,
incorporate the same brown of the Madonna's maphorion.
His robes are also accented with the lapis lazuli blue of
her head scarf and sleeve. The brown is typical of the
Russian preference for a palette consisting primarily of
earth tones. The use of blue unites mother and child in
the traditional symbolism of heaven, or heavenly love and
truth.(12)
     Color symbolism in iconic art is rooted in alchemy.
Therefore, the significance of a color is more than
representational and symbolic. Since icons were often
thought to produce miracles, they were viewed as objects
with spiritual properties. The brown of the Madonna's
maphorion symbolizes the earth. Through the mythology of
alchemy, the brown maphorion therefore invokes the
spiritual properties of the earth as protective,
nourishing mother and haven in death.
     The tilt of the Virgin's head, as well as the
sorrowful expression of her eyes, characterizes her
relationship to Christ. Since the Virgin's gaze is not
focused either upon the child or upon the viewer, she has
a loving but remote and pensive air. Her eyes embody the
traditional Christian symbolism which associates the eyes

with eternal wisdom. The sad thoughtfulness of the
Virgin's gaze suggests that she foresees the ultimate
suffering of her Child upon the cross. Her eyes are the
central feature of her portrait.

The Madonna's gesture of loving protection toward the
Christ child is closely aligned with a second major theme
associated with the Madonna of Russian iconic art: that
of protection or intercession, to which several Russian
cathedrals are dedicated. When Christ of the Cross asked
that St. John become a second son to Mary, St. John became
a symbol of Mary's adoption of humanity. For the Russian
Orthodox Christian, the Madonna represents an intercessor
for man, or, "the last hope of the damned."(13) The true
popularity of the theme of the intercession of the Virgin
originated and developed in Russia rather than in
Byzantium and is vitally important to her image.(14)

Although the Madonna's chin and mouth have a
sculpted, sensual fullness which approaches naturalism,
idyllic or worldly beauty is not a feature of her image.
The iconic style, which rejects naturalism in favor of a
stylized geometric rendering which accentuates the eyes,
derives from a doctrinally based desire to suggest
spiritual rather than worldly realms. Church patriarchs
believed that a sensual rendering of the human form would
focus man's goals in the material rather than in the
spiritual world.(15)

In the Notes, the portrait of Liza is conveyed
entirely through the perceptions of the underground man.
He describes her appearance and records her responses to
the indignities which he inflicts upon her.

The underground man's descriptions of Liza reveal the
ordinariness of her physical appearance. Upon first
meeting her, the underground man states that she has a
"fresh, young pale face with straight dark eyebrows, and
with grave as it were wondering, eyes that attracted me at
once" (Notes, 118).   And a moment later, he adds that
there was something "simple and good-natured in her face,
but something strangely grave. She could not have been
called a beauty, though she was tall, stong-looking, and
well built" (Notes, 118).   Since descriptions of
physical characteristics in the novel are minimal, images
which are repeated are magnified in importance. Liza's
eyes, like the eyes of the iconic Madonna, are the central
image of her portrait, since they are objects of
continuous reference on the part of the underground man.
He conveys Liza's reactions to him by describing her eyes.
These descriptions reveal Liza's inner emotions: He
refers to them as "two eyes scrutinizing me curiously and
persistently." The eyes are always described as having
the same quality of "mournful perplexity" (Notes, 152) and
"heaviness" (Notes, 160).   The descriptions are
important in that they reveal Liza's deeply compassionate
and sympathetic nature. They are the mirrors in which,
like the eyes of the Mother of God, the sorrows of mankind
are reflected. Idealized physical beauty is not a feature
of Liza's image within the novel. Liza's physical
qualities are the qualities of the female form in Russian
iconic art.

As Grossman notes, both the underground man and
Raskolnikov of Crime and Punishment withdraw "into a
private world where they can freely criticize the world's
unshakeable laws in accordance with their own unrestrained
desires."(16)

Through the underground man's self-serving
perspective, the themes and motifs which define Liza are
revealed. The underground man as a societal reject or one
of the damned is metaphorically suggested in his failed
attempt to join the streams of people on the Nevsky
Prospekt. On the Nevsky the underground man attempts to
confront an authority figure, a military officer, simply
to assert his individuality. The attempt fails when he is
brushed aside. And as Matlaw notes, the underground man
"is pushed out of the social strata."(17)

In his humiliation, he desires contact with a woman
who, as a prostitute, cannot reject him. Grossman notes,
that as a prostitute, "Liza is both contrasted to the
lofty and the beautiful and by virtue of her profession
belongs to all men."(18) Both characteristics, in this
human portrayal reflect aspects of the Russian Orthodox
myth of the Madonna. First of all, Liza, like the iconic
Madonna, is not an object of lofty or ideal beauty. But
more importantly, her prostitution, through which she
belongs to all men, does not represent immorality and sin.
It instead represents a form of selfless self-sacrifice
undertaken in order to repay debts and stay alive, prefig-
uring the character of Sonia in Crime and Punishment.
Liza, like the Madonna, belongs to all men as a result of
selfless self-sacrifice. Her sacrifice is an affirmation
of life in the face of enormous suffering; a form of
self-sacrifice that was a supreme virtue in Dostoevski's
thought as epitomized in the figure of Christ.

In his relationship with Liza, the underground man
attempts to define himself by manipulating Liza's
sensibilities. The special qualities of her character are
gradually revealed through her responses to the curious
images with which he taunts her. His manipulations are a
part of a cycle in which he attempts to inflict upon her
all of the suffering that was previously inflicted upon
him by others. He assumes that she will fulfill an
archetypal, feminine role associated with the myth in
which the Madonna, in perpetual sorrow, prays and weeps
for the sins of the world.

The underground man, much in the manner of an
intellectual exercise, seeks to make Liza ashamed of her
prostitution by presenting her with images which are
stereotypes of idyllic family life. Within these mythic
images are a number of suggestions about the nature of
women. The underground man states that out of a woman's
love for man "she would torment him. . . . Women are
particularly given to that..." (Notes, 127). He tells us
that everything a woman does, even torment, is done
through love. For the underground man, the encompassing
love of a woman, epitomized in myth by the Madonna, is
both salvation and tyranny. In resentment, the
underground man tyrannizes Liza by invoking the most
mythically sacred image of ideal family life: mother with

infant son. The underground man taunts, "You know--a
little rosy boy at your breast . . . eyes that look as if
they understood everything" (Notes, 128).
     By contrasting aspects of reality, such as the
necessity of Liza's lifestyle, with aspects of the ideal,
such as a glowing image of motherhood, the underground man
contrasts the idealistic properties of religious myth with
the realities of individual, human existence. Concern
with such contrasts was basic to the development of
Dostoevski's religious thought. Christ was the central
figure of Dostoevski's Christianity, because, as half man
and half god, Christ embodied elements of the ideal and
elements of the real. Dostoevski shared the Russian
peasant religious view which saw the realities of earthly
suffering clearly paralleled in the archetypal sufferings
of the life of Christ on earth. Likewise, Dostoevski's
portrait of Liza blends elements of religious myth with
the sheer human realities of her life.
     The underground man, annoyed by Liza's remark that he
speaks like a book, hopes to demoralize her by suggesting
that, in spite of all earthly suffering, she will find no
final reward in death. He indicates that she is a
disgusting slave who will die of consumption and be buried
in a watery grave filled with filth and wet snow (Notes,
134). Worst of all, she will have no family to mourn
her. Most importantly, he suggests that she will not be
reborn, however she may knock at her coffin lid (Notes,
135). He summarizes his activities by saying "how little
of the idyllic . . . had sufficed to turn a whole human
life at once according to my will. That's virginity, to
be sure! Freshness of soil!" (Notes, 142).
     Here, the underground man expresses the idea that
virginity has to do with an innocence of the mind and the
spirit rather than with the activities of the physical
body. Invoking the earth, here, echoes the ancient,
Russian mythic veneration for the fertility of the soil
associated with the Madonna, who by representing nour-
ishment and protection, perpetuates the worship of Mother
Earth in Russian thought. Through this phrase, Liza is
linked with the eternal. As Fedotov notes, the earth
symbolizes "eternal womanhood . . . mother not virgin,
fertile not pure; and black for the best Russian soil is
black."(19)
     In his last pathetic attempt to manipulate Liza, the
underground man suggests that she will not even have the
joy of knowing that she will be remembered by her children
after death. Here, he attempts to destroy in her any
possible hope for a figurative immortality through the
memories of her children. The underground man expects
Liza to respond to the basic issues associated with
womanhood and with the ancient regard for the cycles of
death, decay, and regeneration.
     The underground man's fantasy of becoming Liza's
salvation as a result of a struggle with her over her life
style is dissolved when she visits his apartment and
perceives that he, unlike the image which he projected, is
emotionally isolated. To cover his humiliation, he
viciously announces that he cared nothing for her salva-

tion. But her response is contrary to his intent to
inflict pain. He describes her response: "What happened
was this: Liza, insulted and crushed by me, understood a
great deal more than I imagined. She understood from all
this what a woman understands first of all, if she feels
genuine love, that is, that I was myself unhappy.... Then
she suddenly rushed to me, threw her arms around me and
burst into tears" (Notes, 157). She embraces him
physically and emotionally with the enveloping and
unconditional love characteristic of a Madonna figure.
The unconditional love and embrace are threats to the
underground man, recalling his earlier allusions to love
as tyranny. In Wasiolek's opinion the underground man
sees "that their parts have been reversed: that she is
now the heroine and he the humiliated creature."(20) But
for his survival, he realizes that he "cannot get on
without domineering and tyrannizing over someone" (Notes,
158). Her expression of selfless love "breaks through the
vicious cycle of hurting and being hurt."(21) But when he
tries to reject her love by a sexual "act of vengeance,"
(rape) the underground man notes that "she warmly and
rapturously embraced me" (Notes, 158).
     In describing Liza's behavior, the underground man
associates an aspect of love with womanhood in general.
He says, "to a woman all reformation--all salvation from
any sort of ruin, and all moral renewal is included in
love and can only show itself in that form" (Notes, 160).
This perspective which Dostoevski himself reiterated in
The Diary of a Writer as noted earlier, characterizes the
Madonna as the last hope of the damned or the intercessor
for man.
     The underground man tries to humiliate Liza further
by giving her money as she leaves, but she refuses it,
thereby indicating her selfless motives. And although the
underground man experiences deep remorse for his actions,
he halts in his attempt to pursue her, realizing that he
would simply continue to repeat his cycle of cruelty.
     To summarize, the issues which the underground man
raises in his relationship with Liza suggest themes and
motifs associated with the mythic and archetypal
conceptions of womanhood epitomized in the figure of the
Russian Madonna. The underground man associates nourishing and redemptive love with the female figure of whom
he says everything is done through love. He describes
motherhood as the most fulfilling of conditions in which a
woman's identity is formed. In other words she is
perceived in direct relation to her child, as the Madonna
is to Christ in the most central image of motherhood in
all mythology. Even her immorality depends upon the
memories of her children. All of these themes have a
clear paradigm in the relationship between the Madonna and
Christ of Russian Christian mythology.
     Physical descriptions of Liza reflect the Russian
conception of the female form in icons of the Madonna.
Descriptions of Liza focus on her pale face, with its
dark, grave, wondering eyes filled with mournful
perplexity. Most importantly, Liza's position in the
novel is pivotal. She is the last figure with whom the

Undergroundman has contact before the confessional
narration of Part I in which he was to have found faith
and salvation in Christ in a section subsequently deleted
from Dostoevski's manuscript by the censors. Regardless,
this series of events invokes the theme of intercession as
a distinct aspect of Liza's characterization.

Icons of the Madonna of tenderness, typified by the
Mother of God of the Don, and the portrait of Liza share
the major physical and thematic attributes associated with
the Russian religious conception of the Christian Madonna;
a Madonna unique to Dostoevski's cultural and religious
heritage.

NOTES

1.   Fyodor Dostoevsky, The Diary of a Writer, trans.
Boris Brasol (New York: George Braziller, 1954), p. 341.

2.   Ibid.

3.   Fyodor Dostoevsky, Notes from Underground, The
Gambler, trans. Constance Garnett (New York: The Heritage
Press, 1967).   This edition is cited throughout.

4.   Robert Louis Jackson, Dostoevsky's Quest for Form
(New Haven, Conn.:   Yale University Press, 1966), p. 214.

5.   Anna Snitkina Dostoevsky, Dostoevsky:
Reminiscences, trans. Beatrice Stillman (New York:
Liveright, 1975), p. 117.

6.   Richard Peace, Dostoevsky: An Examination of the
Major Novels (England: Cambridge Press, 1971), p. 83.

7.   The Virgin of the Don (1392), Theophanes,
double-sides icon.   Dormition on obverse side.   Lime board
and egg tempera, 86 x 76.5 cm., Tretyakov Gallery, Moscow.
See Konrad Onasch, Icons (New York: A. S. Branes and Co.,
1969), pp. 86, 87.

For a complete biography of Theophanes, David and
Tamara Talbot Rice, Icons (Woodstock, N. Y.:   The Overlook
Press, 1974), pp. 101-102.   The respect and admiration
accorded Theophanes' (Greek by birth) works by the Russian
people made him the most powerful influence on the
development of Russian iconic art.

The art historian James Voyce notes that, like El
Greco, who emigrated to Spain, Theophanes reached his
"highest artistic development in his adopted home."

8.   Emile Male, Religious Art: From the 12th to the
18th Centuries (Noonday Press, N.Y. 1972), p. 22.

9.   Sergius Bulgakov, The Orthodox Church (Dobbs
Ferry, N. Y.:   American Review of Eastern Orthodoxy, 935),
p. 139.

10.   George P. Fedotov, The Russian Religious Mind (Belmont, Mass.: Nordland, 1975), Vol. III, p. 376.

11.   Andre Grabar, Christian Iconography (Princeton, N. J.: Princeton University Press, 1968), p. 65.

12.   George Ferguson, Signs and Symbols in Christian Art (London: The Oxford University Press, 1961), p. 151.

13.   James Billington, "The Spirit of Russian Art," The Horizon Book of the Arts of Russia (New York: American Heritage, 1970), p. 20.

14.   M. W. Alpatov, Early Russian Icon Painting (Moscow: Iskusstvo, 1978), p. 9.

15.   For an account of the Doctrine of Images, see Leonid Ousspensky and Vladimir Lossky, The Meaning of Icons (Boston: Boston Book and Art Shop, 1955), pp. 32-33.

16.   Leonid Grossman, Dostoevsky, trans. Mary Mackler (New York: Bobbs-Merrill, 1975), p. 316.

17.   Ralph E. Matlaw, "Structure and Integration in Notes from Underground," PMLA, 73 (March 1958); 101-109.

18.   Grossman, Dostoevsky, p. 314.

19.   Fedotov, Russian Religious Mind, p. 13.

20.   Edward Wasiolek, Dostoevsky: The Major Fiction, (Cambridge, Mass. 1964, M.I.T. Press), p. 53.

21.   Ibid., p. 52.

14.
Dostoevski and Jean-Luc Godard: Kirillov's Return in *La Chinoise*
PETER G. CHRISTENSEN

One of the direct contemporary heirs of Dostoevski's
massive novel on revolution, The Possessed (1872), is
Jean-Luc Godard's La Chinoise, a feature film made in 1967
about a contemporary student revolutionary group in Paris.
The continued interest devoted to this film has often
stemmed from the political attitudes and events of May
1968 which it anticipated. However, it also deserves
study from a literary point of view, since Godard wrote an
excellent screenplay for the film, which was subsequently
published in Issue 114 (May 1971) of Avant Scene du
Cinema.
     That Godard has actively sought a comparison with The
Possessed is apparent through his appropriation of
Dostoevski's Alexei Nilitch Kirillov, the 27-year-old
epileptic civil engineer who after much deliberation kills
himself in order to reconstitute his relationship with the
absolute. In La Chinoise a character named Kirilov (this
time "Serge Dimitri") also commits suicide in a climactic
scene. As Godard takes a far more sympathetic view of
violent social revolution than Dostoevski did, it is
important to examine the transformation of the Kirillov
figure in order to understand our legacy from the Russian
novelist. Although Godard's resurrection of Kirillov as a
Marxist-Leninist artist-revolutionary shows his
dissatisfaction with Dostoevski's brand of religious
existentialism, the naivete of the members of Godard's
quintet prevents the film from becoming a successful
attack on The Possessed. Instead the two works engage in
an important artistic debate on the possibility of social
change, which is not won by either side.
     La Chinoise, Godard's fourteenth feature, is one of
the climactic films of his intensively productive and
increasingly politicized first phase, which covers
1954-1967. During these years he made fifteen features
and about a dozen sketches and shorts. Although his first
feature A Bout de Souffle (1959) was a study of
alienation, its social content was small, and the
alienation was tied to literary motifs, such as the
abortive discussion between the two protagonists concerning Faulkner's The Wild Palms. By the time of his
fifth feature, Les Carabiniers (1963), his concerns were
much more political and in this film a character who

quotes Mayakovsky is shot in the middle of a war-torn
landscape.

The typical Mayakovskian theme of the need for a
synthesis between the making of the revolution and the
desire for a two-person love relationship is a major
element of La Chinoise and constitutes the dilemma of the
two principal characters of the film, Guillaume
(Jean-Pierre Leaud) and Veronique (Anne Wiazemsky).
Guillaume, an actor, and Veronique, one of Francis
Jeanson's philosophy students, have established the
Aden-Arabie circle, a Maoist-oriented Marxist-Leninist
cadre in a pleasant apartment obtained for summer vacation
from Parisian friends. Also in the cell of five are
Kirilov, their slogan painter (played by the Dutch artist
Lex de Bruin); Yvonne (Juliet Berto), a domestic servant
from the provinces and occasional prostitute; and Henri
(Michel Semenianko), a chemist whose views coincide too
closely with those of the French Communist Party and thus
lead to his eventual expulsion from the group. During the
summer the Aden-Arabie circle decides to perform a
terrorist act, the shooting of the Soviet Minister of
Culture. Veronique is entrusted with the deed, but
accidentally kills an innocent man by mistake because she
confuses the digits "3" and "2" in the apartment number of
the victim. She goes back and kills the Minister, or at
least gives the signal for having done so, although the
assassination is never shown. This act represents the end
of the main narrative thrust of the film, for the closing
scenes operate on a system of counterpointed situations
and intertitles.

The scene before the assassination is Kirilov's
suicide. The artist has long talked of killing himself,
but has had difficulty in actually bringing himself to do
it. Finally, he signs a dictated suicide note in which he
claims to have killed the Minister. Guillaume, who
composed the letter, enters his room to coax him to take
his life. No one would doubt here the structural
correspondences which give Guillaume the role of Pyotr
Verkhovensky and the Soviet Minister the role of Shatov.
The Minister's role is of equal interest here because he
is called Michael Cholokhov, a thinly veiled allusion to
the Nobel Prize winning Socialist realist author of The
Quiet Don and Virgin Soil Upturned, Mikhail Sholokhov.

To understand the literary allusions it is necessary
at this point to indicate that La Chinoise is a good
example of one of the so-called new narrative films of the
1960s. In these films the straightforward plots of the
commercial cinema are thwarted by various narrative
devices, some of which have counterparts in the
avant-garde novels of the time. In the case of La
Chinoise the film is interspersed with various interviews
with the cell members, pictorial inserts (usually of
one-shot duration), blue intertitles, red intertitles,
shots of the clapboard, and shots of the cameraman. As a
result the film is self-reflexive and comments on the
nature of art itself. La Chinoise moves from a position
that art is basically mimetic to a belief that art is
meaningful through its illusory nature. It is Kirilov,

who, as a character, is associated with the latter
artistic viewpoint. The change in the narrative
strategies of the film justifies him in spite of his
death.

When Guillaume enters Kirilov's room directly before
his suicide, Kirilov is in the process of painting the
room in thick stripes of color. The stripes continue from
the wall to the chimney, lampshade, and blackboard. As is
typical of Godard's use of interlocking referents, this
type of painting is a recreation of what Alain Jouffroy
calls "the scandalous gesture made by Hundertwasser in
the school in Hamburg --the immense spiral-serpent, the
longest line in the world, with which Hundertwasser
covered the walls, casements, window panes, and radiators
of all the rooms and hallways of the school to denounce
the false liberty ingrained in the teaching of modern
art."(1)   That Western society exists under a pervasively
false type of repressive freedom of expression was an idea
dear to Godard at that time, one even more apparent in his
previous feature, Deux ou Trois Choses que je sais d'elle.

In Kirilov's suicide note this repressive freedom is
connected with the French government's opening of the
University of Nanterre in the Parisian suburbs. It reads
as follows:

> I, Sergei Dmitri Kirilov, claim the murder of
> Mikhail Sholokhov, the current Soviet Minister
> of Culture, now in Paris at the invitation of
> the French government. . . . This murder had the
> following goals: One, to prevent the Soviet
> puppet from attending the dedication of new
> buildings at the University of Nanterre, where
> he was supposed to give a talk on the puppets
> Malraux and Fouchet. Two, this murder is only
> the first of a long series. Violence will be
> the answer to the cultural asphyxiation into
> which the government, willingly, has plunged the
> French universities. Sergei Dmitri Kirilov.
> Aug. 15, 1967.(2)

While Kirilov continues to paint the wall, the camera
moves to the next room to follow Guillaume, who is
rejoining Veronique. Then Guillaume hears the shot, reenters the room, and finds Kirilov on the floor. He
closes the artist's eyes and takes his revolver.

A comparison with The Possessed shows that Pyotr
dictates the note to Kirillov on the spot. This note
reads as follows:

> I, Kirillov, declare that today the --th October
> at about eight o'clock in the evening, I killed
> the student Shatov in the park for turning
> traitor and giving information of the
> manifestoes and of Fedka, who has been lodging
> with us for ten days in Filipov's house. I am
> shooting myself today with my revolver, not
> because I repent and am afraid of you, but

because when I was abroad I made up my mind to
put an end to my life.(3)

At this point Kirillov engages in a heated discussion
with Pyotr about the lack of abuse in the dictated letter.
Kirillov keeps doctoring up the valedictory lines until he
writes down first the famous motto, "liberté, egalité,
fraternité, ou la mort," and then the identificatory
phrase: Gentilhomme, seminariste russe et citoyen du
monde civilisé." After writing these words he snatches up
the revolver and runs off to the next room where he hides
in silence.
     It is from Kirillov, the heir of the French
Revolution, that Godard draws in his version of the
character. Godard has made Kirillov into a terrorist,
whereas, obviously, in The Possessed Kirillov is not one
of the intimate members of Pyotr Verkhovensky's circles.
In La Chinoise Kirilov states the following beliefs on the
day of his death: "I believe in terror. For me, entire
revolutions are made out of terror. A revolutionary
without a bomb is no longer a revolutionary. For the
moment, there are only a few of us, but you will see,
we'll become many. Tomorrow, perhaps, I'll no longer
exist, but I'll be glad and proud of it. Give me a bomb!
Give me a bomb!"(4)
     One may well ask what in Kirillov's thought in The
Possessed suggested to Godard that the character might be
suitable as a revolutionary. The answer appears to be in
the nature of Alexei Kirillov's arguments about the
existence of God. As Kirillov says to Pyotr in their
final confrontation:

     I can't understand how an atheist could know
     that there is no God and not kill himself on the
     spot. To recognize that there is no God and not
     to recognize at the same time that one is God
     oneself is an absurdity, else one would
     certainly kill oneself. If you recognize it you
     are sovereign, and then you won't kill yourself
     but will live in the greatest glory. But one,
     the first, must kill himself, for else who will
     begin and prove it. So I must certainly kill
     myself, to begin and prove it. Now I am only a
     God against my will and I am unhappy.(5)

At the beginning of the film Godard grants Kirilov an
opening line which is a direct response to the engineer's
declarations and doubts. To Yvonne's question, "My God,
why did you abandon me?" he replies, "Because I do not
exist." This is treated as a voice-off, as may be fitting
for a creature who does not exist. Godard's ambiguity is
quite striking since we have yet to see the actor who is
to play Kirilov and because it is readily apparent only
from the screenplay (and not from the film) who is
speaking the lines.
     Is Kirilov the dead God who answers from off stage?
Or, is God dead because Kirilov no longer exists? In
other words, did Dostoevski's character's death turn him

into a God who has subsequently died in the course of
twentieth century history, or did Kirilov's death prove
that he could not become a God?   Perhaps there is really a
third alternative.   It could be that God has turned his
back on man (here, Yvonne) because He did not support
Kirillov in his attempt to become God.   Instead, God
simply allowed Kirillov to die.   That interpretation
should not be totally discounted, even if it seems
fanciful, because it parallels the Crucifixion of Christ
passage in the Kirillov-Pyotr conversation.   "For that is
the miracle, that there never was or never will be another
like Him.   And if that is so, if the laws of nature did
not spare even Him, have not spared even their miracle and
made even Him live in a lie and die for a lie, then all
the planet is a lie and rests on a lie and on mockery."(6)
     In attempting to become the miraculous man who will
kill himself out of selfwill rather than out of despair,
pain, or loneliness, Kirillov in The Possessed is
partially heroic despite the fact that his final act
implicates him in innocent Shàtov's death.   For Godard,
this heroism is extraneous because there is no escape from
death.
     In compensation, Godard's Kirilov returns with a
heroic attitude toward art.   In the published screenplay
there occurs a scene which is not in all the prints of the
film I have studied, but which makes the Dostoevskian
analogies easier to understand.   Here Kirilov throws the
handlebars of a bicycle out of the window.   Yvonne
comments that he is completely mad, but Veronique defends
him.   "No, this worker is inspired.   Look, with a bull's
head he makes a bicycle saddle and handlebars.   That there
is the metamorphosis of the gods, Mr. Malraux."(7)
     Kirillov, the man who unsuccessfully tried to become
God, has been replaced by the man who is capable of
granting the gods a new lease on life through their
metamorphosis.   Nevertheless, the film does not make it
clear whether the bull's head has really become part of a
bicycle or vice versa.   Have the gods been brought down to
earth, or have they been created from human experiences?
Certainly, the latter version of the question relates to
Alexei Kirillov's comments on mankind's desire to create
gods.
     In reference to this question of aesthetics, Kirilov
leads a discussion/lecture:

     "Comrades and friends.   One, the history of
art, for one hundred years, has been the history
of the road traversed by art in the direction of
its own science.   Two, it is not we who close
ourselves up in language; on the contrary, our
society is hermetic and enclosed in the most
impoverished language there is.   Three,
Mayakovski, in poetry, Sergei Eisenstein, in the
cinema, and those who fought for the definition
of a socialist art, were stabbed in the back by
Trotsky and those who, two months after the
storming of the Winter Palace, accepted the
forms of imperialist language, to sign the Peace

of Brest-Litovsk. Art does not reproduce the
visible; it makes visible."
        Veronique [off]: "Yes. Anyway, the
aesthetic effect is imaginary."
        Kirilov: "Yes, but this imaginary is not
the reflection of the real. It is the reality
of this reflection."(8)

The closing reference, as the footnotes to the
sceenplay indicate, is a quotation from Paul Klee.(9)
Kirilov's argument runs in strong contradiction to the
socialist realist art of Mikhail Sholokhov, and therefore,
it is not odd to find a certain justice in Kirilov's
confession to murdering the Soviet Minister.
    The remaining scenes of the film serve to validate
Kirilov's ideas on art. Godard has surely seen himself
implicated in Kirilov's accusations brought against a dead
imperialist language, for he is making a concerted effort
to escape from the tried and true patterns of bourgeois
film production by employing the self-reflexive techniques
that he does in La Chinoise. Godard would agree with
Kirilov, who states, "Works without artistic value,
however advanced they may be from a political point of
view, have no effect. We must fight on two fronts in
literature and in art."(10)
    To prove the limitations of a mimetic concept of
artistic creation, the film proceeds to undercut the
mimetic atmosphere emphasized by the introduction of
Godard's cameraman, Raoul Coutard, into the
revolutionaries' apartment. By allowing the audience to
see the actions filmed, Godard gives the impression that
the action is really underway in the apartment. After
Kirilov's lecture, the interview in the kitchen with Henri
about his expulsion from the cell must logically come
after his expulsion. Yet by panning to Veronique in the
next room and by using her voice while the camera is on
Henri in the kitchen, the audience can only conclude that
cinema verite has been replaced by the enactment of
pre-designed scenarios.
    The artificiality of the later parts of the film is
heightened not only by Veronique's unlikely conversation
with her mentor, Jeanson, or the symbolic murder of
Cholokhov, but also by the introduction of a series of
intertitles. The titles read: "Theatrical vocation of
Wilhelm Meister and his years of apprenticeship and
travels on the road to a true socialist theater."
    The phrase calls to mind the non-mimetic elements of
Goethe's famous experimental novel Wilhelm Meisters
Wanderjahre (1829). We see Guillaume, the Wilhelm Meister
figure of the film, dressed as St.-Just, in a series of
abbreviated scenes which do not directly correspond to the
main plot, but which, instead, suggest the narrative
inserts of the Wanderjahre. Since Kirilov is dead at this
point, Godard is allowing the Wilhelm Meister figure to
take over the reformation of society from him. (Of
course, in the Lehrjahre, it is Hamlet and not St.-Just
who is associated with Wilhelm.)

It seems as if Godard is saying that Dostoevski's
Kirillov can point the way to a better future, but he will
never be able to take us there because he is
self-destructive. Through the figure of Kirillov, Godard
sees Dostoevski as a political and artistic reactionary.
Although Dostoevski was at odds with the realism of his
time, he is still too mimetic for Godard. In his letters
Dostoevski states,

> Ah, my friend! I have completely different
> concepts about reality and about realism from
> our realists and critics. My idealism is more
> real than theirs. Lord! to relate intelligently
> all that we Russians have experienced in the
> past ten years in our spiritual development--now
> wouldn't the realists show that this is a
> fantasy! Yet this is the authentic genuine
> realism! Precisely this is realism, only
> deeper, and they are swimming in shallow
> water.(11)

For Godard, Dostoevski's attitudes toward
characterization and scene arrangement represent part of
the worn-out language of the past. In The Possessed we
must always believe in the characters as real individuals
who move from one intense philosophy-packed encounter to
another while the narrator ticks away real time on his
watch.
Godard's selection of Kirilov as a character, his
imitation of Hundertwasser, his appropriations from Klee,
his relationship with Mikhail Sholokhov, etc., all
indicate Godard's total disrespect for the traditional
concept of characterization. His contradictory scene
arrangements indicate his dissatisfaction with the usual
means of indicating the passage of time. As Alexei
Kirillov told Pyotr, "Time's not an object but an idea.
It will be extinguished in the mind."(12)
However, even Godard does not escape time as an
object. Time is on the side of the Marxist-Leninists. As
Veronique says in the last lines of the film: "I thought
I had made a great leap forward, and I see that really
I've only made the first timid steps on a very long
march."(13) After a fadeout, La Chinoise closes with the
title, "End of a Beginning," a counterpart to the title,
"A Film in the Process of Making Itself."
Had Dostoevski seen this small step forward on the
revolutionary path would he have reacted with the same
hostility as he did to the participants in the Nechaev
affair whom he parodied in the novel? Almost certainly.
At the same time, Godard also treats his revolutionaries
satirically.
From a published interview in Cahiers du Cinema (Vol.
194, October 1967)(14) it is apparent that Godard sided
with the cell with whom he had not yet completely
identified. Nevertheless, their total lack of logical
argumentation and the violence they envisage make one
think of the petty demons around Pyotr. They are all
encased in a dogmatism they never bother to reason out.

In addition, Godard "polyphonically" undercuts his quintet
by the introduction of Francis Jeanson as a character who
plays himself in the film. He tells Veronique that her
plans are not clearly reasoned and will not bring about
the triumph of Marxism.

Although Godard's rejection of Dostoevski is shown
through Kirilov, The Possessed still functions as a
critique of La Chinoise. Speaking of the novel, Geoffrey
C. Kabat says, "almost every character looks forward to an
impending, immediate transformation of his life or in
society.... As in Dead Souls, the characters in The
Possessed collaborate in each others' fantasies to the
point where fantasy becomes the one collective force in
society."(15) Reading The Possessed makes the students'
Aden Arabie fantasies only more apparent. In addition,
the film has no Stepan Verkhovensky to interpret the
meaning of the events, only Guillaume garbed as St.-Just.

In summation, we can see that La Chinoise is an
artistic parody which asks significant questions about the
relevance of Dostoevski's political and religious thought
to our own time. For Godard, assuming a world where God
does not exist, all is indeed possible, even the
transformation of Kirillov into an aesthetician-terrorist
who believes that "If Marxism-Leninism exists, then
everything is permissible."(16) Nevertheless, knowledge
of the deluded thinking of Dostoevski's nineteenth century
iconoclasts (Shigalyov's movement from total freedom to
slavery) makes us realize the ineptness of the Aden-Arabie
circle members and accept the shattering of their dreams
at the end of summer. So, with La Chinoise we have a
parody which does not present a coherent alternative value
system to replace the one it criticizes. Whether one
sides with Dostoevski or Godard on political issues is a
question of personal belief beyond the field of art, one
liable to take us to a dead end. Where Godard and
Dostoevski come together is in a shared dialogue about the
need to abandon realism for other modes of presenting
contemporary political realities. This will not take us
to a dead end; instead, it will remain a crucial theme for
art in the 1980s.(17)

NOTES

1. Jean-Luc Godard, "La Chinoise," Avant Scene du
Cinema 114 (May 1971); 36.

2. Ibid.

3. Fyodor Dostoyevski, The Possessed, trans.
Constance Garnett and F. D. Reeve (New York: Dell, 1961),
p. 636.

4. Godard, "La Chinoise," p. 35.

5. Dostoyevsky, Possessed, p. 634.

6. Ibid.

7.   Godard, "La Chinoise," p. 23.

8.   Ibid.

9.   Ibid.

10. Ibid., p. 24.

11. Robert Louis Jackson, Dostoevski's Quest for Form (New Haven: Yale University Press, 1966), p. 80.

12. Dostoyevsky, Possessed, p. 254.

13. Godard, "La Chinoise," p. 38.

14. "Jacques Bontemps et al., "Lutter sur deux fronts: Conversation avec Jean-Luc Godard," Cahiers du Cinema 194 (October 1967); 13-28, 66-70.

15. Geoffrey C. Kabat, Ideology and Imagination: The Image of Society in Dostoevsky, (New York: Columbia University Press, 1978), p. 136.

16. Godard, "La Chinoise," p. 37.

17. For articles about Godard, see Julia Lesage, Jean-Luc Godard: A Guide to References and Resources (Boston: G. K. Hall, 1979). This bibliography, however, stops at 1976. The most detailed article on "La Chinoise" has appeared since that date. See Jacques Aumont, "This Is Not a Textual Analysis (Godard's 'La Chinoise')," camera obscura, (1983); 131-62.

Statements by Godard about "La Chinoise" can be found as follows:

Alain Jouffroy, "Le Cahier de 'La Chinoise'." Opus international, no. 2 (1967); 12-19. Shooting notes.

Cournot, Michel, "Quelques evidentes incertitudes: entretien entre J.-L. Godard et M. Cournot," Revue d'esthetique, N.S., no. 2-3 (1967); 115-22.

Duvigneau, Michel, "La Chinoise." Telecine 135 (Nov. 1967); 13-27.

"Godard: La Chinoise," Jeune Cinema 25 (Oct. 1967); 16-19.

"Manifeste," Item 116 in Pierre Belfond, ed., Jean-Luc Godard par Jean-Luc Godard (Paris: 1968).

Perles, Yvette, "En marge d'Avignon," Image et son: Revue du cinema 211 (1967).

"Presentation" in Jean Collet, ed. Jean-Luc Godard (New York: Crown, 1970), pp. 138-140.

154   Peter G. Christensen

Program Notes to Accompany Two Godard Premiers ("A
Movie Like Any Other" by Godard and "Two American
Audiences" by Mark Woodward). Philharmonic Hall, Lincoln
Center, December 29, 1968.

15.
Dostoevski and Vladimir Nabokov: The Case of *Despair*

JULIAN W. CONNOLLY

Vladimir Nabokov's attitude toward the work of Fedor
Dostoevski was quite complex. On the one hand, he was
critical of Dostoevski's charged, frenetic style and the
intense emotionality of his characters. He once said of
Dostoevski: "He was a prophet, a claptrap journalist and a
slapdash comedian."(1) However, as is so often the case
when Nabokov expresses a strong opinion on a Russian
author, one must consider his statement with caution, for
he found in Dostoevski's vision of human behavior much of
interest, and in his novel Despair (Otchaianie, 1932,
revised in English, 1966) he creates a rich network of
allusions and references to Dostoevski's fiction that adds
an important layer of meaning to his own portrait of human
dreams and failings.
     There are two main types of allusions to the work of
Dostoevski in Despair. The first type is unstated and
implicit, taking the form of verbal mimicry or the introduction of compositional elements based on episodes from
Dostoevski's fiction. The second type is overt, usually
taking the form of mockery or criticism by the narrator
and protagonist of the novel, Hermann Karlovich, who
refers repeatedly to Dostoevski as he relates to the
reader how he conceived and carried out the murder of a
man he erroneously believed to be his physical double.
These explicit references by Hermann Karlovich are almost
always negative, and it is on the basis of these remarks
that some critics have been quick to pass judgment on the
Dostoevski presence in Despair, regarding it as uniformly
dark and critical. Andrew Field, for example, writes:
"If there is anything held in common between Hermann and
his creator, it is their mutual contempt for the great
Fyodor Mikhailovich who ends as the second, unnoticed
corpse of the novel."(2)   Such a categorical judgment,
however, is unwarranted, for Nabokov's utilization of the
Dostoevski presence is perhaps subtler than Field
recognizes. While Hermann Karlovich outwardly denigrates
Dostoevski and the characters he created, his own words
and behavior unwittingly seem to mirror them, thus
affirming, rather than denying, the relevance of
Dostoevski's vision of human experience. To suggest the
scope and character of Nabokov's interaction with
Dostoevski, this essay will focus on those elements in

Despair which derive from two of Dostoevski's most important works, Notes from the Underground and Crime and Punishment.(3)

Echoes of Notes from the Underground are apparent first of all in the narrative style of Nabokov's work. Hermann Karlovich's idiosyncratic first-person narrative bears a striking resemblance in tone and point of view to the nervous, polemical style of the first-person narrative in Notes from the Underground, and from the outset it is apparent that the reader in both works is dealing with a garrulous, sarcastic, and unreliable narrator who does not hesitate to mislead and bedevil the unwary. For example, early in Despair Hermann Karlovich paints a fanciful picture of his mother and then states, "that bit about my mother was a deliberate lie . . . I purposely leave it there as a sample of one of my essential traits: my lighthearted, inspired lying."(4) This recalls the underground man's confession, "I was lying just now when I said I used to be a nasty official. And I lied out of spite."(5) Both characters then go on to reveal that each has a history of fantasy and invention.(6)

This willingness to lie to an unsuspecting reader and then to confess the lie suggests that the speaker possesses a divided soul, and the narratives of both characters vividly reflect their inner divisions: both works contain multiple shifts and reversals in the narrator's attitude toward the reader. Sometimes the narrator seeks to persuade the reader of the truth of his statements, while other times he professes scorn for the reader's sensibilities. In Notes from the Underground, for example, one finds supplications for credence--"And believe me, ladies and gentlemen, I certainly suffered!" (102)--together with insolent rebuffs to the reader: "I don't care in the least what you think" (98). Similar shifts occur in Despair, from Hermann Karlovich's exclamation, "How I long to convince you! And I will, I will convince you!" (26), to such statements as "Oh, yes, I am going to curse at you, none can forbid me to curse" (31) or "And a damned good fool I have made of someone. Who is he? Gentle reader, look at yourself in the mirror, as you seem to like mirrors so much" (34).

The similarities in attitude toward the reader in Despair and Notes from the Underground are evident. But what lies behind these similarities? Why are both characters so divided in their approach to the outside world? Here, an understanding of the underground man's psyche helps illuminate Hermann Karlovich's soul as well. The underground man is acutely sensitive to the opinions of others. While claiming indifference or even contempt for the "world" of others, he secretly longs for adulation and approval, and he feels vulnerable to outside criticism or interference. Above all, he feels threatened by the outside world and is fearful that he is somehow at its mercy. Consequently, he wavers between pleas for recognition and respect and bitter denunciations or abuse.

The same complex of attitudes can be recognized in Hermann Karlovich's nervous chatter. In fact, the affinities between Hermann and the underground man are so

strong that Mikhaïl Bakhtin's analysis of the underground
man's polemical word and the world-view it reveals strikes
to the very core of Hermann Karlovich's relationship to
the world as well: "In his every thought . . . there is
a struggle of voices, assessments, points of view.   He
senses in everything above all the will of the other
person, the will which predefines him. . .His thought is
developed and constructed as the thought of a person
personally insulted by the world order, personally debased
by its blind inevitability."(7)   These remarks, while
directed at the underground man's "monologue," concisely
define Hermann Karlovich's plight too, the plight of a
being who wishes to control his own destiny (even to the
point of arranging his own "death"), but who fears mightly
the control of anyone else.(8)
       Like the underground man, Hermann longs for
independence of thought and self-assurance in action, and
like Dostoevski's character, he becomes very distressed
when his true vulnerability is exposed to others, for the
loss of control, particularly self-control, is
humiliating.   It is worth noting that both Nabokov and
Dostoevski include in their works scenes in which a moment
of exposure or loss of self-control occurs, and Nabokov,
as if to underscore the basic affinity between his protagonist and Dostoevski's underground man, creates an
exposure scene that seems to draw heavily on a corresponding scene in Notes from the Underground.   In the
latter work, the moment of exposure comes when the
narrator is caught by the prostitute Liza in his room
railing at his inconsiderate servant.   He writes: "And
suddenly, I burst into uncontrollable sobs.   Between my
sobs, I was terribly ashamed, but I couldn't stop. . . .
'Water! Get me some water. . . . Over there!' I mumbled
weakly, knowing full well that I could easily have done
without the water and didn't really have to mumble like
that.   But although my sobbing fit had been quite genuine,
I had to play the part to save appearances" (194).   Here
one finds a characteristic episode in which a moment of
true vulnerability is quickly manipulated by the
calculating narrator to protect his wounded vanity.
       The equivalent scene in Despair depicts Hermann
Karlovich raging at a doctor and a hotel manager who have
come into his room seeking an apology for an earlier
outburst of anger.   He writes:

       I could not stand it any longer, my fit of
       passion passed, but in its stead I felt the
       pressure of tears, and suddenly . . . I fell
       upon my bed and sobbed violently. . . .
          The doctor poured out a glass of water for
       me, offered to bring a soothing drug, stroked my
       shoulder; and I sobbed on and was perfectly
       conscious of my condition, even saw with cold
       mocking lucidity its shame, and at the same time
       I felt all the Dusty-and-Dusky charm of
       hysterics and also something dimly advantageous
       to me, so I continued to shake and heave. . ."
       (197-198).

In both of these passages, one notes uncontrollable sobs,
consciousness of shame, the offering of water, and the
transformation of genuine weeping into the simulation of
tears. On the basis of this kind of evidence it seems
quite likely that Hermann Karlovich has come from the
underground man's overcoat, to paraphrase Dostoevski's
alleged comment about the Russian writer's debt to Gogol.
    Through these resonant echoes of Dostoevski's Notes
from the Underground Nabokov manages both to highlight his
narrator's deep vulnerability beneath his outer shell of
self-assurance and to underscore the importance of the
theme of control in his novel. To Hermann Karlovich, the
need to be in control is paramount; it dominates his every
action, from conceiving the act of murder to writing the
chronicle about the event afterwards. Curiously, both the
act of murder and the act of writing are seen by Hermann
as related pursuits. He regards them both as vehicles to
demonstrate his innate artistic talents, and it is in the
realm of art that he believes his powers of control are
most potent. Indeed, it is his conception of himself as a
writer and the world around him as his manuscript that is
the prime source of conflict and pathos in Despair. As
Field puts it, "Hermann is striving to establish himself
as the primary author of everyone and everything around
him while at the same time freeing himself from any
possible similar control."(9)
    Here again the Dostoevski presence becomes important
in Despair. Puffed up by his image of himself as a gifted
writer and artist who can even treat murder as an
aesthetic matter rather than a moral one, Hermann
Karlovich takes on the great crime novelists of the past,
including Dostoevski, and finds them all inferior to
himself when treating "crime as an art" (131). He writes,
"But what are they--Doyle, Dostoevski, Leblanc,
Wallace--what are all the great novelists who wrote of
nimble criminals . . . what are they in comparison with
me? Blundering fools!" (132). In particular, he
criticizes Dostoevski and the others for a lack of cunning
and imagination, claiming that he possesses a skill as an
artist and criminal that far surpasses that of the earlier
writers. Ironically, however, despite his haughty
criticism of Dostoevski and Crime and Punishment (which he
refers to later as Crime and Slime [187] and "Crime and
Pun" [211]), he fails to recognize that in his own
conception and execution of a crime he actually retraces
basic patterns established in Dostoevski's novel, thereby
demonstrating not that he is a writer superior to or even
equal to Dostoevski, but rather that he is in fact a
literary character whose words and actions are
indisputable proof of the validity and timelessness of
Dostoevski's artistic vision.
    Hermann's unwitting mimicry of patterns in Crime and
Punishment can be detected even in his motivations for
murder, which display strong parallels to Raskolnikov's
motives for murder in Dostoevski's novel. Both characters
are moved by a combination of factors that includes both a
tangible financial motive and a more abstract intention as
well. The financial factor in Raskolnikov's plans is his

hope of finding at the pawnbroker's apartment a
substantial sum of money with which he can help his mother
and sister. Hermann believes that when the police find
his murdered double, they will think that he has been
murdered and will thus award his wife a large insurance
settlement.

More important to each character, though, is the
second, more abstract motive: both men conceive of murder
as a way to validate a personal idea and in particular, to
demonstrate their superiority as human beings.
Raskolnikov conceives of murdering the pawnbroker to
demonstrate that he is a special type, an "extraordinary
man"(10) who has an innate right to transgress or ignore
moral laws in order to fulfill his own ideas. As he tells
Sonya later, "I murdered for myself, for myself alone.
. . . I needed to find out . . . whether I was capable of
stepping over the barriers or not. Dared I stoop and take
power or not?" (402). Similarly, Hermann Karlovich
believes that his act of murder will demonstrate his
superiority too--as an artistic genius. Envisioning the
murder as a work of "creative art," he puts himself in the
class of "inventive geniuses" (132) who stand above the
common public, whom he terms "rabble" (213). Reacting
angrily to the notion that he should be compared with
ordinary criminals, he says, "But to hell with them! They
and I have nothing in common" (203); he longs for his work
to be recognized and appreciated. Thus both, Hermann
Karlovich and Raskolnikov seek to prove that they are
innately higher beings who can commit a crime without
blame or retribution.

Of course, as events unfold, it becomes clear that
neither character has succeeded in attaining his goal and
that both of their schemes are fundamentally flawed.
Significantly, one can observe a rough likeness between
them even in their general physical and emotional
responses to their failures. Both characters, for
example, become prey to spells of self-doubt, disturbing
dreams, and enervating anxiety. Shortly after the murder
one reads of Raskolnikov: "In the first few moments he
thought he must be going mad. . . . He was seized with
such a violent fit of shivering that his teeth chattered
uncontrollably, and every limb shook (84). 'My God!' he
whispered in despair, 'what is the matter with me?'" (85).
One can compare this reaction with that of Hermann
Karlovich who writes: "My hands tremble, I want to shriek
or smash something with a bang. . . . My heart is itching,
a horrible sensation. Must be calm, must keep my head.
No good going on otherwise" (14-15).(11) In this state of
extreme anxiety and nervousness, both characters imagine
at times that they are the subject of ridicule by others
and that they are being toyed with by persecutors who know
more about the crime than they let on.(12)

Furthermore, each character is torn by a conflict of
impulses. Together with an obvious desire to escape
discovery by the police, one detects a deeper, intuitive
recognition that such discovery would be a relief. An
indication of the latter in Crime and Punishment occurs
when Raskolnikov ponders an urge to confess: "Shall I

tell them or shall I not? Oh . . . the devil! I am
tired; oh, to lie down somewhere, or sit . . . soon!"
(164). Likewise, Hermann Karlovich writes at one point,
"But I am dead-tired; the quicker it all ends, the better"
(218). Even the figure of Porfiry Petrovich, the
"paunchy" examining magistrate in Crime and Punishment
with whom Raskolnikov matches wits finds a parodical
counterpart in Despair in the character of the "plumpish"
gendarme who discusses local crimes with Hermann Karlovich
near the end of the novel.(13)

Clearly then, Hermann Karlovich and his plight bear
more than a passing resemblance to Raskolnikov and his
situation. At one point Hermann even seems to be on the
verge of recognizing or admitting this similarity, but he
refuses to entertain the notion for more than an instant.
He writes, "In spite of a grotesque resemblance to
Rascalnikov [sic]--No, that's wrong. Canceled" (199).
However, despite his scorn for Dostoevski's work and
despite his denial of any affinity with Raskolnikov,
Hermann Karlovich does in fact emulate Dostoevski's
character to a surprising degree, thereby attesting to the
continuing cogency of Dostoevski's conception of "crime
and punishment" and demonstrating the fallacy of his own
views on crime and art as well.(14)

In conclusion, it appears that the Dostoevski
presence in Nabokov's Despair is more complex and
significant than previously acknowledged. The
introduction of narrative and structural elements from
Notes from the Underground into Despair accents the
central theme of control in the novel and adds to an
understanding of Hermann Karlovich's fears and
aspirations, while the presence of echoes from Crime and
Punishment unmasks Hermann's limitations as an author and
underscores his status as a character. Moreover, the
subtle interplay between the world of Dostoevski's fiction
and the world created by Nabokov in Despair illuminates
Nabokov's talent for interlacing parody with seriousness
of intent. As Hermann Karlovich criticizes and belittles
Dostoevski and his emotionally charged work, his own
behavior reaffirms the vitality of Dostoevski's vision of
human aspirations and failings. Through his use of a
broad range of Dostoevskian allusions in Despair, then,
Nabokov both exposes the shortcomings of his deluded
narrator and asserts the continued importance of
Dostoevski's legacy in modern Russian literature. Rather
than becoming the "second, unnoticed corpse of the novel,"
Dostoevski thus emerges from Despair not only unharmed,
but perhaps even enhanced.

NOTES

1. Vladimir Nabokov, Strong Opinions (New York: McGraw-Hill Book Company, 1973), p. 42.

2. Andrew Field, Nabokov: His Life in Art (Boston: Little, Brown, 1967), p. 230.

3. Echoes of Dostoevski's The Double are also present in Despair: it is one of the titles that Hermann Karlovich considers using as the title for his own manuscript, and the general notion of having one's identity replaced by one's double is common to both works. However, one should be wary of drawing parallels between these two works because, as Nabokov himself points out, "Felix in Despair is really a false double." "An Interview with Vladimir Nabokov," Wisonsin Studies in Contemporary Literature 8 (Spring 1967); 145.

4. Vladimir Nabokov, Despair (New York: Capricorn Books, 1966), p. 14. All further references to this work will be noted by a parenthetical reference giving the page number from this edition in the text of the essay.

5. Fyodor Dostoevsky, Notes from the Underground, trans. Andrew R. MacAndrew (New York: Signet--New American Library, 1961), p. 91. All further references to this work will be noted by a parenthetical reference giving the page number from this edition in the text of the essay.

6. Hermann Karlovich recalls his childhood: "Not a day passed without my telling some lie. I lied as a nightingale sings, ecstatically, self-obliviously, reveling in the new life harmony which I was creating" (55). In Notes from the Underground the narrator states, "I made up whole stories about myself and put myself through all sorts of adventures to satisfy, at any price, my need to live" (102).

7. Mikhail Bakhtin, Problems of Dostoevsky's Poetics, trans. R. W. Rotsel (Ann Arbor Mich.: Ardis, 1973), p. 198. Original emphasis retained.

8. Hermann's deep aversion to the possibility of being a created one rather than a creator can be seen in his refusal to believe in any "fairy tale" about God. "If I am not the master of my own life, not sultan of my own being, then no man's logic and no man's ecstatic fits may force me to find less silly my impossibly silly position: that of God's slave" (112).

9. Field, Nabokov: His Life in Art, p. 236. For a discussion of Hermann Karlovich's artistic inclinations, see Claire Rosenfield's essay, "Despair and the Lust for Immortality," Wisconsin Studies in Contemporary Literature 8 (Spring 1967); 174-192.

162   Julian W. Connolly

10.   Feodor Dostoevsky, Crime and Punishment, trans.
Jessie Coulson (New York: W. W. Norton, 1964), p. 249.
All further references to this work will be noted by a
parenthetical reference giving the page number form this
edition in the text of the essay.

11.   Dostoevski, Crime and Punishment p. 111; and
Dostoevski, Despair, p. 197.

12.   Raskolnikov asks himself, "what if they know it
all already and were only pretending, mocking me while I
lay here" (120), while Hermann wonders, "who knows, maybe
he was saying all this . . . with a certain design . . .
maybe he was sent to spy . . . ." (199).

13.   In the Russian originals of both works, the word
"pukhlyi" ("plump") is used in reference to these two
characters.   F. M. Dostoevski, Polnoe sobranie sochinene
ii v tridtsati tomakh, 6 (Leningrad: "Nauka," 1973), p.
192; and Vladimir Nabokov, Otchaianie (Ann Arbor, Mich.:
Ardis, 1978), p. 199.

14.   Of course, there are considerable differences
between Hermann Karlovich and Rasholnikov too. In Despair
there is not trace of the religious dimension that is
characteristic of Dostoevski's work, and Hermann is not
converted from his egocentric ways through the
intercession of a soulful female as is Raskolnikov with
the help of Sonya in Crime and Punishment, but such
differences merely serve to point out those areas of
Dostoevski's work which Nabokov found especially
unacceptable--the "mists and mistakes" of mysticism, to
paraphrase the words of G. M. Hyde in his book, Vladimir
Nabokov: America's Russian Novelist (London: Marion
Boyars, 1977), p. 115.

16.
Dostoevski and Richard Wright: From St. Petersburg to Chicago

DASHA CULIC NISULA

The human condition--man's aspirations to understand himself and his attempts to cope within a social framework--is a theme which has appeared in literature for centuries. However, no single author has dwelled upon the subject of the human heart in conflict with itself and with the society within which it exists in more depth and breadth than Fedor Dostoevski. The human condition explored by Dostoevski through the characters of Raskolnikov, Marmeladov, Svidrigailov, Sonya, Stavrogin, and the brothers Karamazov, to name a few, are studies of the basic human psychological framework that transcend geographical, racial, and temporal dimensions. It is then of no surprise that his influence on the minds of readers and writers has been immeasurable. This study of his influence upon a twentieth century black American writer is an example.

The profound impact of Fedor Dostoevski on the work of Richard Wright has been acknowledged in the author's own biographical notes and in several recent studies. In the eyes of Richard Wright, Fedor Dostoevski was "the greatest novelist."(1) Wright studied his works in detail. The full extent of Dostoevski's influence on Wright, however, has yet to be explored. Several studies dealing only with thematic comparisons of Wright and Dostoevski's fiction by Jones(2) and Stanton(3) have appeared recently. However, no single direct comparison between works of these authors has been done. This chapter will therefore attempt to make such a comparison.

Two works by each author will be considered. Dostoevski's Notes from Underground will be compared to Wright's The Man Who Lived Underground, and Dostoevski's Crime and Punishment will be compared to Wright's The Outsider. First, the philosophic thrust of each author as manifested in his earlier works will be treated; a comparison of techniques and ideas elaborated in the novels will follow.

Richard Wright certainly did not hold a covert admiration for the nineteenth century Russian writer. The title of Wright's The Man Who Lived Underground immediately calls attention to Dostoevski's Notes from Underground written almost eighty years earlier. This work represents a union of ideas Dostoevski was to develop fully only later in his novels <u>Crime and Punishment</u>, <u>The Possessed</u> and <u>The Brothers Karamazov.</u>

The writings of Wright may be divided into pre- and post- self-imposed exile of 1947 which he spent in France. His literary career has further been divided by decades. In the thirties his primary concentration was on the oppressed Southern black minority. In the forties his work encompassed an urban setting with a struggling black minority and its attempts to be assimilated by a white Northern society. In the fifties his work reflects a search or quest for personal as well as national identity.

<u>The Man Who Lived Underground</u> falls into the pre-exile period of the forties, a period during which Wright was still a member of the Communist Party. Attracted by the party's championing of Negro rights, Wright joined in 1932 and with its support wrote pieces such as "The Man Who Lived Underground" which appeared in <u>Accent</u> in 1942. As pointed out by Ridenour, however, the concepts of guilt and the individual's responsibility for making himself the man he is, which are treated by Wright in this novella, are totally alien to a proletarian writer and the dictates of Socialist Realism.(4) It is obvious from Wright's work that the Communist Party was unable to hold his attention. He, in fact, gradually realized that the Party was only exploiting the Negroes' oppressive social situation, and in turn used the Party for his own artistic purposes. In 1944, upon completion of <u>The Man Who Lived Underground</u>, he ceased being a member. Three year later, despite growing acceptance of his work in the United States, he exiled himself and went to Paris. It was in exile that Wright began to write his novel <u>The Outsider</u>, a work that was published in 1953. The extended period between the two works may be attributed in part to Wright's long quest for an understanding of his own personal as well as national identity.

The similarities between Dostoevski's works and those of Wright are not only thematic and philosophical, but also structural. The underground motif in both novellas can be seen as the inner world of man, be he white or black, in St. Petersburg or in Chicago. It suggests a hiding from the outside world and a resistance to it. The world outside the underground is in both cases an urban world, dehumanizing and hostile to an ordinary, overly conscious, sensitive man. That our main characters are ordinary people is suggested by the name given to Dostoevski's narrator--Ordinov--taken from the Russian word <u>ordinarnyi</u> meaning ordinary. The narrator, however, remains nameless throughout the text. Wright's protagonist also remains nameless for a good part of the novella and only midway through it, after he has had a chance to steal a typewriter, do we learn his name. He types it as "freddaniels." It may not be a coincidence that Wright chooses this name for his protagonist; the initials F. D. may well stand for Fedor Dostoevski.

Neither in Dostoevski's <u>Notes from Underground</u> nor in Wright's <u>The Man Who Lived Underground</u> is the protagonist presented as a dynamic personality. They are rather static characters; they are stirred to life only by a series of coincidences. In both books, the conflict the characters experience is evident from the start. Notes from Underground opens with a direct reaction against the entire rationalist creed of the nineteenth century, which asserts that man acts in his own best interest. This best exemplifies man's conflict with himself and the world. Basically, man does not act in his own best interest. Dostoevski points out that man must satisfy his whims, and more often than not, the whimsical desires do not correspond to the man's best interest.

In The Man Who Lived Underground Wright introduces us at once to the conflict man experiences by presenting a character pursued by society and forced into the underground, where alone and in despair he broods over his inner conflicts. He finds out that if given the opportunity he enjoys humiliating others and desires to exert power over other men in spite of his strict Christian upbringing.

In the second part of these works the characters make contact with the outside world. In Dostoevski's Notes from Underground the hero tells us of an incident with his former schoolmates and with a prostitute. In relating the story we see him emerge from his underground and initiate contact with the people in his social environment. In Wright's The Man Who Lived Underground, the protagonist also makes his appearance from under the ground. He appears in a grocery store, directly from the sewers and basements into which he had been forced to flee, and flashes through the streets, only to read in paper headlines that the police are still seeking a thief and a murderer. Opportunities arise and he steals jewels, a radio, and money from a safe. A few minutes later he overhears an innocent boy being accused of stealing that very radio and then later he witnesses a beating of an equally innocent watchman. It is only in these contacts with the outside world that he learns more about himself, his existence, and his purpose in life.

Once above ground, the protagonists are exposed to a cycle of power, freedom, and humiliation. And it is only in the underground, isolated from the rest of the world, that they themselves realize their own inherent desire for ultimate freedom, their need for power in order to humiliate, and their own potential to do evil. All this begins to jell in the minds of the heroes. As Dostoevski's hero is humiliated by an officer in the street or by his former schoolmates, he in turn seeks an opportunity for revenge and finds his victims in Liza, the prostitute, and Apollon, his servant.

Fred Daniels also dreams of power. He steals not for the sake of spending the money himself, but rather because he enjoys a brief interlude of power, as he exerts control over the life of an unfortunate night watchman. As the protagonist watches the innocent watchman being beaten and forced into making a confession that later leads to his suicide, Fred Daniels is only reminded of his own recent experience of being chased by the police. For the first time he feels what it is like to have power over others. Fred Daniels's subsequent need to confess his crime is

actually more in line with Dostoevski's Raskolnikov in
Crime and Punishment.

Turning to the subsequent works of these writers,
what immediately becomes apparent is the sudden dynamism
acquired by the static, urban, underground personalities.
In Part One of Crime and Punishment, Raskolnikov plans and
executes a crime; the following five parts constitute the
punishment, his self-examination, with the epilogue
concentrating on his serving a sentence in Siberia, a year
and a half after the murder.

The thematic and structural designs of Wright's The
Outsider are similar to those in Crime and Punishment.
However, it is not The Outsider but Wright's Native Son,
which precedes not only The Outsider but The Man Who Lived
Underground, that has been called the American Crime and
Punishment.(5) In The Outsider, Wright concerns himself
with the issues beyond his protest writing of the
Thirties. These issues are of universal concern to
man--freedom, power, and search and discovery of
self-identity in our modern universe without a God. In
this quest for self-identity Wright's protagonists have
not been overtly conscious of their minority background.
However, we cannot dispense altogether with the black and
white issues in Wright's novel. The issue of race has not
been given a central focus but is used nevertheless to
emphasize the struggle of man for power and control not
only over the forces within himself but also over his
fellow men.

In the first pages of The Outsider the protagonist
carries a sense of guilt much as does Raskolnikov. While
Raskolnikov's is an intellectual guilt, Cross Damon's
guilt is one that emits from the strong Christian
background instilled by his mother. "His dread has been
his mother's first fateful gift to him."(6) And her
religious tirades evoke in him a still stronger desire for
the sensual, "a sin leading to eternal damnation."(7) And
so in the opening pages of the novel, Damon appears in his
"shameful mood of guilt born of desire and fear of
desire."(8) The novel is divided into five books with the
following titles: Dread, Dream, Descent, Despair, and
Decision. (It is interesting to observe here the three
books comprising the Native Son are entitled: Fear,
Flight, and Fate. Again a noteworthy play with the
letters F and D.) For our purposes The Outsider may be
divided into two parts with Book One comprising part one,
and the next four books comprising part two.

Book One in The Outsider can very easily be compared
to Part One of Crime and Punishment. In Book One the
protagonist by mere chance survives a serious subway
accident and takes that opportunity to sever all of his
past relationships by allowing his mother, wife, mistress,
and friends to believe him dead. Damon interprets his
survival as a chance to start a new life and immediately
decides to take advantage of this opportunity to rid
himself of the domestic and financial stress under which
he has been living. Like Raskolnikov he is forced to
abandon his university studies. Now, here is an
opportunity to create his own past and determine his own

future. An urge for control of the self overpowers him
and Damon seizes the opportunity.
        While hiding in a hotel from his family and friends,
Damon runs into his buddy from work, Joe Thomas. In order
to keep his secret of being alive, Damon is forced to kill
him. In killing Joe, Damon actually kills his old self, a
black postal clerk. By the end of Book One, Damon has
freed himself from all previous obligations and pressures.
In order to complete the construction of his new life and
a new self, he boards a train for New York. The next four
books of The Outsider do not, however, constitute self
examination and remorse at what has been done. Rather,
Damon embarks on a path that brings him deeper and deeper
into the realization of the true meaning of life, at the
same time it takes him further away from man, society, and
himself. Damon seeks his new identity as he arbitrarily
picks up different names according to need. On Saturday,
the day after the subway accident, Damon identifies
himself to a prostitute in a hotel as Charles Webb. On
the very next day, as he rents a room across the church to
watch his own funeral, he is John Clark, a visiting
student. On Monday, on the train for New York, he is
Addison Jordan. In this manner Cross Damon becomes any
man and every man. And it is only after he reaches New
York and finds at a graveyard the name of a dead man of
similar age, that he becomes Lionel Lane. He then obtains
Lane's birth certificate and a draft card and almost
overnight resurrects Lionel Lane in his own image.
        Tracing the events, we find that the first murder in
The Outsider occurs within the first three days of the
narrative. The crime in Crime and Punishment also occurs
within three days. However, Wright's complete novel
covers only a week and two days compared to the two weeks
covered in Crime and Punishment preceding the epilogue.
The events in this novel are therefore even more closely
linked than those in Crime and Punishment. We can trace
the time from Friday, when the subway accident occurs, to
Sunday and the murder of Joe Thomas, to Sunday exactly a
week later when Cross Damon is murdered by the Communists.
During that week Damon commits three more murders and
drives Eva to suicide. The role of uncontrollable and
almost unbelievable chance contributes to the fantastic
speed in the first half of this novel. The second half
slows considerably, and the short, pregnant sentences of
the first half become longer, giving a didactic quality to
the rest of the novel. Wright's work has been criticized
precisely for these lengthy monologues that crowd the last
pages.
        The third-person, omniscient narrator present in
Crime and Punishment is also present in Wright's novel.
As he probes the crevices of each character's mind, the
narrator links the character's reminiscences and
juxtaposes the linear progression of the novel with the
character's past and future. Since the psychological time
is again given preference over the linear clock time of
the novel, the reader is given the impression that either
too much or too little time elapses between the recorded
events.

A favorite Dostoevski's literary device, the double, also appears in this work. As mentioned, Joe Thomas is an extension of Cross Damon. The characters with whom Damon identifies the most are Eva Blount and Ely Houston. Viewed as opposite poles of Damon, both of these characters appear in their status as social victims. Eva is an orphan artist and Ely is a hunchback district attorney in New York. Eva represents the creative side which led Damon to seek self control and recreate his own life and identity through Lionel Lane. This creative self is juxtaposed with Ely and the rational self which in the end helps Damon crystallize the meaning of his life. When asked what his life has been like, Damon replies to Ely "horrible"(9) Damon's final utterance reminds us of Joseph Conrad's Kurtz in Heart of Darkness summing up a life of desire, temptation and surrender in "The Horror! The Horror!"(10)

In Crime and Punishment Dostoevski has used his favorite technique of having several characters personify conflicting ideas of the protagonist. For example, the two sides of Raskolnikov are represented by Svidrigailov and Sonya. In Wright's novel, ideas as artistic material are best represented by Gil Blount and Langley Herndon. Gil, as a devout member of the Communist Party, displays the mechanics of this institution in all his relations with the other active and potential members of the Party. Herndon represents the ultimate in conservatism, i.e., Fascism. Both are despised by Damon who quickly surmises the rules of their game. In order to rebel against the ideas represented by these two men, he kills them, and, in killing them, overcomes those who used power over him and in turn makes himself into what he tries to defeat.(11)

Another comparison must be made regarding the manner in which Crime and Punishment and The Outsider evolve from beginning to end. Dostoevski's technique of narrative progression in a spiderweb weaving-fashion sets up Raskolnikov as the nucleus at the beginning of the novel and works out into a net-like pattern ending with Rodion and Sonya in Siberia. Similarly in The Outsider, Wright introduces Damon as the center of a spiderweb weaved by the domestic demands and financial debts. Slowly, every one who comes into Damon's circle or web is eliminated in a series of murders. And each murder in a sense represents a step in search for the self through a painful process of self-annihilation. Damon first eliminates his outward self by pretending he was killed in the subway accident. In killing Joe Thomas he kills his former self, a Christian postal clerk. Then, incognito, he kills Gil and Herndon. Going further toward self-annihilation, Damon kills a free-lance writer, Hilton. All these murders precipitate Eva's suicide. Almost as if all this had not been enough, Damon assumes the ultimate in control and hopelessness in his life when he coldheartedly accepts the news of his mother's death and then denies the presence of his wife and children. In this process, he has actually killed himself. What worse fate could have been bestowed upon him then, than to die at the hands of Communists!

Based upon the material presented here, similarities between the discussed works of Fedor Dostoevski and Richard Wright are substantial and overt. Dostoevski's work evolves as a polemic against the idea of "rational self-interest" advocated by the novelist Nikolai Chèrnyshevski as a means of reeducating man, and thus reforming society. Dostoevski believed that one cannot alter the environment hoping man will change. Man must be taught, changed, and then we can hope for a better society. This idea was taken up by Wright and applied to his twentieth century world. He came up with Fred Daniels, a man who, precisely in his alienation from society and in his own underground world, desolate and in fear, seeks his self-identity. He finds meaning in his existence, realizes man's potential for evil and the guilt that emits from it. He finds truth and freedom not outside himself in society, but alone within himself. Wright shows us a change in Daniels's character that must occur in every man before any change in society can take place. Fred Daniels's vision was Fedor Dostoevski's vision, but the realization and acceptance of that vision in a society is a slow and painful process. Neither of the two characters was able to communicate his newly found truth to the world. Dostoevski's hero from the underground remains in his underground; Fred Daniels is thrown back into the sewer and killed.

As far as the two novels are concerned, the author of Crime and Punishment stresses that sole reliance of man on reason and exertion of his free will lead toward the destruction of his self and of others. Since the hero is saved by Sonya, reliance on some moral code seems indicated. However, the ending of Crime and Punishment does not indicate that any overt change in Raskolnikov's character has taken place. Damon's road to self-destruction begins at the opposite pole. If left to chance, man's nature is such that at the very moment an opportunity presents itself, he rises with a desire to seize whatever he can. The irrational thing in man is precisely this desire which can never be satiated, since it always aims higher and higher. Man's ultimate desire is to be God. Damon's conclusion is that this very desire to control, to be God, is not only proof of man's limitations, but is something that, when left uncontrolled, takes man even further away from God and his fellow men. Society can neither prevent this, nor can it punish an individual who transgresses social law. Man's most severe judge after all is he himself, and man's worst punishment is the torment of his own conscience. Wright realizes this and at the end of the novel has Ely say to Damon: "You are going to punish yourself, see? You are your own law, so you'll be your own judge.... I wouldn't help you by taking you to jail.... It's between you and you, you and yourself."(12)

170   Dasha Culic Nisula

NOTES

1. Richard Wright: Impressions and Perspectives,
ed. D. Ray and R. M. Farnsworth (Ann Arbor: The
University of Michigan Press, 1973), p. 53.

2. Anne Hudson Jones, "The Plight of the Modern
Outsider: A Comparative Study of Dostoevsky's Crime and
Punishment, Camus's L'Etranger, and Wright's The
Outsider," Dissertation Abstracts International 36 (1974).

3. Robert Stanton, "Outrageous Fiction: Crime and
Punishment, The Assistant and Native Son," Pacific Coast
Philology 4 (1969); 52-58.

4. Ronald Ridenour, "'The Man Who Lived
Underground': A Critique," Phylon 31 (1970); 54-57.

5. Kenneth T. Reed, "Native Son: An American Crime
and Punishment," Studies in Black Literature 1 (1970);
33-34.

6. Richard Wright, The Outsider (New York: Harper
and Row, 1966), p. 17.

7. Ibid., p. 18.

8. Ibid., p. 21.

9. Ibid., p. 440.

10. Joseph Conrad, Heart of Darkness (New York: W.
W. Norton, 1963), p. 21.

11. Wright, p. 245.

12. Ibid., p. 430.

17.
Dostoevski and the Catholic Pax Romana

DENNIS DIRSCHERL

No writer has so poignantly expressed his country's
ambiguous and often painful relationship with the West as
Fedor Dostoevski. Indeed, few writers of his era so
deliberately wrestled with the "western problem." His
critique, his final resolution on the Europe of his day,
as is commonly known, focused on what he believed to be
the ultimate source of this alien spirit, that is, the
Roman Catholic Church.

Dostoevski used his most creative genius and "cruel
talent" to portray what he believed to be the spirit
characterizing the mass of humanity beyond the borders of
Russia. Like the true man of his time that he was,
Dostoevski saw the Catholic Church through the eyes of a
long-standing Russian tradition, through the often
polemical and cataclysmic atmosphere built up over the
course of ten centuries.

On June 7, 1862, Dostoevski gave in to the "powerful,
magic, compelling appeal" of Europe. He visited the major
cities, and we know the impression they made on him. His
critique of France makes the case as well as any other.
France, in Dostoevski's estimation, exemplified the heart
of the socialist movement. In that country the picture
was most clear, the crucial factor being that France,
paradoxically, was considered the Catholic country par
excellence. And thus Dostoevski's critique of socialism
really resulted in a propadeutic to a far more important
scrutiny. Socialism, after all, was generated by Roman
Catholicism. "French socialism," he writes, "is nothing
else but a compulsory communion of mankind,--an idea which
dates back to ancient Rome and which was fully conserved
in Catholicism. Thus, the idea of the liberation of the
human spirit from Catholicism became vested there precisely in the narrowest Catholic forms borrowed from the
very heart of its spirit, from its letter, from its
materialism, from its despotism, from its morality."(1)

In Dostoevski's view Roman Catholicism had
degenerated to such an extent in Europe that it was
directly responsible for the materialism and atheism that
was rampant there. Breaking its own association with
Christ, even selling Him for earthly rule, the Catholic
Church had naturally given birth to the monster of
socialism.

In the early stages of his writing career Dostoevski
evidenced only a faint interest in the Catholic Church.
But this intensified while he and his wife remained abroad
from 1867 to 1871. Then he became acutely aware of the
association between European culture and the Catholic
Church. Like Chaadaev, he envisioned Catholicism as the
driving force, the essence of Europe. As Professor
Zenkovsky has written, "not since Chaadaev was there
anyone in Russian literature more conscious of the
religious unity of Western culture than Dostoevski. That
is why he inevitably directs himself to a criticism of
Catholicism, the force which has colored all Western
culture."(2)

Dostoevski's hardnosed critique of Catholicism in his
novels is first revealed in The Possessed. There in the
space of one brief paragraph the trend of his future
observations and convictions is laid bare. Dostoevski
uses Shatov and Stavrogin to reveal the shambles remaining
of authentic Christianity in Europe:

> But you went further--you believed that Roman
> Catholicism was no longer Christian. You
> maintained that Rome had proclaimed a Christ who
> had succumbed to the Devil's third temptation
> and that, by announcing to the world that Christ
> couldn't hold on earth without an earthly
> kingdom, Catholicism had really proclaimed the
> Antichrist and thus was leading the Western
> world to perdition. You actually said that if
> France was suffering it was through the fault of
> Catholicism, because France had rejected the
> decaying Romish god, but had not found another
> to replace him.(3)

Dostoevski becomes more expansive in his subsequent
novel, The Idiot. The "attack" breaks through the surface
in an explosive outburst of the main character, Myshkin.
The incident occurs late in the work in a sudden, almost
traumatic manner. The outburst of Myshkin, the gentle
epileptic, is doubly telling because of the hero's
character and the problem of evil he faces.

Taken aback by Myshkin's disclosures, his fellow
discussants ask for an explanation. Instead he delivers a
lecture:

> Atheism only preaches a negation, but
> Catholicism goes further: it preaches a
> distorted Christ, a Christ calumniated and
> defamed by themselves, the opposite of Christ!
> It preaches the Antichrist. I declare it does,
> I assure you it does!.... Roman Catholicism
> cannot hold its position without universal
> political supremacy, and cries: "Non Possumus!"
> To my thinking Roman Catholicism is not even a
> religion, but simply the continuation of the
> Western Roman Empire, and everything in it is
> subordinated to that idea, faith to begin with.
> The Pope seized the earth, an earthly throne,

and grasped the sword; everything has gone on in
the same way since, only they have added to the
sword lying, fraud, deceit, fanaticism,
superstition, villainy. They have trifled with
the most holy, truthful, sincere, fervent
feelings of the people; they have bartered it
all, all for money, for base earthly power....
Out over there, in Europe, a terrible mass of
the people themselves are beginning to lose
their faith--at first from darkness and lying,
and now from fanaticism and hatred of the Church
and Christianity.(4)

Throughout this brief burst of personal conviction
Myshkin repeatedly denies the suggestion of his listeners
that he has resorted to excessive exaggeration, to an
over-ardent expression of his ideas, or to the spirit of
lethargy that pervades society. Nor is it because of
isolation or excitability. On the contrary, Myshkin
counters that it is due to unsatisfied yearnings, from
"feverishness, from burning thirst."
     The Catholic question continued to haunt Dostoevski,
and with increasing avidity and acceleration he began to
reaffirm and elaborate on his few pithy statements in The
Possessed and The Idiot. Instead of synthesizing in a
major novel his major contentions and convictions that the
Catholic Church had degenerated to a point where it was no
longer even Christian, Dostoevski turned to journalism.
The Diary of a Writer, a massive collection of 1,052
pages, with issues in 1873, 1876, 1877, August 1880, and
January 1881, became his new forum of expression.
     In The Diary Dostoevski gives free expression to all
of his philosophical, political, and theological opinions
and convictions. He makes random remarks on how the West
had dimmed the light of Christ and doomed the West to ruin
and destruction. He also describes the gradual loss of
Christ in history because of the Catholic Church. There
is the demise of both "old and new Rome." Old Rome was
the first to originate and to attempt to practice the
ideal of a universal empire. But the grand plan
disintegrated in time, and when the Pax Romana fell, the
same idea, though not the same formula, was taken over by
western Christianity. Again and again Dostoevski asserts
that the Catholic Church does not need Christ; its only
interest is "universal sovereignty." As a result it will
undertake any campaign or strategy to insure its
livelihood. "It is inspired with a devilish desire to
live, and it is difficult to kill it--it is a snake!"(5)
     If one must consider how an enemy is to be
vanquished, he will naturally look to the source, the
head. In this regard Dostoevski devotes much of his ire
towards the papacy. Aimee Dostoevski offers another
glimpse on the topic. She relates that a Russian writer
and friend of Dostoevski could never understand why her
father could be so interested in "that old fool the Pope."
But she adds, "Now to Dostoevski 'that old fool' was the
most interesting figure in Europe."(6) In Europe
Dostoevski felt that Bismarck alone understood the real

threat behind the papacy. He alone perceived the plight
of Europe with a healthy papacy. Thus from afar
Dostoevski gave moral support to Prince Bismarck in his
endeavor to deal a smashing blow to the attempts at a
Catholic revival in Europe. The scene focused
particularly on the forthcoming death of Pius and the
election of a new pontiff.

> And in Rome it is well known that Prince
> Bismarck is going to use all his power, his best
> endeavors, to deliver the last and most horrible
> blow against the papal authority, exercising his
> utmost influence upon the election of the new
> Pope so as to convert him--if possible with his
> own consent--from a secular sovereign and
> potentate into a Patriarch, and thus, by
> dividing Catholicism into two rival camps, to
> bring about once and forever its disintegration
> and the destruction of its claims and hopes.(7)

Dostoevski noted the insistence with which Pius IX
stared danger in the face, notably on the occasion of
Vatican I (1868-1870) when he boldly proclaimed the
doctrine of infallibility. It was then that Pius finally
revealed "the whole secret," as Dostoevski puts it, about
the Church. The Pope took this resolute stand precisely
when a united Italy was clamoring at the gates of Rome
itself. The Pope, then, was by no means a weak man as
many thought; indeed, he was prepared to fight to the
death for the life of the Church.
The "secret" which Dostoevski refers to is the
allegedly everlasting thrust for power on the part of the
papacy, a theme Dostoevski repeats on numerous occasions.
This, he felt, was made abundantly clear at Vatican I:

> But there always has been a secret: during many
> centuries the Popes have been pretending that
> they were satisfied with their tiny
> dominion--the Papal State; but all this was for
> the sake of mere allegory; still, the important
> point is that in this allegory there was always
> hidden the kernel of the main idea, coupled with
> the indubitable and perpetual hope of papacy in
> the future the kernel would grow into a grand
> tree which would shade the whole world.(8)

Dostoevski depicted the events preceding the
declaration of infallibility as one of hostility and
defeat. Yet, as if getting up from his death bed Pius
announced to the world, "<u>urbi et orbi</u>" the real state of
the question:

> So you thought that I was satisfied with the
> mere title of King of the Papal State? Know
> that I have ever considered myself potentate of
> the whole world and over all earthly kings, and
> not only their spiritual, but their mundane,
> genuine master sovereign and emperor. It is I

who am king over all kings and sovereign over
all sovereigns, and to me alone on earth belong
the destinies, the ages and the bounds of time.
And now I am proclaiming this in the dogma of my
infallibility.(9)

For Dostoevski this triumphant declaration was merely
a belated confession, a mere resurrection and repetition
of the old Roman imperial idea, and it marked the complete
sale of Christ for the kingdoms of this world. Faith in
God has been at once replaced by faith in the Pope. In
the process the vertical or transcendental element of
religion and the spiritual life had been exterminated to
assure temporarily the survival of the Church.
     As far back as 1868 Dostoevski laid plans for a book
to be entitled "The Life of a Great Sinner." In this
project he intended to draw up a sweeping comparison
between Catholicism and Jesuitry, on one hand, and
Orthodoxy on the other. Along with the material
accumulated during the laboratory period of the Diary,
Dostoevski used these ideas as the molding force of his
last novel. As planned, The Brothers Karamazov pitted
faith versus atheism. The most striking and compelling
part of this novel is unquestionably "The Grand
Inquisitor." In the space of some twenty pages Dostoevski
surpasses the traches of his previous creative artistry.
     There have been many debates over the purpose and
intent of Dostoevski's "Grand Inquisitor." But what
Dostoevski does, and this is obvious in all his published
material, is to maintain a consistent, immovable view of
the Catholic Church. He follows a persistent pattern
throughout his literary career in this regard, and the
insistence of his critique grows with the years. In this
instance Zenkovsky has the more accurate appraisal of the
purpose and scope of the Grand Inquisitor: "Dostoevsky
purposely chose the form of a legend to express his most
concentrated and incisive criticism of the Catholic idea,
which he considers to be the basis of European culture.
What is important for him is the true meaning of the
spirit and idea of Catholicism, rather than its individual
expressions or exact formulas."(10)
     As in his previous novels, letters, and Diary, so too
in his last creative work does Dostoevski follow the
pattern of highly condensing his sharp barbs toward the
Catholic Church. By comparison with the bulk of the work,
moreover, the space allotted to the Catholic idea is
minimal and sporadic. Dostoevski is merely being
consistent.
     Before the actual episode of the Grand Inquisitor,
Dostoevski cleverly manipulates the psychological dilemma
of Ivan's alleged inability to accept the problem of evil
in this world, notably the suffering of innocents. Here
Dostoevski marshals forth the basest cruelty that man can
unleash on helpless children. He depicts "artistically
cruel" adults in action: Turks blowing out the brains of
a baby, a general setting his dogs on a young boy, tearing
him to pieces before his mother's eyes, parents beating
unmercifully their five-year-old daughter and locking her

up in a frozen privy after they smear her with human
excrement. This account of suffering innocents is
shrewdly calculated to make the episode of the Grand
Inquisitor all the more soul-searching under the glimpse
of Ivan.

From the problem of innocent suffering, Ivan leaps
into the problem of global suffering, all mankind. At
first he focuses on a small cross section, those heretics
in Seville during "the most terrible time of the
Inquisition, when fires were lighted every day to the
glory of God."(11)

In this incredible scene Jesus Christ makes his
second appearance on earth where just a day previously and
in His honor, "ad majorem gloriam Dei," a hundred heretics
were burned to death "in the presence of the king, the
court, the knights, the cardinals, the most charming
ladies of the court, and the whole population of
Seville."(12) In effect Ivan has successfully transposed
his theme of inhuman suffering from little children to
adults. The guilt, moreover, now rests with the Catholic
Church, not with some unknown parents or adults.

Ivan paints a compelling contrast between Christ and
the Grand Inquisitor. Jesus, except for the two
words--"Maiden, arise!"--is absolutely silent throughout
the interlude. He is passive and submissive to all that
takes place there in Seville. The "old man" of ninety,
tall and erect with his withered face and sunken eyes, on
the other hand, is in complete control of the entire city.
He has, for all practical purposes, condemned Jesus to
silence.

Jesus has come to "hinder" the work of his followers,
but the Grand Inquisitor will not allow any change in the
strategy. As Ivan points out to Alesha, Jesus doesn't
have the right "to add anything to what He has said of
old."(13) Ivan then proceeds to make one of his most
telling blows: "One may say it is the most fundamental
feature of Roman Catholicism, in my opinion at least.
'All has been given by Thee to the Pope,' they say, 'And
all, therefore, is still in the Pope's hands, and there is
no need for Thee to come now at all. Thou must not meddle
for the time, at least.' That's how they speak and write
too--the Jesuits, at any rate. I have read it myself in
the works of their theologians."(14)

It is important to pause here, however briefly, to
highlight Dostoevski's personal convictions concerning the
Jesuits. The author had more than a passing interest in
the "Pope's army." Indeed, Dostoevski's entire corpus of
articles and novels is dotted with sarcasm, satire, and
vituperation toward the Society of Jesus. There are no
benign words in his quiver for this branch of the Catholic
Church. In the Diary for January 1877, for instance,
Dostoevski states that in France "The Jesuits and atheists
there are the one and the same."(15) In The Idiot Myshkin
refers to "atheism," "jesuitism," and "nihilism" in the
same breath.(16) In the Diary for November 1877 he
associates the Jesuits with the philosophy and program 'of
every means for Christ's cause."(17) The Jesuits, then,

are plotters par excellence, notably for their casuistry, cunning, and conspiratorial nature.

At last the Inquisitor reveals his own terrible "secret" to Jesus. He has been abandoned altogether. It is not so much a question, therefore, of "correcting" His work but of giving allegiance to an alien power:

> We are not working with Thee, but with him--that
> is our mystery. It's long--eight centuries--
> since we have been on his side and not on Thine.
> Just eight centuries ago, we took from him what
> Thou didst reject with scorn, that last gift he
> offered Thee, showing Thee all the kingdoms of
> the earth. We took from him Rome and the sword
> of Caesar, and proclaimed ourselves sole rulers
> of the earth, though hitherto we have not been
> able to complete our work. . . . Mankind as a
> whole has always striven to organize a universal
> state. . . . For who can rule men if not he who
> holds their conscience and their bread in his
> hands? We have taken the sword of Caesar, and
> in taking it, of course, have rejected Thee and
> followed him.(18)

Dostoevski here is undoubtedly suggesting, as far as the time frame is concerned, that the Catholic Church sold out in the eighth century during "the donation of Pepin" in 756 and the rise of papal supremacy over the Church. Included in this era and later would be the slow, imperceptible rift between western and eastern Christianity.

The episode of the Grand Inquisitor closes Dostoevski's sweeping critique of Roman Catholicism. In it he reached the heights of his creative mastery and struck with the utmost force at what he considered the heart of the Catholic idea. In essence the symbolic content of the story represents the breakdown and corruption of Rome. In the process the Inquisitor's spirit, more specifically the Antichrist, had replaced Christ in the West. Dostoevski's insistence, moreover, that the Church of the West was locked on a path taking it further and further away from the pristine faith of early Christianity could not be put more painfully than Ivan's closing remark to Alesha: "Surely you don't suppose I am going straight off to the Jesuits, to join the men who are correcting His work?"(19)

A BRIEF REFLECTION

As we have seen, Dostoevski's sometimes unattractive
personality mightily reflected itself in his political and
philosophical views. As a man Dostoevski was intense,
nervous, pessimistic, and very often intolerant. To be
sure, Dostoevski lived in an age that struggled under
unusual stress. Old structures were crumbling, new and
vital forces were attempting to assert themselves. It was
the age of rampant nationalism when nations proclaimed new
destinies for themselves.
        For all practical purposes Dostoevski betrayed only a
relentless hatred for the Europe of his day, a Europe that
deserved to be destroyed because of its self-seeking
egotistical individualism, its worn out morals, and its
autocratic Church that was losing its grip over its flock.
        In his critique of the Catholic Church Dostoevski
simply went beyond the realms of historical reality. In
this respect he was a victim of his own times. Masaryk
points to a parallel in the Russian thought of
Dostoevski's day, that is, Russian thought could be negative, but not critical: "In everything we see the lack of
criticism, of the cautious gradation."(20)
        In the final analysis Dostoevski's messianic hopes
and aspirations were turned inside out. Third Rome became
the Third International. "Dostoevsky and the Bolsheviks
represent extremes in their respective viewpoints, yet
there is a deeper affinity in their goal and methods than
is sometimes recognized."(21) Or as Simmons wisely
observes, "The curious fact is that if one substituted
communism for his conception of the mission of the
Orthodox faith, and world world revolution for his notion
of a Pan-Slavic war against Europe, the identity of his
whole position with that of modern Soviet Russia would be
striking."(22)
        We still must face the final realization. Dostoevski
is no straw man that can be reduced to ashes in a couple
of paragraphs. He was a creative genius, a master of his
craft, indeed, destined to be unequaled in many ways. He
did truly find and surface many important issues that
continue to stand in our paths both here and in the
future. He forced his readers to think, to reflect, to
choose. The Catholic Church of the nineteenth century was
not always a pretty sight, as in other centuries as well.
As strong and as extreme as his critique may have been, we
can still learn from this thinker even when his ideas
carried him to the limit of reality. We are still the
wiser for it.

NOTES

1. Fyodor Dostoevsky, The Diary of a Writer, trans. Boris Brasol (New York; Scribner 1949), II, 563.

2. V. V. Zenkovsky, Russian Thinkers and Europe (Ann Arbor, Mich.: J.W. Edwards 1953), p. 168.

3. Fyodor Dostoevsky, The Possessed, trans. Andrew R. MacAndrew (New York; Signet 1962), p. 236.

4. Fyodor Dostoevsky, The Idiot, trans. Constance Garnett (New York; Macmillan 1948), pp. 532-533.

5. Dostoevsky, The Diary of a Writer, II, 738.

6. Aimee Dostoevsky, Fyodor Dostoyevsky (New Haven; Yale University Press 1922), p. 255.

7. Dostoevsky, Diary, II, 825.

8. Dostoevski, Diary, I, 255-256.

9. Ibid., 256.

10. Zenkovsky, Russian Thinkers, p. 167.

11. Fyodor Dostoevsky, The Brothers Karamazov, trans. Constance Garnett (New York; Vintage 1950), p. 295.

12. Ibid.

13. Ibid., p. 297.

14. Ibid.

15. Dostoevski, Diary, II, 563.

16. Dostoevski, The Idiot, p. 535.

17. Dostoevski, Diary, II, 911.

18. Dostoevski, The Brothers Karamazov, pp. 305-306.

19. Ibid., p. 312.

20. Hans Kohn, Pan-Slavism: Its History and Ideology. (Notre Dame, Ind.: University of Notre Dame Press, 1953), p. 286.

21. Hans Kohn, Prophets and Peoples (New York: Macmillan, 1946), p. 135.

22. Ernest J. Simmons, Dostoevsky: The Making of a Novelist (New York: Oxford University Press, 1940), pp. 327-328.

18.
Rebirth and the Cognitive Dream: From Dostoevski to Hermann Hesse and C. G. Jung

PHYLLIS BERDT KENEVAN

It has been said that Dostoevski the prophet overshadows
Dostoevski the novelist. However one may judge that fact
esthetically, it is Dostoevski the prophet who stirs and
fascinates us. Perhaps only Nietzsche saw as profoundly
the moral and spiritual implications of the death of God.
Yet it is not those implications, however significant they
may be, that are my present concern. Nietzsche's madman
and Ivan Karamazov express that anguish only too clearly.
What I would like to examine, instead, is the aftermath of
that anguish. For Dostoevski also prophesied the rebirth
of humanity through a renewed spirituality. Because at
first glance that spirituality seems tied to the influence
of the Russian Orthodox Church, and history has not
validated that influence, it appears to be the case that
Dostoevski grossly misread the future.
    The Brothers Karamazov, for instance, is infused with
an almost Biblical atmosphere of expectation; "this star
will rise in the East" is a theme frequently encountered
in the novel.
    How are we to assess his expectation? Was Dostoevski
caught up in a world of pure religious fantasy? For,
instead of a new spiritual brotherhood, the star which
rose in the East and spread its message throughout the
world in the twentieth century has been unequivocally a
Red one, flanked by a hammer and sickle. Did Dostoevski
predict a world to come whose reality turned out to be the
antithesis of his vision?
    It is the thesis of this chapter that not only did
Dostoevski not fail as a prophet, but that his vision of
spiritual rebirth is even now emerging into our
consciousness.
    In support of this thesis I would like to draw upon
an article by Hermann Hesse,(1) which gives a unique
interpretation of Dostoevski's ideal. According to Hesse,
this is not the ideal of the Russian Orthodox Church, nor
is it typical of Classical European Rationalism. It is,
Hesse claims, an "asiatic ideal." He suggests that the
phenomenon of the "madman seer" with his holy vision lurks
behind the prophetic insight of Dostoevski; and as
Asiatics recognize and honor the vision of their madmen,
so does he honor the vision of Dostoevski. According to
Hesse, then, Dostoevski's ideal of rebirth and universal

brotherhood comes out of a return to deep unconscious
sources. From this point of view the term "asiatic" is
defensible; for if modern European man has been dominated
by Classical European Rationalism, then a return to
unconscious sources would be a return to what has been
excluded from Western consciousness, but embraced and
developed in the East. The return to the unconscious
would then be an opening to "the East."
     Under this interpretation, it is interesting to look
at Zosima's relationship to the Church in The Brothers
Karamazov. Zosima, associated with the clerically unpop-
ular Elder System, is in conflict with the church
establishment. His spirituality is not that of the
conventional church. In fact, in Dostoevski's description
of the Elder System, there is an open admission of
connection with Eastern esoteric schools. He writes;
"This institution of elders is not founded on theory, but
was established in the East from the practise of a thousand years."(2) As a midwife of spiritual rebirth, Zosima
sends Alesha out of the monastery, away from conventional
spirituality, and into the world. The strongest message
he gives is conveyed in the metaphor of the corn of wheat:
"Except a corn of wheat fall into the ground and die, it
abideth alone; but if it die, it bringeth forth much
fruit."(3) The Sufis, for instance, say man is asleep,
and must die before he can awaken. This is precisely the
"Eastern" emphasis which Alesha carries to the world. He
goes forth to awaken men to the need to die before they
can be reborn.
     According to Hesse, then, the death that Dostoevski
is describing is a return to the inner depths of chaos, to
the unconscious, where psychic transformation is made
possible through a birth of new values.
     From Hesse's viewpoint this is where Dostoevski is
most prophetic; for the return to the creative unconscious
in a search for new values is one of the most prominent
characteristics of our time. Freud, with his largely
negative view of the unconscious and his distrust of
spirituality, feared and wanted to stem what he called the
"black tide of mud of occultism."(4) But our conception
of the unconscious has altered since Freud, and in a more
Jungian frame of mind we look upon the unconscious as a
creative source and a center for harmonious balance. Out
of that changing view of the unconscious have come many of
the popular movements of our time, from the frankly occult
to the most venerable Eastern religions. Europe and the
United States have become the marketplaces for new
spiritual frontiers; martial arts, Sufi schools, Yoga,
Zen, T.M., parapsychology, Castaneda, Shamanism, hypnosis,
"life before life," "life after life," and reincarnation,
among others. The opening of the unconscious for modern
Western man has uncovered a new Route to the East. Freud
may have been justified in his fears; for he is the
twentieth century Marco Polo who has opened to us far more
exotic spices than he intended.
     If Hesse is right, however, then this creative source
is precisely the route to a spiritual rebirth; and if
Jung, as a twentieth century diagnostician can be trusted,

this influx of the East through our own creative transformation is the means to a new spiritual health.

If we approach Dostoevski's prophetic vision in this light, then we must take a new look at his novels. From this point of view, the significance he gives to dreams as a source of self-knowledge and transformation emerges with startling clarity. It is one hundred years since Dostoevski wrote these novels, but only now are we seeing a growing respect for the function of the dream. Modern interest in dreams began with Freud's Interpretation of Dreams in 1900. By 1945 Jung was calling the dream "the most common and most normal expression of the unconscious psyche."(5) More recently the dream has been put into the experimental laboratory as well.

In the light of this recent respect for the dream, Dostoevski's novels are indeed prophetic. But it is not only his understanding of the dream as a source of self-transformation which is so modern; it is also his recognition of what Jung calls the "Great Dream," a dream which has collective significance. In fact, it is Dostoevski who taps so profoundly our most persistent "Great Dream"--the ideal of universal brotherhood, that haunting and elusive collective dream we call today the coming of the Aquarian Age.

Taking Dostoevski's account of the dream as an example of his prophetic vision, I would like to argue in support of my thesis that his vision has not failed and that it would be premature to identify his star with the red one. In my defense of this thesis I would like to stress, first, his use of the dream as a source of individual transformation and, second, the dream in its collective significance as the prophetic ground for the new ideal of universal brotherhood. Both the personal transformation and the collective ideal involve, in Hesse's sense, an encounter with the unconscious--the East in us, from which comes our rebirth, both personal and, we hope, collective.

I have chosen the term "cognitive dream" very deliberately to signify that these dreams bring new knowledge to the dreamer. But this is cognition of a very special kind, for it is one which invades the whole being of a person in such a way that it disarms the rigid, ruling prejudices of the intellect. We see repeatedly in Dostoevski's characters the danger of an intellect divorced from the feeling and intuitive parts of the psyche. For it is in those depths that moral knowledge resides; and intellect cut off from spirit spells moral disaster. How can such an anomalous situation correct itself? Too clever an intellect offers infinite ratio-nalizations that seal off more and more profoundly the healing sources of spiritual love. Obviously, only crisis situations can cut through those barriers, if at all. But there is another way, through the symbolism of dreams. Dream symbols, since they do not speak to the rational intellect, elude the limiting concepts of intellectual prejudices and take the whole person unawares. They give substance to certain semi-conscious beliefs which the intellect holds at bay, and if the symbols are powerful

enough, they transform the psyche as a conversion does.
It is not that the problems of the rational intellect are
solved; rather, one is no longer interested in them. The
focus has shifted. I justify calling the dreams
"cognitive," then, because the dream symbols are catalysts
of new values and meanings which spring up as the lived
world is transformed. In his presentation of the
transformative power of dreams Dostoevski is strikingly
modern. For instance, Jung, who has written extensively
about this process claims that dreams compensate our
conscious attitudes and give us a totally different point
of view.(6)

Two examples of the transformative capacity of dreams
can be seen in The Brothers Karamazov. Dmitri's dream of
the hungry babe changes him from an egocentric, self-
indulgent personality despairing over his inner division
to a more grounded self recognizing the difference between
the relative and the absolute. Like Kierkegaard's knight
of infinite faith he recognizes that what really matters
is his new spiritual life; that the greatest loss would be
not his physical freedom, but his new-found spiritual
freedom which has opened to him, simultaneously, the
absolute worth of his relationship with God and his shared
responsibility for all humanity. The symbolism of the
starving babe brings to Dmitri the realization of Father
Zosima's teaching that "we are all responsible for all."
In that realization his old problems pale into
insignificance.

Alesha, too, gains new understanding through a dream.
Deeply anguished, in rebellion against injustice, he falls
into a troubled sleep at the coffin of Father Zosima.
When he awakens, his rebellion is gone. Again, the dream
does not resolve the problem of the injustice of Zosima's
stinking corpse. But Alesha's rebellion fades away in the
face of the powerful symbolism of the wedding feast where
the message that "there is no living without joy" is given
meaning through the miracle of the transformation of water
into wine, and the union of opposites in marriage. None
of this symbolism seems directly connected with what
Alesha does upon awakening. But one can follow the
meaning which the dream symbols carry to his consciousness
by the fact that he is carrying out an earlier directive
of Zosima almost as though it were a posthypnotic
instruction. What Zosima had said was; "Love to throw
yourself on the earth and kiss it. Kiss the earth and
love it with an unceasing, consuming love. Love all men,
love everything. Seek that rapture and ecstasy. Water
the earth with the tears of your joy and love those tears.
Don't be ashamed of that ecstasy, prize it, for it is a
gift of God and a great one; it is not given to many but
only to the elect."(7)   Alesha, upon awakening from his
dream, leaves the room abruptly. "Alyosha stood, gazed,
and suddenly threw himself down on the earth. He did not
know why he embraced it. He could not have told why he
longed so irresistibly to kiss it, to kiss it all. But he
kissed it weeping, sobbing and watering it with his tears,
and vowed passionately to love it, to love it for ever and

ever. 'Water the earth with the tears of your joy and
love those tears,' echoed in his soul...."(8)
     With Ivan Karamazov we have the remarkable "waking
dream" (what Jungians call "active imagination") in which
he engages in a dialogue with the devil. In active
imagination, according to Jungians, there is a deliberate
encounter with one's fantasies in an unstructured and
highly individual effort to increase inner awareness.
Ivan knows very well that the devil is a figment of
himself, and that he cannot evade the negative self-image
which is coming to him from his own unconscious. The
devil is a shadow figure, torturing Ivan with a relentless
insistence that he reexamine all his own former ideas and
ideals as though they were coming from someone else. It
is no accident that someone appears shabby and
supercilious. In this way Ivan is forced into an
objectivity in regard to himself that is painfully
humiliating. Yet Ivan is not so easily conquered by this
symbolic devil. Neither a waking nor a sleeping dream, at
this point, can break through the barriers of his
intellect. Alesha recognizes instinctively, in his first
real conversation with Ivan, that this "corn of wheat"
will not "die easily," for the trouble lies not with the
death of the spirit but with the tenacious life of a proud
ego. Ivan's encounter with the unconscious is therefore
inconclusive. The symbols of transformation have not yet
emerged; only the symbols of chaos which precede
transformation.
     A similar struggle dominates the character of
Raskolnikov in Crime and Punishment. Also a proud man of
intellect, he has two significant dreams. The first
transformation is aborted when the dream symbols prove to
be an ineffective match for his conscious obsession. It
is only after profound suffering and a physical illness
that Raskolnikov finally has the transformative dream.
When it comes, it is remarkable. This is a dream Jung
might call a "Great Dream" because it has collective
significance. The Great Dream is one which foretells the
destiny of mankind. These dreams, and the visions which
often accompany them, appear repeatedly in Dostoevski's
novels. It is through these dreams that we recognize what
Hesse describes as a return to the primitive depths in
order to bring forth new beginnings. For they all concern
the rebirth of the human spirit to a new kind of love and
a transformed consciousness. This process is most
sparingly described in Raskolnikov's dream. Another
version of it is expressed with more complexity through
Versilov's dream in A Raw Youth, and the fullest account
is presented in the vision of Zosima's mysterious visitor
in The Brothers Karamazov.
     These Great Dreams are characterized by three stages:
1. The new age is preceded by a period of chaos and
    nihilism, expressed as relativity in values,
    materialism, and extreme individualism.
2. The struggle for salvation comes through the work of a
    small number of elect.

3.   The elect usher in a new Golden Age of universal love,
      brotherhood, and a new spiritual consciousness. Using
      the three stages as a guiding thread, I would like to
      trace very briefly this development of the Great
      Dream.

THE FIRST STAGE--NIHILISM

The "microbe dream" of Raskolnikov describes very
dramatically the period of nihilism. In that dream the
whole world becomes diseased with microbes which infect
people with relativism. "Each thought that he alone had
the truth.... They accused one another, fought and killed
each other. There were conflagrations and famine. All
men and all things were involved in destruction...."(9)
In A Raw Youth Versilov describes his awakening from
the dream of a Golden Age into the reality of a nihilistic
Europe. "They are doomed," he states, "to strife for a
long time yet, because they are still too German and too
French and have not yet finished struggling in those
national characters. And I regret the destruction that
must come before they have finished.... Oh they are doomed
to pass through fearful agonies before they attain the
kingdom of God."(10)
In The Brothers Karamazov it is Zosima's visitor who
brings the vision of the new age. But he describes,
first, the "period of isolation" which precedes the new
age. He says:

> the isolation that prevails everywhere, above all in
> our age--has not fully developed, it has not reached
> its limit yet. For everyone strives to keep his
> individuality as apart as possible, wishes to secure
> the greatest possible fullness of life for himself;
> but meantime all his efforts result not in attaining
> fullness of life, but self-destruction, for instead
> of self-realization he ends by arriving at complete
> solitude . . . he has trained himself not to believe
> in the help of others...."(11)

THE SECOND STAGE--SALVATION THROUGH THE ELECT

Raskolnikov's dream ends with the following cryptic
reference to an elite who are destined to save the world.
"Only a few men could be saved in the whole world. They
were a pure chosen people, destined to found a new race
and a new life, to renew and purify the earth, but no one
had seen these men, no one had heard their words and their
voices."(12)
In A Raw Youth the elite is identified as the one
thousand aristocratic Russians, i.e., those Russians who,
by being most truly themselves, are the proponents of
universal brotherhood. Only these Russians are truly
"European," truly identified with humanity.
In The Brothers Karamazov Alesha is singled out as
one of the elect, and he accepts that responsibility. His
immediate response to his dream is to leave the monastery
for the world, and his first work as a member of the elect

is to convert Kolya and thereby reach all the boys.
"Hurray for Karamazov" both ends the book and signals the
beginning of the new universal brotherhood of man.
      But there is also the Russian Monk as described by
Zosima, who is not just any Russian monk. He is the
disciple of an Elder, an elect within an elite. It is the
task of this elect to keep the ideal alive. Zosima says:
"Sometimes even if he has to do it alone, and his conduct
seems to be crazy, a man must set an example, and so draw
men's souls out of their solitude, and spur them on to
some act of brotherly love, that the great idea may not
die."(13)

THE THIRD STAGE--THE REBIRTH OF HUMANITY

      The rebirth of humanity is only a prediction in
Raskolnikov's dream. But in A Raw Youth Versilov
describes a complex development. It begins with a dream
of the Golden Age, a primitive society of three thousand
years ago, the "cradle of Europe." Here was the earthly
paradise of man, where people lived happy and innocent
lives, filled with "simple-hearted joy and love."
Although the paradise is lost, it remains as a powerful
ideal. Versilov describes the new sensation with which he
awakened from that dream as "the love of all humanity."
That dream is followed by the vision of the "last day of
civilization" already described. Renewal, however, does
not immediately follow the nihilism. Instead, Versilov
pictures humanity undergoing a melancholy moment of truth
and coming to terms with its loss of the sustaining image
of God. Without the great idea of immortality all the
love and passion formerly accorded to God is turned upon,
he says, "the whole of nature, on the world, on men, on
every blade of grass: they would inevitably grow to love
the earth and life as they gradually became aware of their
own transitory and finite nature."(14) There is an
unmistakable similarity between the above passage and
Alesha's "loving the earth and watering it with his
tears." But the full meaning of this love does not emerge
until after humanity has learned to feel compassion for
all life; for it is only then that humanity is reborn and
God returns.
      Although at first glance this epic seems
uncharacteristic of Dostoevski, it is clearly a version of
the dream of the mysterious visitor in The Brothers
Karamazov. In this dream, as in the transformed humanity
of Versilov's vision, "all are responsible to all for
all." The most important prophecy in regard to this
rebirth of humanity is contained in the following passage:

      Believe me, this dream, as you call it, will
      come to pass without doubt, it will come, but
      not now, for every process has its law. It's a
      spiritual, psychological process. To transform
      the world, to recreate it afresh, men must turn
      into another path psychologically. Until you
      have become really, in actual fact, a brother to
      everyone, brotherhood will not come to pass....

> You ask when it will come to pass; it will come
> to pass, but first we have to go through the
> period of isolation.(15)

Zosima uses a metaphor to express the common tie between
all living beings, "All is like an ocean, all is flowing
and blending; a touch in one place sets up movement at the
other end of the earth." His message to Alesha to "love
the earth, birds, animals, trees" is an expression of this
connectedness. As in Versilov's vision, it is not until
this love becomes a reality that mankind becomes
transformed, and only then does the divine mystery become
manifest. Although the culmination of Versilov's vision
is the reappearance of God, Zosima is far less orthodox.
In fact, his mythology is more suggestive of science
fiction. He says: "Much on earth is hidden from us, but
to make up for that we have been given a precious mystic
sense of our living bond with the other world... the roots
of our thoughts and feelings are not here but in other
worlds... God took seeds from different worlds and sowed
them on this earth ... what grows lives and is alive only
through the feeling of its contact with other mysterious
worlds."(16) Universal love "alters one's consciousness."
This is the secret behind the transformation of Versilov's
mythical civilization, and the aim of Zosima's teaching.
Alesha, weeping and kissing the earth, experiences the
mystic unity described by Zosima. Through his ability to
love all creation, Alesha has connected with the invisible
worlds which confirm him as one of the elect.
    In this projection of a future Golden Age there seems
very little of traditional Christianity. Rather, it
suggests an evolutionary possibility. In other words, the
"altered state of consciousness" experienced by Alesha, as
one of the elect, is an intimation of the potentialities
of the human race. The injunction to love all creation
is, to twentieth century ears, an increasingly appropriate
corrective for a past which has culminated in our
threatening not only all life on this planet, but the very
earth itself. Thus Alesha's ecstatic experience with the
earth speaks directly to modern man as a crucial and
necessary requirement for his own renewal. The
implication for us is that when that responsible caring
for everything permeates human consciousness, then the
psychological transformation which the mysterious visitor
describes as a "law" will bring about the rebirth of
humanity to a new understanding of universal brotherhood.
    For the above reasons I would argue that Dostoevski's
prophetic vision is not to be identified with a
traditional Christian viewpoint, nor is it one which we
have outgrown. In fact, his vision of a future universal
brotherhood is embodied in the proliferating popular
literature of today. The Aquarian Age we are awaiting in
the twenty-first century promises just such a breakthrough
to new levels of consciousness. With the added threat of
a nuclear holocaust we have an even greater need for a
defense which stresses the interconnectedness of all life.
The period of isolation which Dostoevski described is with
us today. But the dream of a rebirth of humanity gives us

a limit to the isolation, and the hope of transforming
fate into destiny.

At the least we can point to the significance of the
dream itself as evidence that Dostoevski read the future
correctly. For we are looking with increasing interest to
the dream as a source of self-knowledge. In a recent book
Montague Ullman, one of the most prominent workers in the
field of dream experimentation, argues that dreams heal
because they give us information through metaphorical
images which allow us to recognize our mistaken
attitudes.(17) But even more pertinent is the fact that
he offers support for Dostoevski's characterization of the
Great Dream:

> When we go to sleep and start to dream, we begin
> to focus, not on our separateness, but on
> shortening this emotional space.... It is as if
> our dreaming self is still concerned with
> certain fundamental facts that we seem to have
> neglected down through the course of human
> history: that we are all members of a single
> species; that the essence of being human is
> being connected with other humans; and that the
> schisms we have set up have kept us from
> realizing that vision when we are awake, a
> vision that has never been lost while we
> dream.(18)

We must agree, then, with Hesse when he names Dostoevski
the prophet of the renewal of Western man. Such a renewal
is certainly behind Jung's claim that modern man is
fascinated by his own unconscious, searching within
himself for the missing God. In any event, we cannot deny
our present preoccupation with the unconscious, which is
also the language of our dreams.

Nietzsche predicted it would take two hundred years
to work through the implications of the death of God. If
we take his timetable, we have still one hundred years in
which to learn the healing love which Dostoevski tells us
will transform our consciousness and bring us to the new
age of universal brotherhood. If we listen to our dreams,
as he suggests and Montague confirms, we should become
increasingly aware of the inter-connectedness of all life,
that "it is all like an ocean." Dostoevski saw our
predicament one hundred years ago. For that alone he has
earned our respect. But he also saw our solution and had
the courage to tell us, even if it meant that he was only
"keeping the great idea alive." What more can one ask of
a prophet?

NOTES

1. Hermann Hesse, "The Brothers Karamazov, or the "Decline of Europe," in My Belief (New York: Farrar, Straus and Giroux, 1974).

2. Fyodor Dostoevski, The Brothers Karamazov, trans. Constance Garnett (New York: Modern Library, 1950), pp. 26, 27.

3. Ibid., Frontispiece, pp. 339, 370.

4. C. G. Jung, Memories, Dreams, Reflections (New York: Vintage Books, 1961), pp. 152-155.

5. C. G. Jung, Dreams (Princeton: Princeton University Press, 1974), p. 73.

6. Ibid., pp. 30, 31.

7. Dostoevski, Brothers Karamazov, p. 387.

8. Ibid., pp. 436, 437.

9. Fyodor Dostoevski, Crime and Punishment, trans. Constance Garnett (New York: Random House, 1956), pp. 488, 489.

10. Fyodor Dostoevski, A Raw Youth, trans. Constance Garnett (London: William Heinemann Ltd., 1916), p. 462.

11. Dostoevski, Brothers Karamazov, p. 363.

12. Dostoevski, Crime and Punishment, p. 489. An interesting comparison might be made between the extraordinary man of Raskolnikov's earlier theory and the spiritual and moral elite of his dream, i.e., is Raskolnikov reinterpreting his theory from a different center of reference?

13. Dostoevski, Brothers Karamazov, p. 364.

14. Ibid., pp. 466, 467.

15. Ibid., pp. 362, 363. In Psychology Today, August 1980, is the following article: "The Age of Indifference. . . . Survival demands collective action, yet the cancer of isolation is spreading across the land."

16. Ibid., pp. 384, 385.

17. Montague Ullman and Nan Zimmerman, Working with Dreams (New York: Delacorte Press, 1979).

18. Ibid., pp. 89-90.

19.
Between Heaven and Hell: The Dialectic of Dostoevski's Tragic Vision
ANTHONY S. MAGISTRALE

That Dostoevski belongs to the tragic tradition can be accepted with little argument. For tragedy, at its most significant and broadest level, is not simply death and suffering. Nor is it simply any response to these events. Rather, it is concerned with locating man's relation to himself, to other men, and to the larger universe. The central difference between the world of classical and Shakespearean tragedy, and the tragic world, prophetic of our own time, which Dostoevski envisioned, consists of the place of man in the scheme of the universe. In Dostoevski's fiction, the problem is not one of values or loyalties--as is the case with an Oedipus or Othello--but of a complete bankruptcy of all values and loyalties, a bankruptcy which leaves the individual with little or no sense of cosmic integration. Dostoevski's tragic heroes do not have the satisfaction of clear and present opponents--an unjust divinity, ungrateful daughters, or an oppressive social and religious code. His major characters struggle not so much with a crisis as with a condition; and this condition is the contemporary confusion of values and the dilemma within man's soul.(1) This helps to explain the incessant struggle within Dostoevski's most engaging characters: these individuals seek to define their identities whether through rebellion against the traditional values of social man, which is in keeping with the modern spirit, or by passive acceptance of the Christian axiom that suffering and surrendering to godly justice corrects all transgressions. His characters are so vivid precisely because Dostoevski himself, in contrast to the Greeks or Shakespeare, was never able to resolve completely this conflict between two antithetical positions. No classical or Elizabethan hero was ever "lost" in the sense that occurs in Dostoevski.

To illustrate the complexity of Dostoevski's tragic scheme, let us examine in some detail two representative characters. Raskolnikov and Myshkin are emblematic of the two most obsessive concerns in the novelist's canon: the intellectual rebel, a figure that includes Ivan Karamazov, the underground man, and Nikolai Stavrogin; and the sainted figure, in whom Sonya Marmeladov, Alesha Karamazov, and Father Zosima would be seen as Myshkin's spiritual kin.(2) Because the worlds of <u>The Idiot</u> and

Crime and Punishment are radically different, it is impossible to speak of Dostoevski's conception of tragedy as
the same in both books. Yet there is at the center of
these two novels a fundamental artistic conflict that
results in tragedy. The struggle between good and evil is
at the core of every Dostoevski novel. Again and again
the writer felt compelled to delve more deeply into it.
And he did so, granting more and more stature to his
antagonists, in order to test the Christian belief which
states that man is capable of rising above sin. As
Dostoevski developed as a novelist and a theologian, he
came to recognize the need for man to establish a
difficult, but necessary balance between the forces of
good and evil contained within himself. When tragedy
occurs in Dostoevski's fictional world, it is because this
precarious balance has been disturbed. Raskolnikov's
superman theory and Myshkin's innocent purity are the two
extremes in the writer's dialectic. They both give birth
to tragedy because each position lacks an effective and
adequate counterpoint.
     Outwardly, Raskolnikov resembles characters embodying
classical qualities of the tragic hero. Like Sophocles's
Antigone, or Milton's Satan, Raskolnikov is rebelling
against both society and established morality. He is akin
also to Shakespeare's Macbeth or Byron's Manfred in
asserting his own godliness in the face of the universe.
Like the tragic heroes of the Greeks and Shakespeare,
Raskolnikov is endowed with a certain degree of free will.
He is able to exert his will upon circumstance:
Raskolnikov decides to kill, he is not driven to do so.(3)
On the other hand, while the tragic hero acts freely, we
sense that, at certain points, he is helpless to alter the
course of his destruction. Desdemona, for example, loses
her handkerchief at the worst possible time. Similarly,
throughout Crime and Punishment, it seems that accident or
chance, not logic, prompts Raskolnikov to action. For
example, Raskolnikov elects to murder the pawnbroker after
accidentally learning that Lizaveta will not be home.
Moreover, he avoids immediate capture after committing the
crimes because fate happened to place an empty apartment
under the pawnbroker's. The difference between
Raskolnikov and the figures of classical tragedy lies in
the intensity of suffering and self-disgust that
Raskolnikov feels from the moment he conceives of his
crime. If Raskolnikov moved in the realm of Lear,
Othello, or even Oedipus, the suffering he is forced to
undergo would produce a corresponding spiritual cleansing.
The tragic world of Crime and Punishment, however, is more
complicated, less easily resolved, and Dostoevski himself
less sure of where he stood in the war that tears at
Raskolnikov's soul. We are left with only a sense of
movement toward the direction of Raskolnikov's future
life. And even this must be severely qualified in light
of a superimposed Epilogue and Raskolnikov's own belief
that "he was further than ever from seeing that what he
did was a crime."(4) While it is true that both the
influence of the other characters (especially Sonya) and
Raskolnikov's personal struggles with good and evil give

some substance to the promise of resurrection that
Dostoevski projects in the Epilogue, it is equally
important to remember that Raskolnikov never believes he
is wrong in formulating his extraordinary man theory. He
believes he has a right to transgress moral laws when he
lies in his attic room, when he kills the moneylender,
when he goes to follow Sonya's advice and "seek his
punishment" and, finally, when he commences his sentence
in Siberia. Raskolnikov actively seeks punishment from
the moment he commits the crime; but his repentance is
indeed another issue, and one which Dostoevski leaves
unresolved.

     We run into similar problems in the character of Ivan
Karamazov. Like Raskolnikov, he begins to move into doubt
and suffering. His "gentleman-devil" appears--in a role
similar to Porfiry's in Crime and Punishment--to help him
articulate the "other side" of his personality: the side
that yearns to believe with the simple-hearted faith of a
peasant. His complete physical and mental breakdown is
symptomatic of a moral collapse as well as an indication
of the suffering he is undergoing in re-evaluating his
earlier "everything is allowed" theories. However, just
when the light of salvation appears to break through this
internalized dialectic to create a synthesis, Dostoevski
removes Ivan from the scene. We do not witness the dawn,
and the unconscious, feverish Ivan we leave at the end of
The Brothers Karamazov is not given positive hopes for
recovery (Epilogue, chapter one). Even if Ivan should
revive physically, there is no evidence that he will ever
come to embrace the position represented by Father Zosima
and Alesha. Once again, as in Crime and Punishment, we
are left with movement, but no resolution. Ivan's future,
like Raskolnikov's, is left decidedly open.

     Everywhere in Dostoevski, argues Andre Gide,
characters achieve the kingdom of heaven only by the
denial of mind and will and the surrender of
personality.(5) Two other highly respected scholars of
Dostoevski's work, Mochulsky and Berdyaev, similarly
stress the significance of the redemptive theme in his
canon. Berdyaev's notes: "Men . . . learn from inner
experience the nothingness of evil, how it defeats and
destroys itself while it is being experienced, and when
they have purged themselves of it they reach the light.
. . . At the same time it must be recognized that nobody
has fought against the principle of evil and the powers of
darkness more courageously than Dostoevski did."(6) If we
assume that these critics are correct in evaluating
Dostoevski as working on the side of the angels, fighting
against "the principle of evil and the powers of
darkness," why was he never able to consign his
intellectual rebels to a position that went beyond
implication, to a point at which a secure resolution,
based firmly on the side of goodness, is uncovered and
dramatized? When one examines the strength and
persuasiveness with which Dostoevski infuses his rebels,
the impossibility of having them wholly renounce their
theories, value systems, and allegiances becomes not only
an artistic concern of accuracy in relation to character

portrayal, but enlarges to focus on Dostoevski's
conception of man, a being caught in a moral contest in
which the need for humility and the rejection of self-will
is in constant conflict against the powers of darkness.
Dostoevski, perhaps like Blake's Milton, was unable to
relinquish his fascination with evil because he knew that
mortal man could not. This is why it is as impossible for
Raskolnikov or Ivan Karamazov as for their creator to
resolve the duality of human nature by accepting either
route as an absolute solution: the path of blood and
crime to power or the road of submission and suffering to
a Christ-like transcendence. Furthermore, this position
of transcendence that Raskolnikov and Ivan Karamazov seem
to be looking toward at the end of each respective book,
is the very region where Prince Myshkin lives and moves.
It is an internal realm in which there exists no duality,
a realm where evil thrives only outside the mind of the
Prince. But it is the magnitude of this evil, and the
inability of the Prince himself to project a workable
alternative to it, that ultimately conquers the purity of
Myshkin and leads him and those immediately connected to
him into a descent to destruction.

In perhaps no other Dostoevski novel is the power of
darkness more effectively revealed than in The Idiot. The
novelist's diaries, notebooks, and letters leave no doubt
that Myshkin was conceived as a Christ-figure. He not
only physically resembles the image of Christ in Russian
icons, but is also involved in a "spiritual mission" that
posits nothing less than a Russian moral reawakening
through the virtues of love and humility. Each time the
Prince begins to expound on these virtues or attempts to
put them into practice, however, he invariably creates
discord within other people, whose usual reaction is to
dismiss him.

Although the Prince is completely honest and desires
only happiness for the individuals he has become involved
with, contact with him for any protracted period of time
inevitably ends in disaster. It is of course his dark
brother, Rogozhin, who finally commits the murder that
brings Nastasya her "release" from a life of humiliation
and deceit, but Myshkin, because of his excess of
compassion rather than love, is equally responsible for
the act. Like King Lear, Myshkin suffers from self-
blindness. But the Prince's tragedy arises out of pity
rather than love. He "loves" both Nastasya and Aglaia,
yet his love encompasses neither of them.(7) Asexual, he
is incapable of understanding Nastasya, at least on a
human level. And Nastasya recognizes that, although he
will always pity her, he will never be capable of giving
her love.

The question, then, is how can a "positively good
man" fail so tragically? Perhaps the reason for his
failure is found in this very definition of a man who is
"positively good." Myshkin is totally unable to interact
with anyone on a human plane--he is the embodiment of a
Divine love which the rest of the world can neither
understand nor is prepared to accept. Aglaia and Nastasya
yearn for his strength and endurance, but he can give them

only superhuman pity and subhuman affection. Like
Quixote, to whom he is often compared, and out of date in
an age no longer chivalrous, Myshkin is equally
inappropriate as a saint in a fiendish world. As
Dostoevski illustrates, Myshkin's struggle is useless:
both his methods and his aims are futile. The Prince
remains incapable of achieving the highest level of
expression available in Dostoevski's oeuvre; for in his
fiction, in order to ascend one must first descend. It is
for this reason that Myshkin's "mission," like Christ's,
ends in failure. Had either "succeeded" in his goal of
spiritual reformation, man would relinquish those dual
aspects of good and evil, and his free will would be
meaningless. Rather, man would take on the kind of
one-dimensional characterization that the Grand Inquisitor
so effectively outlines. In Dostoevski's tragic realm,
the passive example of goodness is not sufficient as a
guide to salvation; an active immersion is also necessary
if man is to retain his human dualism and thereby
recognize his bond, to borrow from Hawthorne, with the
"electric chain of humanity." As Hawthorne and Dostoevski
both knew, this "chain" possesses within it the potential
for moral growth, but this potential is realized only
after the individual has gained an active awareness of
sin.
        Dostoevski's characters were never able to resolve
the coexistence in their own natures of what Dmitri
Karamazov labelled the "ideal of Sodom" and the "ideal of
the Madonna." Dostoevski's own search for God led him
into the same vein of doubt that runs through his
intellectual rebels. While his intellect sympathized with
the profound casuistry of an Ivan Karamazov or a
Raskolnikov, who feel there can be no loving God in a
world of meaningless suffering, his heart empathized with
the precepts of his sainted characters, Sonya, Myshkin,
Alesha, and Zosima, who believe that salvation can be
achieved only through suffering and love. Thus,
Dostoevski's notion of tragedy, unlike that of the Greeks
and the Elizabethans, did not tend toward the
reconciliation of opposites, toward wholeness and
affirmation. Rather, like Nathaniel Hawthorne and
Flannery O'Connor, Dostoevski felt that while antithetical
positions might be synthesized in Christ, the mortal
sphere has not yet become His realm, and that, although
there may be wholeness in a domain beyond the earthly one,
ultimate solutions are not appropriate in the human world.
        For the length of his tenure on earth, man, in
Dostoevski's eyes, is at best incomplete. There exists a
recognition of moral direction and an evolving sense of
self-awareness available to characters such as Raskolnikov
and Ivan Karamazov, but these are always qualified by an
awareness of evil that constrains man in a precarious
balance between heaven and hell. The only certainty
available to man in Dostoevski's tragic realm arises from
the paradoxical principle of equipose: balancing the evil
in one's nature through love, humility, and suffering.
This is Myshkin's real problem in The Idiot: he can never
attain equipose (or even establish a movement toward this

balance) because he does not contain an evil principle.
The spiritual conflicts in Dostoevski represent the most
vital element in his fiction. Yet his final statements at
the conclusions of his best work usually result in
severely qualified moral development, ambiguity, or
ethical impasse. This has bothered many readers who seek
a sharper, more definitive stance in relation to those
moral and philosophical concerns that the novelist chose
to explore. The evil of Raskolnikov's superman theory or
the goodness of Myshkin's humility are the two extremes,
but they are by no means complete in themselves. For
Dostoevski's work, like Rembrandt's, is bathed in shadow,
and the shadows are essential. There are flashes of
light, transient moments of illuminating awareness, but
this is all. The reader must always return, like Jacob
and the angel, to struggling within the darkness.

NOTES

1. Richard Sewall, The Vision of Tragedy (New Haven:
Yale University Press, 1959), p. 110.

2. While it is appropriate to make connections
between Myshkin and Alyosha, we must never forget that
Dostoevski's first attempt to portray a "positively good
man" in The Idiot, failed to satisfy the writer. In The
Brothers Karamazov, Dostoevski once again drew a portrait
of moral perfection. But unlike the earlier Myshkin, who
is a holy fool, epileptic, and completely out of place in
an unholy world, Alyosha is a Karamazov, and thus contains
an active principle of worldly evil. It is because of
this aspect of his Karamazov nature that he matures beyond
the Prince and becomes a part of the human world.

3. There exist several mirror characters to
Raskolnikov in Crime and Punishment; they represent the
unique and sometimes contradictory aspects of his personality. Svidrigailov reflects the student's penchant for
violence and evil, while Sonya embodies his capacities for
performing good. To some extent, Dostoevski creates the
character of Razumihin so that the latter might provide
yet another mirror to Raskolnikov in relation to the
subject of determinism. Razumihin faces almost the same
problems as Raskolnikov; nevertheless, he solves them
differently. He gives lessons and translates articles to
remain self-sufficient. Even Raskolnikov recognizes that
he too could earn a living in the same manner. He says so
to Sonya after the murder: "Razumihin works! But I
turned sulky and wouldn't" (375). Unlike Raskolnikov,
Razumihin does not have to contend with illusions of
intellectual superiority or the frustrations of a
poverty-stricken family.

4. Fyodor Dostoevski, Crime and Punishment, trans.
Constance Garnett (New York: Random House, 1950), p. 466.

5. Andre Gide, Dostoevski (New York: New Directions, 1961), p. 90.

6. Nicholas Berdyaev, Dostoevski (New York: World Publishing, 1957), pp. 92-93.

7. Richard Curle, Characters of Dostoevski (New York: Russell and Russell, 1966), pp. 88-89.

20.
Dostoevski and George Sand:
Two Opponents of the Anthill
ISABELLE NAGINSKI

The death of George Sand on June 8, 1876 marked the end of
an era. With the exception of Victor Hugo, who died in
1885, she was the last of France's great Romantic
prosateurs.(1) In the funeral oration which Hugo composed
for Sand, he stressed the symbolic meaning of the event.
He placed her in a generation which included Barbes,
Balzac, Lamartine, Quinet, and Michelet: "Each time one
of these powerful human creatures dies, we can hear
something resembling the enormous noise of wings;
something goes off, something unexpectedly takes place ...
the torch, which was a man or a woman and which became
extinguished in this form, lights up again in the form of
an idea."(2) It was precisely as an idea that George Sand
interested the Russian intelligentsia, specifically
Dostoevski. Reactions to the news of Sand's passing were
not confined to the French literary world, or indeed to
Western Europe. In distant Petersburg Dostoevski offered
his readers two whole articles devoted to Sand. His Diary
of a Writer provided the platform for voicing his
reactions to the loss of this "poet-innovator," as he
called her. The two articles, "The Death of George Sand"
and "A Few Words About George Sand," are crucial to our
understanding of several points in the literary traffic
between Russia and France in the nineteenth century.
First, they delineate the meaning of Sand's writing for
the various Russian intellectual milieux of the 1830s and
1840s. Second, they articulate the ideological kinship
between the two writers. Finally, they provide an insight
into the literary relationship between Sand and
Dostoevski.
    In tracing the impact of Sand on an entire generation
of intelligenty, Dostoevski emphasized the nurturing
effect of Sand's early works on a young emerging writer of
the 1840s, himself:(3)

>   Many will smile perhaps when they read of the
>   significance which I attribute to George Sand;
>   but such people would be mistaken to make fun of
>   me ... everything that in the appearance of this
>   poet constituted a "new word," everything that
>   was "all-human," all this at the time made on
>   us, on our Russia, a strong and deep impression,

did not escape us and thus demonstrated that
every poet-innovator in Europe, every poet
appearing there with a new idea and a new force,
cannot help but become immediately a Russian
poet, cannot escape Russian thought, and cannot
help but become practically a Russian force.(4)

The remarkable power of George Sand's voice in Russia
can be explained partially by the fact that, since 1825,
virtually every foreign book concerned with social
questions was forbidden entry into Russia; works by
Fourier or Saint-Simon, for instance, had to be smuggled
in and read secretly. But there was a loophole in the
censorship: foreign novels could be imported. Thus
George Sand's works became a medium through which social
ideas from the West could infiltrate Russia. For Russian
intellectuals she became "the propagandist of the new
ideas from the West, ideas of humanitarian socialism and
the emancipation of women."(5) In his articles,
Dostoevski confirms this ideological appeal of George
Sand's works for the Thirties and Forties:

George Sand . . . immediately assumed among us
practically the first place among an entire
Pleiad of new writers who, at the time, had
suddenly risen to fame and become famous
throughout Europe. Even Dickens, who appeared
in Russia practically at the same time as her,
was not as popular . . . . The main thing was
that the reader was able to extract even from
novels everything against which he had been
warned. At least in the mid-forties in Russia,
even the majority of readers knew, if only
partially, that George Sand was one of the most
brilliant, strict and authentic representatives
of that category of new people from the West who
had appeared at the time and had begun by
directly negating those "positive" acquisitions
by which the bloody French (or rather, European)
revolution had ended its work at the end of the
18th century. Once the revolution was over
(after Napoleon I), new attempts were made to
express new longings and new ideals.(6)

Although the dominating tone of his two articles is
overwhelmingly positive, Dostoevski nonetheless judged
that Sand's impact on Russian thought had been restricted
to two decades. His denial of the lasting effect of this
"idealist of the thirties and forties"(7) can be discerned
in the following passage:

by the mid-forties George Sand's glory and the
faith we all had in her genius stood so high
that all of us, her contemporaries, expected
from her something incomparably greater in the
future, some new word which had not yet been
heard, even something decisive and definitive.
These hopes were not realized; it seemed at the

time, i.e. at the end of the forties, that she
had already said everything that she had been
destined to express.(8)

Dostoevski sees Sand as an artifact of the 1840s, as a
writer whose influence was short-lived because her thought
could not grow, could not keep up with the surge of that
"powerful, self-confident and . . . sick century."(9)
Sand, that "sphinx with the golden gaze,"(10) to use
Flaubert's formula, could no longer see the world in its
true light. Her task accomplished, the towering idol was
destined to fall.

Dostoevski, here, is partly reflecting the
stereotypical attitude toward Sand in the late nineteenth
century. Even Henry James, though generally well-disposed
and often laudatory toward Sand, expressed a similar
severe judgment: "Realism had been invented, or rather
propagated; and in the light of Madame Bovary, [Sand's]
own facile fiction began to be regarded as the work of
some sort of superior Mrs. Radcliffe. She was antiquated;
she belonged to the infancy of art."(11) The sub-textual
issue here is the tension between the values of
Romanticism and those of Realism. Henry James, although
an admirer of Sand, was convinced of the superiority of
the latter movement, and thus could make neat categories
in which to fit the "infancy" and "adulthood" of art.

But Dostoevski, rather than actually restricting
Sand's importance to the Romantic era, as he first claimed
to be doing, found that her so-called antiquated opinions
and values were still valid in the 1870s. Indeed, by
stressing the ever- present power of Sand's ideas on his
own ideological development, he undermined his earlier
statement just quoted. Thus Dostoevski's articles in a
sense "recuperated" George Sand's ideology of the 1840s
and "recycled" it into something still valid thirty years
later. By expressing his feeling of solidarity with her,
Dostoevski made Sand into a fellow-opponent of what he so
pointedly called the Anthill. In Notes from Underground
and elsewhere he used this term to deconstruct the
symbolic meaning of that architectural structure which
the Socialists so grandly called the Crystal Palace, a
building signifying Brotherly Love and Harmony for the
Socialists, but only totalitarian terrorism for
Dostoevski. In The Diary of a Writer he made Sand his
ally and, in so doing, an enemy of Chernyshevski's utopian
phalanstery: "George Sand was, perhaps, one of the most
perfect confessors of Christ.... She based her Socialism,
her convictions, hopes and ideals on the moral feeling of
human beings, on the spiritual thirst of humankind, on its
striving toward perfection and purity, and not on
"ant-necessity" (murav'inaia neobkhodimost')."(12) The
formula "ant-necessity" makes clear that, for Dostoevski,
Sand was an enemy of systems which in the name of justice
and equality create limitless despotism.(13) This
ideological alliance between the two writers is based on
their common belief in the spiritual essence of mankind.

Furthermore, by insisting on Sand's prophetic voice,
Dostoevski updated her message, so that her "new word,"

directed at France in the 1840s, retained validity for the
Russia of the 1880s. When Dostoevski claimed that George
Sand "was one of the most clairvoyant foreseers (odna iz
samykh iasnovidiashchikh predchuvstvennits) . . . of a
happier future awaiting humankind,"(14) he was in fact
already striving toward a definition of what he later
called "Russian socialism." In the last installment of
The Diary of a Writer, he gave an expanded version of this
ideal socialism:

> I am now referring to our Russian "socialism",
> whose goal and final outcome is a church of all
> peoples and all the universe, established on
> earth. . . . I am talking about the constant and
> inherent thirst of the Russian people for a
> great, universal, brotherly fellowship in the
> name of Christ. . . . Not in communism, not in
> mechanical forms does the socialism of the
> Russian people consist: The people believe that
> they will be saved at the end of time by the
> universal union in the name of Christ. That is
> our Russian socialism.(15)

By stressing Sand's universality ("everything in the
appearance of this poet ... that was all-human), by
insisting on the religious aspects of socialism,
Dostoevski transformed Sand into an ideological ally apres
la lettre.
     In The Diary of a Writer Dostoevski was primarily
interested in collecting raw material--facts, faits
divers, events, anecdotes, reflections--to incorporate
into his literary system of ideas. As deeply and
sincerely as he felt the loss of George Sand, his two
articles were not so much necrologies as the expression in
rough form of ideas or theories which he expressed again
later in a more polished form and in other texts. That
major portions of The Diary of a Writer served as
preliminary notebooks for The Brothers Karamazov, for
instance, is generally recognized. We know that the
profuse materials on children in the Diary were a
foundation-text for The Brothers Karamazov.(16) As early
as January 1876, Dostoevski was writing in the Diary that
he was contemplating "writing a novel about present-day
children and about their present-day fathers in their
present-day mutual interrelations."(17) I think, however,
that the George Sand articles also have a connection with
the Brothers Karamazov, a connection which is difficult to
discern because Dostoevski is not very clear, either
deliberately so as to cover his tracks, or more likely,
because he is unconscious of the connection. In any case,
the two Sand articles are fascinating not only for what
they reveal, but for what they conceal about the concrete
artistic impact of Sand on the Russian writer.
     In the first of the Sand articles, Dostoevski only
once tries to identify the literary impact of a Sand text
on his own writing. What he identifies are character
types: "Many ... of her heroines represented a type of
such elevated moral purity that it could not have been

imagined without a great moral quest in the soul of the
poet herself."(18)   As Dostoevski describes the heroines
in Sand's Venetian novels, L'Uscoque and La Derniere
Aldini, in her pastoral tale, Jeanne, and in "the
magnificent story,"(19) La Marquise, the reader
experiences an uncanny feeling that the women described
resemble the characters of a Dostoevski novel.   They
possess "proud chastity," thirst for "magnanimous
sacrifice," and display "strength of innocence, honesty
and purity."(20)   Robert Jackson, in his most recent book
on Dostoevski, has proposed a link between this evaluation
of Sand's characters and the writer's own heroine in "A
Gentle Creature: "Without any question, Dostoevsky's
story 'The Gentle Creature', which appeared in the
November 1876 issue of Diary of a Writer, less than half a
year after his articles on George Sand, gives evidence of
his veneration of the French writer."(21)
     But although Dostoevski acknowledges the literary
impact of Sand's early archetypical heroines on his own
creative imagination, these have little bearing on
Brothers Karamazov.   Sand's "influence" on Dostoevski's
last novel must be understood in a larger, more fluid
sense.   In his late years Dostoevski was returning to the
influences of his youth, casting a backward glance on the
literary models of his apprentice years.   By filtering his
admiration through his own rich experience as an
accomplished writer, he repossessed and creatively
transformed such influences.   "A Gentle Creature" attests
to Sand's lingering presence in Dostoevski's mind for
months after he had composed his necrologies.   In view of
this, we can only suppose that the two Sand articles
allowed certain Sandian themes to come to the forefront of
his literary reflections.   Dostoevski's remarkable memory
for print and his masterful assimilation of all that he
read encourage me to speculate that George Sand
undoubtedly did inspire certain aspects of Brothers
Karamazov, but not in the restricted sense the Sand
articles might suggest.   Rather, there is an uncanny
series of correspondences between Dostoevski's masterwork
and a novel by Sand which he does not even mention.
Paradoxically, the novel in questions does not contain a
single woman character.   The novel is Spiridion and in the
space that remains I will examine the possible connections
between Sand's obscure and remarkable novel and
Dostoevski's well-known and likewise remarkable work.
     We cannot even assert unequivocally that Dostoevski
read Spiridion.   However, circumstances strongly suggest
that he had.   For one thing, as Joseph Frank notes in the
first volume of his biography, "we know that Dostoevsky
read [Sand's] L'Uscoque, which was published in the Revue
des deux mondes in 1838.   Spiridion began to appear in the
same publication the very same year and the eminently
respectable journal was certainly available in the French
library to which Dostoevsky was a subscriber."(22)
Secondly, the Soviet critic, Leonid Grossman, believes
that Spiridion must have been on Dostoevski's mind as
early as the end of 1868, when he was contemplating his
epic novel, Atheism, and again in the spring of 1870, when

he had renamed the work "Life of a Great Sinner" (the Russian zhitie, life, with its hagiographic connotations, immediately calls to mind the genre of a saint's life):

> In Belinski's circle in the early 1840s, an original and fascinating book by George Sand, Spiridion, was very much appreciated. Panaev had translated parts of it especially for Belinski and Nekrasov. It is quite possible that, filled with enthusiasm for George Sand's works, Dostoevski read this novel in his youth and discerned in it then a new, original and daring genre, which combined contemporary politics with religious and philosophical problems which, undoubtedly, corresponded to some hidden creative tendencies in the young writer. He valued this attempt at an ideological and contemporary epic and turned to it at the time he was planning his book on atheism, and ten years later, when he was planning his last novel, The Brothers Karamazov.(23)

In fact, the basic problems posed in Spiridion are so close to Dostoevski's own concerns that it is hard to imagine that he would not have been much impressed by Sand's novel: "[Spiridion] posed the essential problem of the time: socialism or Christianity? This problem already agitated Dostoevski in his youth and it lay, though from a different perspective, at the basis of his last novel. On the whole, Spiridion was a large-scale critique of Catholicism against a background of Utopian socialist ideas."(24)

In terms of plot-structure, the correlations between Spiridion and Brothers Karamazov are remarkable. Inasmuch as Spiridion corresponds to the plan for Dostoevski's masterwork, it could be subtitled "Confessions of a Great Sinner." The novel takes place in the eighteenth century and ends in the midst of the violence of the French Revolution. The hero is the monk Alexis who recounts his spiritual biography to a young novice. His narration of the journey from traditional faith to philosophical doubt, then to despairing atheism, and finally to a form of humanitarian and pro-revolutionary deism constitutes a veritable "encyclopedia of beliefs,"(25) comparable to what Dostoevski had dreamed of producing in Atheism. The spiritual itinerary of one tortured soul who tracks down the truth by reading exhaustively liturgical, heretical, and philosophical texts and proceeds to inform the reader of his ideological travels by means of an oral confession to his spiritual heir--this rhetorical formula is one which would have pleased Dostoevski's literary sensibility. In fact, it is interesting that Spiridion which begins as a first-person narrative in the voice of the young novice, Angel, soon gives way to a dialogue between the novice and his teacher, and then is quickly taken over by Alexis whose monologue is both a philosophical and ideological testament.

The dialogue form leading into monologue is
reminiscent of a Dostoevskian device. Ippolit's
monological confession in The Idiot, for example, emerges
from the general drawing-room conversation. Ivan's
"Legend of the Grand Inquisitor" grows out of a
conversation with his brother. The character who becomes
a narrator within the novel, such are Alexis in Spiridion
and countless protagonists in Dostoevski's novels. What
Bakhtin has called "the motif of the speaking person" in
the novel,(26) a motif most often identified with
Dostoevskian discourse, is already worked out extensively
in Spiridion and constitutes one of the main rhetorical
devices of the novel.
    For the reader who is only distantly acquainted with
George Sand's literary output, and who contents himself
with stereotypical notions of what constitutes a Sand
novel, Spiridion will seem quite untypical. Even more
surprising is the importance Sand herself ascribed to the
book. In Histoire de ma vie she went so far as to say:
"If I had wanted to show the serious foundation [of my
life], I would have told a life which resembled more the
life of the monk Alexis (in the novel . . . Spiridion)
than the life of Indiana, the passionate Creole girl."(27)
    Spiridion, then, is a multifarious text,
incorporating elements of autobiography (one could point
to parallel passages in the novel and Histoire de ma vie),
part philosophical treatise (the theories of Pierre
Leroux play an important role), part Gothic tale (certain
fantastic decors are straight out of Walpole's Castle of
Otranto or Ann Radcliffe's Mysteries of Udolpho), part
novel of initiation, a fertile genre in French literature
which includes Balzac's Seraphita, Nerval's Aurelia, and
Rimbaud's Une Saison en enfer.(28)
    Spiridion has no plot to speak of. The novel, set in
a monastery, is entirely made up of monologues and
dialogues between monks. The text is of one piece, with
no chapters or parts to halt the growing rhetorical power
of the book. Nothing truly happens--no events, no
adventures, no intrigues; no love interests--no one goes
anywhere or does anything. The novel's main theme is the
power of spoken and written words: conversations,
speeches, confessions (both oral and written), diaries,
prayers, religious and heretical texts, Alexis' "livre
blanc" whose writing is invisible, Spiridion's manuscript
buried in his tomb, voices of phantoms reciting prophetic
and cryptic words, oral doctrines passed on from father to
spiritual son. As such, the tone of the novel is strongly
reminiscent of the monological philosophical narratives in
Dostoevski's novels. The major areas of convergence of
Brothers Karamazov with Spiridion are its inserted
narratives, primarily Zosima's "Notes of the Life of God"
and Ivan's "Legend of the Grand Inquisitor."
    The relationship between Alesha and Zosima in
Brothers Karamazov is comparable to that of Angel and
Alexis. Like Zosima, Alexis is an old monk who lives
apart from the rest of the members of the monastery. Both
men are venerated yet viewed with suspicion by the other
monks. Both are encountered in the last months of their

lives and we see them choose heirs who care for them with
love and devotion. Both young men are left with some kind
of holy text. Alesha preserves in writing his last
conversations with Zosima. The narrative in Spiridion
contains the last conversations between Alexis and Angel.
The confessions of the two old monks are built around the
notion of conversion, from atheism to a fluid kind of
Christianity. Their final religious philosophy resembles
each other's more than either strict Orthodoxy or Roman
Catholicism. Their theological positions are strikingly
similar. They stand against rigid interpretations of
religious dogma, question the need for a hierarchical
church, favor a religion based on understanding with the
heart rather than the intellect, reserve an important role
for mystery, support the individual's quest for truth and
the need for freedom of choice. Both distinguish between
license and freedom, insist on the responsibility of each
for all. The life of the spirit is all-encompassing, with
death defined as a new life. These two parallel passages
will make apparent the resemblances between the two
articulations of doctrine. In Spiridion Alexis spells out
his idealist beliefs:

> "I believe," says Alexis, "in a perpetual
> engendering of souls which does not obey the law
> of matter or the ties of blood, but obeys
> mysterious laws and invisible ties.... For us
> there are two immortalities, both are material
> and immaterial; one is of this world and
> transmits our ideas and feelings to humanity
> through our works and deeds; the other is
> registered in a better world through our merit
> and our sufferings and preserves a providential
> power over men and things of this world."(29)

Zosima's words in Brothers Karamazov seem to echo
Alexis:

> Much on earth is hidden from us, but to make up
> for that we have been given a precious mystic
> sense of our living bond with the other world,
> with the higher heavenly world, and the roots of
> our thoughts and feelings are not here but in
> other worlds.... God took seeds from different
> worlds and sowed them on this earth, and His
> garden grew up and everything came up that could
> come up, but what grows lives and is alive only
> through the feeling of its contact with other
> mysterious worlds.(30)

Furthermore, one of the ideas which Alexis develops
in Spiridion is that man's fundamental nature is neither
materialistic nor rational. Although he stands in favor
of "the gigantic work of the French Revolution," he
insists that is main task is spiritual:

> It was not, it could not be, only a question of
> bread and shelter for the poor; it was a much

loftier goal ... which this Revolution, in fact,
was aiming for. Not only did it have to give a
legitimate well-being to the people, it had to,
it still must ... accomplish fully the task of
giving freedom of conscience to the entire human
race ... this soul which torments me, this
thirst for the infinite which devours me, will
they be satisfied and appeased because my body
is safe from want ... will the life of this
world suffice for men's desires, and will the
earth be vast enough for men's thoughts?(31)

At the end of the novel, Alexis is attacked and killed in
a church by revolutionaries. His final words are of
forgiveness for those who do not know what they are doing.
The mission of the Revolution is expressed in religious
terms: "We are only images that are being shattered
because they no longer represent the ideas which made
their strength and their holiness. This is the work of
Providence, and the mission of our executioners is sacred,
although they themselves do not understand it yet.
Nevertheless, they said these words and you heard them:
it is in the name of the sans-culotte Jesus that they are
desecrating the sanctuary of the church."(32)
     The theme of "not by bread alone" and the use of a
religious vocabulary to articulate the meaning of the
Revolution--two notions which Dostoevski expounded in
Brothers Karamazov and Diary of a Writer. When, in "The
Legend," the Grand Inquisitor accuses Christ of putting
the spiritual over the material, he is defined by
Dostoevski as a builder of "one unanimous and harmonious
anthill":

You did reply that man lives not by bread alone.
But do You know that for the sake of the earthly
bread the spirit of the earth will rise up
against You and will strive with You and
overcome You ... Do you know that the ages will
pass, and humanity will proclaim by the lips of
their sages that there is no crime, and
therefore no sin; there is only hunger? "Feed
men, and then ask of them virtue!"... You did
promise them the bread of Heaven, but I repeat
again, can it compare with earthly bread in the
eyes of the weak, ever sinful and ignoble race
of man?(33)

Christ makes no answer to this but merely kisses his
tormentor. Alexis's words in Spiridion about his
tormentors seem to provide the answer Christ might have
given in "The Legend," so close are their two respective
positions.
     Finally, both the Grand Inquisitor and Donatien, the
prior of the monastery in Spiridion, two men in positions
of great spiritual power, share the same secret: they
have lost faith and are in alliance with the Other, with
Satan. Indeed, Dostoevski seems to be referring

specifically to <u>Spiridion</u> in his Sand article when he says:

> [Sand] believed unconditionally in the human
> personality (and even in its immortality), she
> magnified and developed its manifestation during
> her entire life, in each of her works and
> thereby became identified in thought and feeling
> with one of the basic tenets of Christianity,
> i.e. with the recognition of the human
> personality and its freedom.... And it may well
> be possible that there was no thinker or writer
> in the France of her time who possessed such a
> clear understanding that "man shall not live by
> bread alone."(34)

Despite Dostoevski's opinion, then, that "by the end of the 1840s [Sand] had already said everything that she was destined and predestined to express," we can see the vital impact that Sand's writing and thought had on the Russian writer's last novel, an impact that resuscitated her from the dead and made her a living voice in the late nineteenth century. Through the Dostoevski of the late 1870s, Sand still speaks to us today. He could not have paid her a higher compliment.

NOTES

1.   Stendhal had died in 1842; Balzac in 1850; Nerval in 1855; Merimee in 1870; and Theophile Gautier in 1872.

2.   Victor Hugo, "Obseques de George Sand," <u>Oeuvres completes</u> (Paris: Club francais du livre, 1970), vol. 15, p. 1382.

3.   Dostoevski refers to the following works by George Sand in his own writings: <u>La Marquise</u> (1832), <u>Leone Leoni</u> (1834), <u>Andre</u> (1835), <u>Les Maitres mosaistes</u> (1837), <u>Mauprat</u> (1837), <u>La Derniere Aldini</u> (1838), <u>L'Uscoque</u> (1839), <u>Jeanne</u> (1844), <u>Teverino</u> (1845), <u>Le Meunier d'Angibault</u> (1845), <u>Lucrezia Floriani</u> (1846), <u>L'Homme de neige</u> (1859), <u>Les Dames vertes</u> (1859), <u>La Confession d'une jeune fille</u> (1865), <u>Cesarine Dietrich</u> (1871), <u>Journal d'un voyageur pendant la guerre</u> (1871), <u>Flamarande</u> (1875), <u>Les Deux freres</u> (1875). It is hard to believe he had not also read: <u>Indiana</u> (1832), <u>Lelia</u> (1833), <u>Jacques</u> (1834), <u>Lettres d'un voyageur</u> (1834-36), <u>Horace</u> (1841), <u>Consuelo</u> (1842), <u>La Comtesse de Rudolstadt</u> (1843), and portions of <u>Histoire de ma vie</u>. He also translated most of <u>La Derniere Aldini</u> into Russian in 1844, only to find, to his great disappointment, that a translation had already been done. Cf. Joseph Frank, <u>Dostoevsky. The Seeds of Revolt, 1821-1849</u> (Princeton: Princeton University Press, 1976), p. 129. I am grateful to Joseph Frank whose encouragement to embark on a study of Sand and Dostoevski has been invaluable to me.

4. F. M. Dostoevski, Dnevnik pisatelia za 1876 god (mai--oktiabr'). Polnoe sobranie sochinenii v tridtsati tomakh (Leningrad: Izd. Nauka, vols. 1-25: 1972-1983), vol. 23, p. 32. The emphasis is mine. This volume will henceforth be referred to as Dnevnik pisatelia in the notes, followed by the volume and page numbers. This edition of Dostoevski's complete works will be referred to as PSS.

5. O. Watzke, "George Sand et Dostoevski," Revue de litterature comparee, (avril- juin 1940): p. 165.

6. Dostoevski, Dnevnik pisatelia, vol. 23, pp. 33-34.

7. Ibid., vol. 23, p. 30.

8. Ibid., vol. 23, p. 36. The emphasis is mine.

9. Ibid., vol. 23, p. 30.

10. Gustave Flaubert et George Sand, Correspondance, Alphonse Jacobs, ed. (Paris: Flammarion, 1981), p. 348.

11. Henry James, French Poets and Novelists (London, 1884); cited by Curtis Cate, George Sand. A Biography (New York: Avon Books, 1975), p. 724.

12. Dostoevski, Dnevnik pisatelia, vol. 23, p. 37.

13. This is precisely the point which the revolutionary Shigalov expresses in The Possessed: "Starting with unlimited freedom, I ended up with unlimited despotism" (Dostoevskii, Besy. PSS, vol. 10, p. 311).

14. Dostoevski, Dnevnik pisatelia, vol. 23, p. 32.

15. Dostoevski, Dnevnik pisatelia za 1877, 1880 i 1881 gody. Polnoe sobranie khudozhestvennykh proizvedennii (Moskva/Leningrad: Gosudarstvennoe izd., 1929), vol. 12, p. 436.

16. Cf. notably the entries for July, August, and December, 1877.

17. Dostoevski, Dnevnik pisatelia za 1876 god (ianvar'--aprel'). PSS, vol. 22, p. 7.

18. Dostoevski, Dnevnik pisatelia, vol. 23, p. 35.

19. Ibid., vol. 23, p. 36.

20. Ibid.

21. Robert Louis Jackson, The Art of Dostoevsky. Deliriums and Nocturnes (Princeton: Princeton University Press, 1981), p. 259.

22. Joseph Frank, Dostoevski, p. 130.

23. Leonid Grossman, Dostoevski (Moskva: Molodaia gvardiia, 1962), p. 434.

24. Ibid.

25. Ibid.

26. M. M. Bakhtin, "Discourse in the Novel," in Michael Holquits, ed., The Dialogic Imagination, (Austin: University of Texas Press, 1981), p. 347.

27. George Sand, Histoire de ma vie. Oeuvres autobiographiques, ed., Georges Lubin, (Paris: Pleiade, 1971), vol. 2, p. 160.

28. Jean Cassou, "George Sand et le secret du XIXe siecle," in Parti pris; essais et colloques (Paris: Michel, 1964), p. 70.

29. George Sand, Spiridion. Oeuvres de George Sand, nouvelle edition (Paris, Garnier freres, 1851), vol. 7, pp. 394-395.

30. I am using the revised Garnett translation of Dostoevski, Brothers Karamazov (New York: Norton, 1976), p. 299. For the original, see Dostevski, Brat'ia Karamazovy. PSS, vol. 14, p. 290.

31. Sand, Spiridion, p. 396.

32. Ibid., p. 444.

33. Dostoevski, Brothers Karamazov, pp. 233-234; Dostoevski, Brat'ia Karamazovy, pp. 230-231.

34. Dostoevski, Dnevnik pisatelia, vol. 23, p. 37.

Note: All translations from the French and the Russian are my own, unless other wise noted, and I have used the Library of Congress system for the trans literation of Russian.

HOFSTRA UNIVERSITY

HEMPSTEAD, NEW YORK 11550

Dostoevski and the Human Condition
After a Century

An International Conference
On the Occasion of the 100th Anniversary of His Death

THURSDAY, FRIDAY, SATURDAY
APRIL 9, 10, 11, 1981

Guest of Honor

HENRI PEYRE

CONFERENCES AT HOFSTRA UNIVERSITY

George Sand Centennial - November 1976   Vol. I - available

Heinrich von Kleist Bicentennial - November 1977   Vol. II - available

The Chinese Woman - December 1977

George Sand: Her Life, Her Works, Her Influence -   Vol. III - 1982
     April 1978

William Cullen Bryant and His America - October 1978   Vol. IV - 1982

The Trotsky-Stalin Conflict and Russia in the 1920's -   Vol. V
     March 1979

Albert Einstein Centennial - November 1979   Vol. VI

Renaissance Venice Symposium - March 1980   Vol. VII

Sean O'Casey - March 1980

Walt Whitman - April 1980   Vol. VIII

Nineteenth Century Women Writers - November 1980   Vol. IX

Fedor Dostoevski - April 9, 10, 11, 1981   Vol. X

Gotthold Ephraim Lessing - November 12, 13, 14, 1981   Vol. XI

Franklin Delano Roosevelt: The Man, the Myth, the Era -   Vol. XII
     March 4, 5, 6, 1982

Johann Wolfgang von Goethe - April 1, 2, 3, 1982   Vol. XIII

James Joyce - October 1982   Vol. XIV

Twentieth Century Women Writers - November 5, 6, 7, 1982   Vol. XV

Jose Ortega y Gasset - April 1983   Vol. XVI

Romanticism in the Old and the New World - Celebrating   Vol. XVII
     Washington Irving, Stendhal, and Vasilii Andreevich
     Zhukovskii -- 1783-1983 - November 1983

"Calls for Papers" -- available upon request

FEDOR MIKHAILOVICH DOSTOEVSKI

1881-1981

Dostoevski and the Human Condition After a Century

An International Conference
On the Occasion of the 100th Anniversary of His Death

THURSDAY, FRIDAY, SATURDAY
APRIL 9, 10, 11, 1981

Guest of Honor

HENRI PEYRE

PROGRAM

CONFERENCE DIRECTORS:	Frank S. Lambasa Valija Ozolins
DIRECTOR: UNIVERSITY CENTER FOR CULTURAL & INTERCULTURAL STUDIES (UCCIS)	Joseph G. Astman
ASSISTANTS TO THE DIRECTOR:	Natalie Datlof Alexej Ugrinsky Conference Coordinators
COOPERATING INSTITUTIONS:	Audio Brandon Films Mount Vernon, NY Nassau County Office of Cultural Development Roslyn, NY Nassau Library System Uniondale, NY New Community Cinema Huntington, NY

GREETINGS

I wish you every success with your venture.

Joseph Brodsky
American Academy in Rome
Rome, Italy

I am certain that your gathering will be a notable occasion.

Joseph Frank
Princeton University
Princeton, NJ

I wish your conference every success while regretting my inability to join you at that time.

David I. Goldstein
Paris, France

With best wishes for all success.

Helen Muchnic
Cummington, MA

Best wishes for the success of your conference.

Alexander Solzhenitsyn
Cavendish, VT

UNIVERSITY CENTER FOR CULTURAL & INTERCULTURAL STUDIES
HOFSTRA UNIVERSITY
HEMPSTEAD, NEW YORK 11550

Thursday, April 9, 1981   David Filderman Gallery, Dept. of Special Collections
                            Hofstra University Library - 9th Floor

11:00 a.m. - 1:00 p.m.   Registration and Opening Ceremonies

12:00 noon   Greetings from the Hofstra University Community

                            Joseph G. Astman, Director
                            University Center for Cultural & Intercultural Studies

                            Robert C. Vogt, Dean
                            Hofstra College of Liberal Arts & Sciences

                            Opening Address: Pete Hamill, Journalist
                                              New York, NY

                            "Dostoevski: The Poet and the City"

                            Opening of Gallery Exhibit and Reception

                            "Fedor Mikhailovich Dostoevski: Artist, Philisopher,
                               Russian - 1881-1981"

                            Greetings: Marguerite Regan
                                        Assistant to the Dean of Library Services

1:00 - 2:00 p.m.   Lunch - Student Center Cafeteria, North Campus

2:00 - 3:30 p.m.   PANEL I - THE SHORTER FICTION - David Filderman Gallery

                            Moderator: Mary Emery
                                        Professor Emerita
                                        Dept. of Comparative Literature & Languages
                                        Hofstra University

                            "The Russian Iconic Representation of the Christian
                            Madonna: A Feminine Archetype in Dostoevski's
                            Notes from Underground"
                            Patricia Flanagan Behrendt, Pennsylvania State University
                            University Park, PA

                            "The Nature of Referent in The Double"
                            Asya Pekurovskaya, Reed College
                            Portland, OR

                            "Notes from Underground One Hundred Years after the
                            Author's Death"
                            Rado Pribic, Lafayette College
                            Easton, PA

3:30 p.m.   Coffee Break

Thursday, April 9, 1981 (cont'd.) - David Filderman Gallery - 9th Floor

4:00 - 5:00 p.m.   PANEL II - THE "DEVIL" AND "NAPOLEON" AS CONCEPTS

                                    Moderator: Vera Von Wiren-Garczynski
                                                Dept. of Germanic & Slavic Languages
                                                The City College-CUNY
                                                New York, NY

                                    "The Function of the Devil in the Artistic World of
                                        Dostoevski"
                                    Michel Aucouturier
                                    Université de Paris - Sorbonne
                                    Paris, France

                                    "The Dynamics of the Idea of Napoleon in Crime and
                                        Punishment"
                                    Shoshana Knapp
                                    Virginia Polytechnic Institute & State University
                                    Blacksburg, VA

5:00 - 7:00 p.m.   Dinner - Student Center Cafeteria, North Campus
                                    $4.25 - Prix fixe   (unlimited)

7:00 p.m.   Hofstra School of Law - Room 238, South Campus

                                    "Re-Reading Crime and Punishment"
                                    Sophia H. Sulowska
                                    Columba High School
                                    Coatbridge, Scotland

7:20 p.m.   Film Showing

                                    CRIME AND PUNISHMENT - USSR, 1970

                                    In Russian with English subtitles - 220 minutes

                                    Intermission - Coffee Break

Friday, April 10, 1981   Dining Rooms ABC - Student Center, North Campus

8:30 - 9:30 a.m.   Breakfast - Student Center Cafeteria - North Campus

9:00 a.m. - 4:00 p.m.   BOOK FAIR - Student Center Mezzanine - North Campus

9:30 - 10:30 a.m.   Greetings: Valija Ozolins
                                        Conference Co-Director

                            PANEL III - THE IDIOT

                            Moderator: Andrej Kodjak
                                        Dept. of Slavic Languages & Literature
                                        New York University
                                        New York, NY

                            "The Idiot: A Feminist Analysis"
                            Olga Matich, University of Southern California
                            Los Angeles, CA

                            "Narcissus Inverted: Fantastic-Realism as a Way of
                                Knowing in Dostoevski's The Idiot"
                            Dennis P. Slattery, Southern Methodist University
                            Dallas, TX

10:30 a.m.   Coffee Break - Student Center Mezzanine

11:00 - 12:00 noon   Special Address: Robert L. Jackson
                                              Yale University
                                              New Haven, CT

                            "Dostoevski in the Twentieth Century"

12:00 - 1:30 p.m.   Lunch - Student Center Cafeteria

1:30 - 2:30 p.m.   Keynote Address: Henri Peyre
                                              The Graduate Center - CUNY
                                              New York, NY

                            "Gide and Dostoevski: A Reappraisal"

2:30 p.m.   Coffee Break - Student Center Mezzanine

ON THE SCREEN:

Fedor Dostoevski's

Crime and Punishment

USSR, 1970. Black and white.
In Russian with English subtitles.
220 minutes
Lev Kulidjanov, Director

STORY:

Obsessed by the notion of committing a perfect crime, Raskolnikov, an impoverished student living in a rooming house in St. Petersburg, kills an old pawnbroker and her stepsister with an ax and steals some jewelry from their apartment. Raskolnikov's guilty behavior arouses the suspicions of Inspector Porfiri, who questions him about the crime. In answer, Raskolnikov expounds his theory that superior individuals need not obey the law. Later, Raskolnikov visits Sonia, the daughter of a friend killed in a traffic accident. He confesses his crime to the girl, a prostitute. Confronted by Porfiri, Raskolnikov confesses and surrenders to the police. Sentenced to eight years in Siberia, Raskolnikov is followed there by Sonia, who inspires his regeneration.

CAST:

Raskolnikov	Georgi Taratorkin
Porfiri	Innokenti Smoktunovsky
Sonia	Tatyana Bedova
Dunia	Victoria Fyodorovna
Svidrigaliov	Yefim Kopelyan
Marmeladov	Maia Bulgakova
Mrs. Raskolnikov	Irian Gosheva

THURSDAY, APRIL 9, 1981

Hofstra School of Law
7:00 p.m. — Room 238

Admission - Free	UCCIS
Limited Seating	Hofstra University
For Information:	Hempstead, NY 11550
	(516) 560-3296 or 3359

Sponsored by:
Hofstra College of Liberal Arts and Sciences
Robert C. Vogt, Dean

ON THE STAGE:

JACK POGGI

in

DOSTOEVSKI'S FORGOTTEN PEOPLE

Translated and Performed by Jack Poggi
Actor, Author and Professor of Theater at C.W. Post Center -LIU
Greenvale, NY

FRIDAY, APRIL 10, 1981

8:30 p.m.

STUDENT CENTER THEATER

North Campus

"...one of the most one-man, one-man shows ever invented...."
Leo Seligsohn, *Newsday*
"...a first-rate and thoroughly professional evening in the theater...."
"...classics with guts and compassion...."
Robert Heide, playwright, New York, NY

Admission - Free	UCCIS
Limited Seating	Hofstra University
For Information:	Hempstead, NY 11550
	(516) 560-3296 or 3359

Sponsored by:
Nassau County Office of Cultural Development
Marcia E. O'Brien, Director

Friday, April 10, 1981 (cont'd.) - Student Center Theater - North Campus

3:00 - 5:00 p.m.   PANEL IV - NINETEENTH AND TWENTIETH CENTURY RELATIONSHIPS

                              Moderator: Edward J. Czervinski
                                           Dept. of Germanic & Slavic Languages
                                           SUNY at Stony Brook
                                           Stony Brook, NY

                              "Nabokov and Dostoevski: The Case of Despair"
                              Julian W. Connolly, University of Virginia
                              Charlottesville, VA

                              "From St. Petersburg to Chicago: The Human Condition
                                  After a Century"
                              Dasha D. Culic, University of Southern California
                              Los Angeles, CA

                              "Two Opponents of the Ant-Hill: Dostoevski and
                                  George Sand"
                              Isabelle Naginski, Bard College
                              Annandale-on-Hudson, NY

                              "Dostoevski and America's Southern Women Writers:
                                  Parallels and Confluences"
                              Temira Pachmuss - Univ. of Illinois - Urbana-Champaign
                              Urbana, IL

5:30   RUSSIAN BANQUET   Dining Rooms ABC

                                    Cash Bar

RUSSIAN BANQUET

Dining Rooms ABC - 5:30 p.m.

GUEST OF HONOR

HENRI PEYRE

Ambassador and Plenipotentiary
to the World of the French Language,
its Literature, Civilization, Culture,
Influences and Affinities

Award Ceremony

Greetings: James M. Shuart, President
            Hofstra University

            Alex Szogyi
            French Department
            Hunter College-CUNY and
            The Graduate Center-CUNY
            New York, NY

            Hughes de Kerret
            Cultural Attaché
            Cultural Services of the French Embassy
            New York, NY

Musical Interlude

The Brothers Kallaur play Slavic Melodies

Gregory, Michael and Daniel Kallaur
Accompanied by Arlene Kallaur

Dramatic Presentation - Student Center Theater, North Campus -- 8:30 p.m.

Greetings: Marcia E. O'Brien, Director
            Nassau County Office of Cultural Development
            Roslyn, NY

DOSTOEVSKI'S FORGOTTEN PEOPLE

Translated and Performed by Jack Poggi
Actor, Author and Professor of Theater

Sponsored by: Nassau County Office of Cultural Development
               Marcia E. O'Brien, Director

Saturday, April 11, 1981   Dining Rooms ABC - Student Center, North Campus

8:00 - 9:00 a.m.   Continental Breakfast

9:00 - 10:30 a.m.   Greetings: Frank S. Lambasa
                                               Conference Co-Director

                                  PANEL V - THE BROTHERS KARAMAZOV

                                  Moderator: Constantine Kallaur
                                               Dept. of Foreign Languages
                                               Nassau Community College
                                               Garden City, NY

                                  "Rebirth and the Cognitive Dream"
                                  Phyllis Berdt Kenevan, University of Colorado
                                  Boulder, CO

                                  "The Legend of the Grand Inquisitor: The Death
                                       Struggle of Ideologies"
                                  Thelma Z. Lavine, The George Washington University
                                  Washington, DC

                                  "Murder and Suicide in The Brothers Karamazov:
                                       The Double Rebellion of Pavel Smerdiakov"
                                  N. Norman Shneidman, Erindale College-Univ. of Toronto
                                  Mississauga, Ontario, Canada

10:30 a.m.   Coffee Break

11:00 a.m. - 1:00 p.m.   PANEL VI - THE POSSESSED

                                  Moderator: Marina Astman
                                               Dept. of Russian
                                               Barnard College-Columbia University
                                               New York, NY

                                  "Kirillov's Return as Artist"
                                  Peter Glenn Christensen, SUNY at Oswego
                                  Oswego, NY

                                  "Kirillov, Stavrogin, and Suicide"
                                  Roger L. Cox, University of Delaware
                                  Newark, DE

                                  "The Demon of Irony: Stavrogin the Adversary at Tihon's"
                                  Reed B. Merrill, Western Washington University
                                  Bellingham, WA

                                  "The Aesthetics of Dostoevski as Reflected in
                                       The Possessed"
                                  Valija Ozolins, Hofstra University
                                  Hempstead, NY

Saturday, April 11, 1981 (cont'd.)

1:00 - 2:00 p.m.   Lunch - Student Center Cafeteria, North Campus

2:00 - 4:00 p.m.   Room 142 - Student Center

                                   PANEL VII - HISTORY AND FICTION

                                   Moderator: Lucy Vogel
                                               Dept. of Germanic & Slavic Languages
                                               SUNY at Stony Brook
                                               Stony Brook, NY

                                   "Dostoevski and the Catholic Pax Romana"
                                   Denis Dirscherl, S.J., Georgetown Preparatory School
                                   Rockville, MD

                                   "Nihilists and Idealists in the Novels of Dostoevski"
                                   Edwin L. Hetfield, State University College at Buffalo
                                   Buffalo, NY

                                   "Between Heaven and Hell: The Dialectic of Dostoevski's
                                      Tragic Vision"
                                   Anthony S. Magistrale, University of Pittsburgh
                                   Pittsburgh, PA

                                   "Thorns Among the Laurel: Dostoevski's Speech on
                                      Pushkin"
                                   Alan P. Pollard, Rhode Island College
                                   Providence, RI

4:00 p.m.   Roundtable Discussion

                                   Wine and Cheese Reception

                                   Closing Remarks: Frank S. Lambasa

DOSTOEVSKI CONFERENCE

Book Fair

<u>Participants</u>

Brentano's
289 Sunrise Mall
Massapequa, NY   11758

Four Continent Book Corporation
149 Fifth Avenue
New York, NY   10010

New American Library, Inc.
1633 Broadway
New York, NY   10019

Russica Book Shop
80 East 11th Street
New York, NY   10003

Nel Panzeca
Director, Book Fair

CREDIT for the success of the Conference goes to more people than can be named on
    this program, but those below deserve a special vote of thanks:

HOFSTRA UNIVERSITY OFFICERS: James M. Shuart, President
                               Harold E. Yuker, Provost
                               Robert C. Vogt, Dean, HCLAS

ARA Slater: Joan Murray

DAVID FILDERMAN GALLERY: Department of Special Collections
                           Marguerite Regan, Assistant to the Dean of Library Services
                           Nancy Herb
                           Anne Rubino

DEPARTMENT OF COMPARATIVE LITERATURE & LANGUAGES: Alice Hayes, Senior Executive Secretary

DRAMA DEPARTMENT: Richard France, Chairman
                    John De Vito, Production Assistant

HOFSTRA LIBRARY ASSOCIATES: Walter Fillin, President

HOFSTRA SCHOOL OF LAW: Charlotte Hoffer, Assistant to the Dean

HOFSTRA UNIVERSITY LIBRARY: Charles R. Andrews, Dean

OFFICE OF THE SECRETARY: Robert D. Noble, Secretary
                           Armand Troncone & Staff
                           Doris Brown & Staff

SCHEDULING OFFICE: Margaret Shields

TECHNICAL AND MEDIA SERVICES: Albert Nowicki & Staff

UCCIS: Marilyn Seidman, Conference Secretary
         Conference Assistants: Karin Barnaby
                                  Alexander Lake
                                  Nel Panzeca
                                  Stuart Weber
                                  Nikolai Ugrinsky

UNIVERSITY RELATIONS: Harold Klein, Director
                        Brian Ballweg, Assistant Director

And to the very talented performers of Slavic music: Richard Berman   Gregory Kallaur
                                                       Helen Greenwald   Michael Kallaur
                                                       Arlene Kallaur   William Zito
                                                       Daniel Kallaur

Index

DARLA KOWALSKI

Aucouturier, Gustave, 115
Backes, Jean-Louis, 115
Bakhtin, Mikhail, Problems
  of Dostoevsky's
  Poetics, 87, 89-91,
  125, 127, 157, 205
Bakunin, Mikhail, 15
Balzac, Honore de, 2-3,
  117, 120-121, 124, 128,
  199, 205
Beckett, Samuel, 6
Beethoven, Ludwig van, 128
Belinski, Vissarion, 15,
  204
Bennet, Arnold, 118
Berdyaev, Nicholas, 117,
  193
Bismarck, Otto von, 108,
  173-174
Blackmur, R.P., 63
Blake, William, 194
Brecht, Bertolt, 13
Bulgakov, Mikhail, 136
Byron, George Gordon,
  Lord, 91-92, 192
Camus, Albert, (The Myth
  of Sisyphus, 95), 124,
  129
Catteau, Jacques, 115
Cerny, Vaclav, 96
Cervantes, (Don Quixote,
  195)
Chadaev, P.Y., 172
Chandler, Raymond, 3
Chernyshevsky, Nikolai,
  (What's to be Done?,
  58, 122), 107, 169, 201
Chirkov, N.M., 24
Claudel, Paul, 115,
  123-124, 128
Conrad, Joseph, 116,
  (Heart of Darkness,
  168)
Corneille, 2, 124, 128
Dickens, Charles, 3, 6,
  121, 200
Dostoevski, Aimee, 173

Dostoevski, Fedor
  Mikhailovich Works:
A Raw Youth, 6-8, 24, 117,
  185-187
Atheism (Life of a Great
  Sinner), 175, 203-204
The Brothers Karamazov, 4,
  13-20, 23-28, 79, 81,
  89, 116, 118, 122, 128,

  133, 164, 175, 181-182,
  184-187, 193, 203,
  205-207
The Citizen, 59
Correspondence, 126
Crime and Punishment, 4,
  31-40, 79, 81, 94, 116,
  128, 139, 156, 158-160,
  163-164, 1660-169, 185,
  192-193
Diary of a Writer, 59,
  61, 133, 141,
  173, 175-176, 199, 201,
  ("The Gentle Creature,"
  202), 203
The Demons, 122, 124
The Double, 41-51, 63
The Idiot, 4, 8, 53-59,
  61-68, 81, 116, 120,
  122, 124, 128, 134,
  172-173, 176, 191,
  194-195, 205
Life of a Great Sinner,
  see Atheism
Memoirs from the House of
  the Dead, 3
Notebooks, 126
Notebooks on The Idiot, 65
Notes from Underground, 5,
  7, 71-77, 81, 89, 94,
  117, 133-142, 156-158,
  160, 163-165, 201
Poor Folk, 3
The Possessed, 4, 79, 82,
  84, 87-88, 99-109, 145,
  147-149, 151-152, 164,
  172-173
"A Busy Night," 81
"A Few Words About George
  Sand", 199, 202-203
"At Tihon's" ("Stavrogin's
  Confession,"), 83, 89
"The Death of George
  Sand," 199, 202-203
"The Dream of a Ridiculous
  Man," 84,89
"The Eternal Husband",
  124
"The Faint Heart," 6-7
"The Grand Inquisitor,"
  81, 89, 175, 205, 207
"The Little Hero," 134
"Mr. Shchedrin or Schism
  Among the Nihilists,"
  102

Characters in the works
  of:

Alexandra Petrovna, 57
Andrey Filippovich, 42-45
Apollon, 165
Arkady, 6
Darya Pavlovna, 85
Dasha, 91
Dunya, 37-39
Epanchin, 57, 64
Epanchin, Aglaya, 54-57,
    64, 194
Mrs. Epanchin, 54-55
Euphorion, 101
Ferdyshchenko, 58
Ganya, 54, 56, 58
Golyadkin, 42-47, 63
Grand Inquisitor, 1,
    13-20, 81, 89, 175-177,
    195, 207
Grigorii, 23
Ippolit, 57, 89, 205
Ivolgin, general, 54,
    57-58
Mrs. Ivolgin, 57-58
Ivolgin, Varya, 54, 57-58
Karmazinov, 107-108
Karamazov, Alesha, 17, 25,
    79, 85, 87, 117, 125,
    176-177, 182, 184-188.
    191, 193, 195, 205-206
Karamazov, Dmitri, 25, 27,
    87, 184, 195
Karamazov, Fedor, 1,
    23-25, 27
Karamazov, Ivan, 8-9, 17,
    24-27, 79, 85, 87-89,
    92, 117, 127,
    176-177, 181, 185, 191,
    193-195, 205
Kirillov, Alexei Nilitch,
    79-85, 91, 145,
    147-149, 151
Klara Olsufyevna, 45
Kolya, 187
Lebedev, 58
Lebedev, Vera, 54, 57
Lebyadkin, Mary
    Timofeevna, 94
Lembke, Juliya Mikhailovna
    von, 100, 103, 105-109
Liputin, 79
Lizaveta Petrovna, 57,
    74-77, 91, 94, 133,
    136, 138-142, 157, 165,
    192
Lyamshin, 108
Madame M., 134
Marey, 85

Marfa, 23
Marie, 65
Matryosha, 83, 85, 89, 91,
    94
Mermeladov, Sonya, 31,
    35-39, 94, 120, 139,
    159, 163, 168-169,
    191-193, 195
Myshkin, Prince Lev, 1-2,
    8, 54-57, 62-67, 87,
    123, 125, 172-173, 176,
    192, 194-195
Nastasya Filippovna,
    54-56, 58, 62-67, 125,
    134, 194
Petrushka, 47
Porfiry Petrovich, 32-34,
    36, 38-39, 160, 193
Prince S., 57, 67
Ptitsyn, 58
Queen of Festives, 42
Raskolnikov, Rodion, 1,
    8-9, 26, 32-40, 79, 85,
    94, 117, 120, 139,
    158-160. 163, 166,
    168-169, 185-187,
    192-196
Rogozhin, Parfyon, 54-55,
    62-67, 125, 194
Dr. Rutenspitz, 42, 45-46
Shatov, Darya, 82, 91, 96,
    122, 146-147, 149
Shatov, 172
Shchedrodarov, 102
Shigalyov, 80, 85, 91,
    122, 152
Smerdiakov, Pavel, 23-28
Smerdiashchaia, Lizaveta,
    24-24
Snegirov, Iliusha, 23
Stavrogin, Nikolai, 1,
    79-85, 87-96, 105, 116,
    163, 174, 191
Stavrogina, Marya, 91
Stavrogina, Varvara
    Petrovna, 100-107
Svidrigailov, 31, 38-39,
    85, 163, 168
Father Tihon, 83, 87-96
Totsky, 54-55, 57
Underground Man, 5, 7-8,
    71-77, 90, 94, 120,
    133, 138-142, 156-158,
    191
Verkhovensky, Pyotr
    Stepanovich, 80-82,
    91-92, 105, 108, 122,
    146-149, 151

Verkhovensky, Stepan
    Trofimovitch, 88, 91,
    100-109, 152
Versilov, 89, 185-188
Vladimir Semyonovich,
    42-45
Yevgeny Pavlovich, 55-57
Father Zosima, 26, 79, 87,
    117, 125, 182, 184-188,
    191, 193, 195, 205-206

Doskoevski and/on:

Anti-Christ, 14, 17, 91,
    125, 172, 177, 185,
    207,
Art, 99-110, 136
Beauty, 56, 63-64, 99-110,
    134
Christ, 13-14, 62, 65-66,
    79, 89, 96, 122, 136,
    139-140, 149, 171-173,
    175-177, 194, 201-202,
    207
Christian Apocalyptism,
    14, 17, 19
City, the, 1-9
Communism, 15, 17-19
Concept of "two", "double"
    and "Doppelganger",
    41-51, 61-68, 168
Confession, 35, 39, 42,
    75, 84, 87, 89-92,
    94-95, 120, 122, 124
Decadence, 54
Dialectic, 191-192, 195
Dreams, 183-187, 189
English People, 5
Existentialism, 7, 13, 145
Fantastic-Realism, 61-68,
    126
"Femme Fatale" characters,
    53-59
French People (dislike of,
    5), 171
Humor, 7, 90, 124
Icons, 13, 17, 19-20
Idealogies, 13-20
Irony, 87-96, 100, 124
Leitmotifs, 101
Liberalism (Western),
    17-20
Marxism and Marxist
    Ideology, 7, 13-14,
    18-20
Murder, 23-28, 159,
    192-193

Narrator, 100
Nihilism, 20, 56, 87-89,
    91-92, 102, 176 185-187
Parricide, 25-27
Pax Romana, 171-178
Petrashevsky Circle, 15
Psychology, 124, 163
Redemption, 80
Religion, 4, 13-14, 19,
    57, 81-82, 89-94, 96,
    102, 120-123, 128,
    133-142, 145, 171-178,
    181-182, (spiritual
    conflicts in the works,
    191-196), 202, 204
Romanticism, 41-42
    (German, 100), 101, 201
St Petersburg, 1-5, 7, 16,
    101-102, 105
Socialism, 14-16, 171,
    201-202, 204
Suicide, 23-28, 55, 79-85,
    95, 145
Tragedy, 191-192, 194-195
the West, or Western
    Culture, 17-19,
    171-173, 177, 189,
as Prophet, 181-183,
    188-189
Women, 53-59, 125, 133-142

Dostoevski, Mikhail
    (brother of Fedor), 1-2
Eikhenbaum, B.M., 43
Eliot, T.S., 118, 125, 128
Ellison, Ralph, Invisible
    Man, 8
Enlightenment, Age of,
    18-20
Epokha (1864), 102
Euclid, 17
Faulkner, William, 145
Flaubert, Gustave (Madame
    Bovary, 55, 201), 118
Frank, Joseph, 203
Freud, Sigmund, 7, 28,
    46-47, 182
    (Interpretation of
    Dreams, 183)
Galsworthy, Hugh, 116
Garnett, Constance, 2
Garnett, Richard, 116
Gide, Andre, 115, 118-129,
    193
Godard, Jean-Luc, 145
Goethe, Johann Wolfgang
    von, (Faust, 100), 127,
    129, (Wilhelm Meisters

Wanderjahre, 150)
Gogol, Nikolai, 43, 45
   48, (Dead Souls, 152),
   158
Goncharov, I.A., 53
Grossman, Leonid, 71, 139,
   203
Hamilton, Edith, 64
Hawthorne, Nathaniel, 195
Hegel, Georg Wilhelm
   Friedrich, 15-16, 18,
   20
Heidegger, Martin, 109
Herzen, Alexander, 15
Hesse, Hermann, 181-183,
   185, 189
Hingley, Ronald, 4-5
Hitler, Adolf, 2
Holbein, Hans, 66
Homer, 42
Hugo, Victor, 120, 125,
   199
Isayeva, Mariya Dmitrievna
   (Fedor M. Dostoevski's
   wife), 4-5
Ivanov, Viatcheslav, 127
Jackson, Robert Louis,
   133-134, 203
James, Henry, 116-201
Jouffroy, Alain, 147
Jung, Carl Gustav, 7, 183,
   185, 189
Kabat, Geoffrey C. 152
Kierkegaard, Soren, 47,
   89-90, 93, 184
Kramarenko, M., 47
Kramskoi, Ivan
   Nikolaevich, 23
Kukol'nik, Nestor
   Vasil'evich, 101
Las Cases, E. de, 39
Lawrence, D.H., 116
Lermontov, Mikhail, A Hero
   of Our Time, 91
Levinson, Andre, 117
Lorraine, Claude, 85
Lyngstad, Alexandra H.,
   27
The Madonna, 103, 105-108,
   133-142
Magretta, Jean, 63
Malraux, Andre, 115
Mann, Thomas, 121
Marx, Karl, 16, 18-19
Mayakovsky, V.V., 146
Menninger, Karl, 28
Milton, John, (Paradise

Lost [Satan], 192)
Mirsky, Prince D.S.,
   History of Russian
   Literature, 117
Mochulsky, Konstantin, 31,
   89, 193
Mohammed, 40
Murray, John Middleton,
   116
Nabokov, Vladimir,
   (Despair, 155-160)
Napoleon I, 31-40, 200
Napoleon III, (Louis
   Napoleon Bonaparte), 32
Narcissus, 61-68
Nietzsche, Friedrich, 88,
   (The Birth of Tragedy,
   94), 95-96, 118, 124,
   129, 181, 189
O'Connor, Flannery, 195
Omsk, Siberia (place of
   Fedor Dostoevski's
   deportment), 3, 15, 18
Orlando, Francesco, 46
Ovid (Metamorphoses, 63)
Pascal, Pierre, 115, 125
Peace, Richard, 134
Petronius, (Satyricon,
   127)
Pinter, Harold, 6
Plato, 19-20
Porter, Lawrence, 66
Pozner, Vladimir, 116
Proust, Marcel, 115, 121,
   124-126
Pushkin, Alexander, 2,
   ("The Queen of Spades,"
   31), 42, 53, 102, 117
Racine, 2, 117
Radcliffe, Ann, 201, 205
Raphael, 103-104, 107-108
Rembrandt,6, 196
Remizov, Alexis, 121
Rimbaud, A., 95, 205
Riviere, Jacques, 128
Rousseau, Jean Jacques, 5,
   123
Sade, Donatien Alphonse
   Francois, comte de, 88
Sand, George, 120, 199-208
Sartre, Jean Paul, 13, 20,
   109, 121
Schiller, Friedrich von, 2
   ("The Robbers," 27)
Shakespeare, William,
   (Hamlet, 84, 91, 150),
   103-105, 117, 125,
   191-192, 194

Scholokhov, Mikhail, 146
Socrates, 62
Sophocles, 191-192
Stalin, Josef, 2, 4, 8,
    122
Steiner, George, 28
Stendhal pseud. of Marie
    Henri Beyle, (The Red
    and the Black, 31), 127
St. John, 80, 138
St. Paul, 82
Strakhov, Nikolay, 62, 125
Stravinskij, Igor, 47
Suslova, Appollinariya, 5
Tate, Allen ("What is
    Traditional Society,"
    61)
Teniers, David, 107
Tolstoi, Leo, 6, 116, 118,
    121, 126
Troyat, Henri, 116
Turgenev, Ivan, 2, 6, 53,
    108
Ullman, Montague, 189
Vinogradov, Viktor
    Vladimirovich, 47
Vogue, Eugene Marie
    Melchior, vicomte de,
    115, 120, 127
Voltaire, F.M.A. de, 5
Wilde, Oscar, (The
    Picture of Dorian
    Gray, 95), 118
Wright, Richard, 163-169
Zenkovsky, V.V., (Russian
    Thinkers and Europe),
    172, 175
Ziolkowski, Theodore, 63
Zola, Emile, 6

About the Editors and Contributors

PATRICIA FLANAGAN BEHRENDT is Instructor and Coordinator of the Introduction to Theatre Arts Program, University of Nebraska-Lincoln. She is recipient of the Fling Fellowship to complete dissertation research at the Bodleian Library, Oxford University, and has a special interest in theories of interdisciplinary study with publications on this theme ranging from the cult of Dionysus in Roman scenographic painting to patterns of classical myth in Zola and Ibsen.

PETER G. CHRISTENSEN is Adjunct Lecturer of English, State University of New York at Binghamton. He has published articles on Marguerite Yourcenar and John Dos Passos. He has also written forthcoming essays on Italo Calvino, Jean Cocteau, Paul Nizan, and B. Traven. He is currently at work on a series of essays on D. H. Lawrence.

JULIAN W. CONNOLLY is Associate Professor of Slavic Languages and Literatures, University of Virginia. He is author of *Ivan Bunin*, and has published numerous articles on Vladimir Nabokov and other twentieth-century Russian authors.

ROGER L. COX is Professor of English and Comparative Literature, University of Delaware and a member of the International Dostoevsky Society. He formerly taught at Bates College and DePauw University. He is author of *Between Earth and Heaven: Shakespeare, Dostoevsky, and the Meaning of Christian Tragedy*; and his essays on Dostoevsky have appeared in *Forum International, Dostoevsky Studies*, and *Canadian Slavonic Papers*.

DENNIS DIRSCHERL is Chaplain in the U.S. Air Force Reserve and book reviewer for Best Sellers and NC News Service. He has published many articles and book reviews. For years he has been a student of the Russian language.

PETE HAMILL is Contributing Editor to the *Village Voice*. He was formerly Contributing Editor for *New York Magazine* and Syndicated Columnist for the *New York Times*. He is author of *A Killing for Christ*, *The Gift*, *Flesh and Blood*, *Dirty Laundry*, *The Deadly Piece*, *The Invisible City*, and *A Rational Ravings*.

PHYLLIS BERDT KENEVAN is Associate Professor of Philosophy, University of Colorado. Her principle research interests are in the areas of existentialism, philosophical psychology, and philosophy in literature. Her publications include articles on Sartre, Nietzsche, Dostoevski, and Jung.

SHOSHANA KNAPP is Associate Professor of English, Virginia Polytechnic Institute and State University. She has written numerous journal articles, and is currently completing a book-length study of the intellectual friendship of George Eliot and Herbert Spencer.

FRANK S. LAMBASA is Professor of Comparative Literature and Languages, Hofstra University. He has also taught at University of Michigan and at East China Normal University, Shanghai. He is author of books and articles on European authors.

THELMA Z. LAVINE is Robinson University Professor in the Humanities, George Mason University. She was previously Elton Professor of Philosophy and chair of the Philosophy Department at George Washington University. She has written extensively for philosophic and social scientific journals, and is author of *From Socrates to Sartre: the Philosophic Quest* and co-author of *History and Anti-History in Philosophy*.

ANTHONY S. MAGISTRALE is Assistant Professor of English, University of Vermont. He is the author of *Writer's Guide: Psychology*, *The Moral Voyages of Stephen King*, and various journal articles.

OLGA MATICH is Associate Professor of Russian Literature, University of Southern California. She is editor of *The Third Wave: Russian Literature in Emigration* (1984), proceedings of the first major conference on contemporary Russian literature in exile, and author of *Paradox in the Religious Poetry of Zinaida Gippius*.

REED MERRILL is author of numerous articles on the modern novel in such publications as *Modern Fiction Studies*, *Comparative Literature Studies*, *Mosaic*, and *The South Atlantic Quarterly*. He is co-author of a bibliography on Arthur Koestler, and has recently completed a critical study of the novel and philosophy.

ISABELLE NAGINSKI is Assistant Professor of French and Comparative Literature, Tufts University. She has published numerous articles on nineteenth-century French and Russian literature and is currently completing a book entitled *Literary Traffic: The Impact of French Fiction on the Russian Novel.*

DASHA CULIC NISULA is Adjunct Professor of Composition and Literature, Saginaw Valley State College. Her current research focuses on translation and analysis of works by several poets from Yugoslavia. She recently completed a bilingual edition of *Selected Poems by Vesna Parun.*

VALIJA K. OZOLINS is Professor of Russian Language and Literature, Hofstra University. She specializes in Dostoevsky and nineteenth-century Russian literature.

ASYA PEKUROVSKAYA is teacher of Russian, University of California at Santa Cruz, and was formerly Professor and Head of the Russian Department at Reed College.

HENRI PEYRE, now Emeritus, was for many years Chairman of the French Department and Distinguished Professor, Yale University, and later at the Graduate Center of the City University. He is author of many volumes of criticism and literary history.

RADO PRIBIC is Associate Professor of Languages, Lafayette College. He is author of *Bonaventura's "Nachtwachen" and Dostoevsky's "Notes from the Underground": A Comparison in Nihilism* and has written numerous articles and reviews dealing primarily with Germano-Slavic literary and cultural relations.

N. N. SHNEIDMAN is Professor of Russian and Soviet Literatures, University of Toronto, Canada. He has lectured and published extensively on problems of Russian literature and Soviet society in Europe and North America. He is the author of *Literature and Ideology in Soviet Education, The Soviet Road to Olympus: Theory and Practice of Soviet Physical Culture and Sport, Soviet Literature in the 1970s: Artistic Diversity and Ideological Conformity,* and *Dostoevsky and Suicide* (1984).

DENNIS PATRICK SLATTERY is Professor of English, Southern Methodist University and a member of the Teacher's Advisory Board, The Dallas Institute of Humanities and Culture. He is the author of *The Idiot; Dostoevsky's Fantastic Prince. A Phenomenological Study* and has written many journal articles and book chapters. He is currently working on another book on Dostoevsky.

ALEXEJ UGRINSKY is Assistant Professor of German at Hofstra University and Acting Co-Director of the Hofstra University Cultural Center. His earlier works have appeared in the *Journal of Long Island Bookcollectors* and the *Acta of the Congress of the International Association of German Studies*. He is editor of *Lessing and the Enlightenment* (Greenwood Press, 1986).